War and Slavery in Sudan

The Ethnography of Political Violence

Cynthia Keppley Mahmood, Series Editor

A complete list of books in the series
is available from the publisher.

War and Slavery in Sudan

Jok Madut Jok

PENN

UNIVERSITY OF PENNSYLVANIA PRESS

Philadelphia

Copyright © 2001 University of Pennsylvania Press
All rights reserved
Printed in the United States of America on acid-free paper

10 9 8 7 6 5 4 3 2

Published by
University of Pennsylvania Press
Philadelphia, Pennsylvania 19104-4011

Library of Congress Cataloging-in-Publication Data
Jok, Jok Madut.
  War and slavery in Sudan / Jok Madut Jok.
      p.   cm. — (The ethnography of political violence)
  Includes bibliographical references and index.
  ISBN 0-8122-3595-9 (cloth : alk. paper) —
  ISBN 0-8122-1762-4 (pbk. : alk. paper)
  1. Slavery—Sudan.   2. Sudan—History—Civil War, 1983–
3. Racism—Sudan.   I. Title.   II. Series.
HT1381 .J65   2001
305.8′009624—dc21   00-052774

Contents

Preface

> The Murahileen chain people
> as the fisherman chains his catch with a rope
> The Murahileen take us into servitude in their land
> The Murahileen drag us on the surface of our land
> but we will not let go of our land
> Sudan is our land

This verse is from a Dinka song that describes the experience of the people of South Sudan and the Nuba of central Sudan with the recently revived slavery and slave trade. It was in some ways inevitable that I would focus on this area of study. I am a South Sudanese anthropologist who has been studying Sudan all my academic life. I now teach at a university in the United States. My career as a Sudanist, without a doubt, began with the knowledge I acquired from personal experience as a native son. But this knowledge became more specialized after 1993 when I undertook field study in South Sudan for my doctorate at the University of California, Los Angeles. That research project examined the impact of the unresolved North-South civil war on the family, gender relations, and reproductive health in northern Bahr el-Ghazal in southwestern Sudan.[1] Moreover, while I was in Bahr el-Ghazal conducting research, I also worked for a humanitarian relief agency, and this role enabled me to travel extensively in the areas that have now become the subject of this book.

Having been seriously understudied due to war, which made travel in the region difficult, South Sudan presents an ambitious researcher with the temptation to do it all. Therefore, while I was documenting the interaction between the behaviors and attitudes of militarized youth, on the one hand, and traditional gender relations, on the other, during my first period of fieldwork, my research extended into more issues than I had planned. Such topics as household decision making regarding pregnancy, abortion, sexuality and sexual violence, sexually transmitted diseases, childbirth, care for the young, and other reproductive health issues took the center stage of my dissertation research.[2] Yet, the temptation to document other tragedies such as government militia raiding, displacement, loss of assets, preemptive migration, and the dismal future of the family was far too great to resist. By 1995, about twelve years after the second round of the civil war began, South Sudan had lost a third of its population to war, famine, and displacement to the North or neighboring countries. Suffering abounded and there was an immediate need to understand it. Basic services were almost completely nonexistent and mortality rates were extremely high. The traditional structure of the family was so reconfigured that the individual person was left without the care that the society had always provided in times of need. People were in a state of almost total despair, and there was no end to this misery in sight. There is still none.

I returned to California in 1995 with loads of notebooks on varied topics after two years of dissertation research. I went back to South Sudan every summer thereafter. The topic for the present study became clear in my mind in 1998 because of my own interest in questions of ethnic nationalism and nation building and the need to expose the tragic human rights situation in Sudan.

This book chronicles the current wave of slavery in Sudan. The history of slavery in Sudan goes as far back as the earliest alien encroachment, but the current revival began in 1983 with the beginning of the second round of North-South conflict. Northern Sudanese Arabs capture and sell (or exploit in other ways) large numbers of African Sudanese, primarily the Dinka, Nuer, and Nuba of central Sudan. The Arab slave raiders, although traditionally hostile to Nuer and Dinka, are currently engaged in slave taking for slightly different reasons than before the civil war. Since the beginning of the war, successive governments in Khartoum have sought different means to exploit the traditional animosity between the Dinka and the Arabs and have supported the Arab side in order to fight the war by proxy. These cattle-herding Arab tribesmen, known as the Baggara, were recruited as a low-cost counterinsurgency militia and deployed against the southern opposition force, the Sudan Peoples' Liberation Army (SPLA). However, instead of confronting the SPLA, the militia force waged war against the civilian population of northern Bahr el-Ghazal, which the Sudanese government considers the support base for the SPLA. Soon after the initiation of the militia system, the Baggara discovered a very effective method of suppressing the rebellion in the South: destroying civilian villages and frightening the population into deserting their homes. But mere suppression of the southern revolt only satisfied the government; the Baggara received only meager government assistance. It was more lucrative to capture large numbers of women, children, and any able-bodied men they could subdue and take them into slavery in their northern provinces of Darfur and Kordofan. In addition to benefiting from the slave labor, the Bagarra hoped that helping implement the government's military strategy would earn them extra government resources. This book explains the intricacies and nuances of how a counterinsurgency militia became a slave-taking army.

The problem with writing this book is that its topic is controversial. When one writes from the perspective of one's own people and when one has a responsibility toward the whole country, there is a certain degree of ambivalence involved. There is no doubt that I will be seen as focusing on the concerns of Southerners, but if I do not focus on the victims of the crisis I am studying I could also be blamed for trying to marginalize the very people whose agony I am trying to expose. I am conscious of the possibility that my having only worked in the South could bias my views. But I have made an equally conscious attempt to be objective in presentation. While no one writing on Sudan's tumultuous and tragic history can claim absolute neutrality, I have tried to express the concerns of Southerners without being anti-North.

Many South Sudanese living under the Sudan government's oppression have asked and encouraged me to write about their suffering and its history. They long for a voice, and I have agreed to lend them mine. An academic factor that strongly influenced my decision to write this book was the existence of an excellent body of anthropological, historical, and journalistic material on important aspects of how the war has triggered the revival of slavery. Robert Collins has written extensively and perceptively on the history of slavery and the slave trade on the Upper Nile, the role of the current war on the reemergence of slavery, and relations between Arab Northerners and African Southerners.[3] He has also recently authored an insightful analysis of why the Baggara raid the Dinka.[4]

The Dinka historian, the late Damazo Dut Majak, a native of northern Bahr el-Ghazal from the Malwal section, conducted a historical survey throughout the region in the 1980s and wrote a compelling dissertation and numerous articles on the history of alien encroachment in his home region.[5] His work provides a detailed ethnographic and historical analysis of the arrival of Arab traders who later became the slave traders in Bahr el-Ghazal, and is complete with genealogies and maximal family systems. He gives examples of the families that were at the forefront of confrontations with the Arabs, the French, and the British, and provides an overview of economic activities before and during the occupation of the region by slave traders (1821–98)—the Turkiyya (1821–81) and the Mahdist era (1881–98)—and under the Anglo-Egyptian Condominium rule (1898–1956).

Historians Martin Daly and Douglas Johnson have both written instructive accounts on how the colonial governments dealt with the question of North-South relations and the role of slavery in these relations.[6] A North Sudanese, Ahmed Sikainga, has also written important books on the relationship between Bahr el-Ghazal and Darfur in terms of slavery and trade as well as exchanging cultures.[7] In more recent times, a great deal of ethnographic research has been devoted to changing circumstances in war-torn South Sudan. In the anthropological literature, Sharon Hutchinson's book on how the Nuer are coping with the war and the state is most compelling.[8] Francis Mading Deng, a Dinka legal anthropologist, has been an authority on North-South relationships and the debate on the identity of the country, particularly the relationships between the Baggara and his native Dinka section of Ngok.[9]

In the field of journalism, the *New Yorker,* the *Washington Post,* the *Washington Times,* the *New York Times,* the *Los Angeles Times,* the *Boston Globe,* the South African *Mail and Guardian,* as well as a number of European and Canadian magazines and newspapers have all carried extensive accounts of slave raiding since 1995. Many of them have tried to expose the role of the government in slave taking. They have also debated the issue of slave redemption discussed later in this book—that is, the practice whereby Christian and antislavery groups from the Western world purchase the freedom of slaves and return them to their home villages in the South. Another issue for these newspapers and magazines has been the disturbing silence of the international community, especially powerful industrial countries. But the most systematic and instrumental journalistic writing on slavery in Sudan has been that by Sudanese journalist and former government minister Bona Malwal. He pioneered the campaign to expose this tragic practice in the 1980s as editor of the *Sudan Times,* the only English-language newspaper in Khartoum at the time. When he went into exile in England, Malwal started publishing a newsletter, the *Sudan Democratic Gazette,* which focused on the slavery issue.

Although it has been mostly South Sudanese who have spoken out against slavery, there have been a few North Sudanese who have felt that slavery cannot be tolerated in a modern nation-state that is seeking to build its identity on ethnic, religious, and racial diversity. Among these very few Northerners were two courageous university professors who risked their lives to write candidly to expose this inhuman practice they thought had only remained as a bad mark on the pages of history but no longer existed in their country. Having read numerous reports in the *Sudan Times,* Ushari Mahmud and Suleiman Baldo traveled to ed-

Da'ein in Darfur in order to ascertain the rumors they had heard about slavery, only to return with disheartening accounts of a massacre of some two thousand Dinka by the Baggara Arabs. Their booklet *Human Rights Abuses in the Sudan, 1987: The Diein Massacre: Slavery in the Sudan* caused an outcry among rights activists, South Sudanese, and the government. The activists and citizens of South Sudan were outraged at the government's complicity, and the government was furious at the two professors for "defaming" the good name of the country. The authors were accused of being "fifth column" and supporters of the southern rebel army, and were classed as traitors.

More and more such reports prompted the United Nations Commission on Human Rights to send a Special Rapporteur to Sudan in 1994 and 1995 to examine the allegations of human rights violations by the Islamist regime in Khartoum. Special Rapporteur Gaspar Biro wrote a detailed report centering on the question of slavery.[10] He documented how the militia force operates and how the army violates all the known conventions on the conduct of war. He also described the kind of destruction both the regular army and the militias mete out in the Dinka areas, and the fate of the captives, who are physically and emotionally abused and sold as slaves or forced to work under conditions amounting to slavery. The response of the government of Sudan to this report was one of fury. Gaspar Biro was accused of harboring anti-Islam and anti-Arab sentiments, and the government made a request to the High Commissioner for Human Rights to remove Biro as the Special Rapporteur on Sudan. In 1999, another Special Rapporteur for Sudan, Argentinian lawyer Leonardo Franco, was appointed. He also produced a detailed examination of the question of slavery incriminating the government of Sudan.[11]

Many historians, anthropologists, and journalists have worked or traveled in the communities where most of my research for this book was done. And I am pleased to report that numerous people mentioned them to me as soon as I said that I was writing a book on the issue of slavery. I heard many stories filled with praise for the journalists and human rights investigators. I also took copies of magazine articles and newspaper clippings with me to the field and discussed their main findings with people who had provided the information to the researchers. I found that these local people almost always agreed with what I told them the researchers had recorded. As it is with all literate South Sudanese cut off by war from any sources of reading material, the people of Bahr el-Ghazal were overjoyed when I brought these materials. They also lamented that although these works were the foundation of a history of modern South Sudan, the seventeen years of war had deprived several generations of South Sudanese of education so that no one will write that history and most South Sudanese will not comprehend what outsiders write about them. Still, at a time when many academics in social sciences and humanities are quick to criticize the production of journalistic literature as historical evidence, I found that many journalists familiarize themselves with the anthropological literature and have an understanding of Sudanese cultures before traveling to Sudan. I therefore find these sources to have value, not just for me but also for the local people. In preparation for this work I compiled (with the appreciated assistance of many aid agencies) a large body of documents, reports, unpublished papers, student theses and dissertations, and scholarly publications, which have informed this study directly or indirectly; those works most directly relevant are appropriately cited in the notes. I have also drawn on my own knowledge as a Sudanese.

This study began in a serious and systematic sense in 1998, when I collaborated with Sharon Hutchinson on a research project funded by the Harry Frank Guggenheim Foundation to investigate the militarization of Nuer and Dinka ethnic identities since the split of the SPLA in 1991, and the violence against civilians that ensued from the split. That research consisted of concurrent surveys, with Hutchinson working in the Nuer areas and I in the Dinka areas, with the aim of establishing a list of factors that the people thought fueled the ethnic conflicts between the two groups, and possible ways to mitigate them. One of the important factors in conflicts among South Sudanese ethnic groups that I investigated further for the present project was the role of the central government in fanning these ethnic wars as a way to weaken these groups in their confrontation with the North. Significant results from that research are instrumental to the present study. Also, my travels throughout northern Bahr el-Ghazal in the summers of 1998 and 1999 allowed me to administer interview schedules for this study; I thus gained more than a total of six months of firsthand experience in observing the aftermath of the slave raids. Most of my time during these trips was spent at various relief stations and market towns in Aweil East, Aweil West, and Tuic Counties.

During most of these trips, I had either set out to do research on a topic other than slavery or to work as a consultant, but the issues surrounding slavery were always paramount for my respondents, and there was no way to brush them aside simply because I had come to do something else. I remembered Cynthia Nelson, my professor at the American University in Cairo, commenting that if an issue is of obvious importance to one's research subjects, then that issue should be the topic of one's research.[12] I established contacts with local officials, traditional administration (chiefs and headmen), SPLA officers and commanders, spiritual leaders, laypersons, and former slaves who either had escaped from bondage or had been freed through redemption programs. All of them invariably regarded slave raiding to be the most tragic experience they have had during the civil war.

My most intensive and systematic data gathering took place between June and August 1998 and during June 1999. As on previous visits, I concentrated my work in the areas just a day or two days' walk to the Dinka-Baggara border, which include the villages of Gok Machar, Manyiel, Majak Baai, Marial Baai, Warawar, and Beech, all in Aweil West and Aweil East Counties. I also traveled and conducted well over a hundred interviews in Tuic County, where both the Tuic people and the displaced Ngok have suffered constant assault by the Baggara. Most of the people with whom I spoke in these parts of northern Bahr el-Ghazal were either displaced from the border areas, returnees from displacement, or living in dilapidated villages destroyed during the raids. My interviews also included people from other parts of northern Bahr el-Ghazal who had either witnessed the destruction themselves or were host to thousands of others who were displaced from their villages. I have also interviewed local civilian officials, SPLA military personnel, chiefs, and clan leaders. The interviews about slavery focused on the experience of enslavement or bondage itself, the volume of the slave trade, the local efforts to redeem the slaves, and attempts to rebuff the militias and prevent the capture of slaves. I also probed the respondents about the fate of ex-slave children or women who have been returned to their villages but who had lost their families, and about people's rationalizations of the resurgence of slavery. I have also conducted interviews on local perceptions of Arab and African relations and the cultural differences, racial tensions, and history of contact between these groups; why these relations create conflicts; and how these conflicts might be mitigated. The most important interviews, in my opinion, were those conducted with former slaves, for without their testimonies and narratives of what happens to the slaves, there would be no substance for this book.

Altogether, I conducted and recorded more than two hundred interviews on the topics of militia raiding and slavery over the entire period of my research stay in Bahr el-Ghazal since 1993. Some interviews were confined to individual respondents and others were done in a group setting. Each interview lasted between half an hour and one hour, not including time I spent answering respondents' questions about America, how I got there, and why other South Sudanese in diaspora do not go back to visit their homeland as I do.

The interviews were conducted with men, women, and children. They were open-ended exchanges in which we discussed a particular topic to a point of saturation. The specific topics we explored varied but always related to war, militia raids, and their upheavals. Some interviews focused on insecurity, disruption of trade networks between North and South, food shortages as people have lost their crops and livestock to raiding, and the aftermath of the raids. Others dealt with history, the relationship between government and people, the state power or lack thereof, and SPLA administration compared to the prewar government. Still others revolved around identities, race relations, local ideas about the status of a South Sudanese person in the constitution, the state laws, and whether or not the people of South Sudan feel that they are represented in the center. The interviews with former slaves focused on their experiences while in captivity, how they got their freedom, and how they are fitting back into their communities.

I need to insert a note at the outset about three terms that are used throughout this book. They are the Kiir River, South Sudan, and Sudan. Kiir is the Dinka name for the river that the reader will find on maps as Bahr al-'Arab, which is the Arabic name for the same river and means "Arab Sea." The valleys of this river serve as the dry season pastures for both groups and have historically been the source of confrontation. As I am writing from the perspective of the Dinka, I use the Dinka word for the river.

My use of "South Sudan" (instead of "southern Sudan," used by most writers) reflects the views of my informants, who believe that the expression South Sudan confers a distinct and bounded national identity for the people who live in this region. It has a secessionist connotation, and most people I interviewed, including SPLA personnel, talked about a future nation comprising the three southern regions of Upper Nile, Equatoria, and Bahr el-Ghazal separate from the North.

My use of "Sudan" rather than "the Sudan" reflects both my ideological standpoint and a historical fact. "The Sudan" is a colonial term coined during the scramble for Africa to distinguish between the country as we know it today and the rest of bilād as-sūdān, the term used by Arab traders in reference to the whole region stretching from Senegal to the Nile Valley. Because the rest of Africa that was included in the Sudan has long been carved up into different countries, only one place bears the name, eliminating the need for the definite article.

I covered a great deal of complex material under serious time constraints and from a vast territory where travel is extremely difficult and where security is a constant concern. I was able to do this because of my association with relief agencies, without whose assistance this project would have been impossible. I have flown in aid agency aircraft from the northwestern Kenyan town of Lokichokio, where the relief consortium Operation Life-line Sudan (OLS) is based, to northern Bahr el-Ghazal. From whichever bush airstrip I was dropped off, I again relied on the hospitality of aid agency field staff for accommodation, vehicle rides, or bicycle loans. The enthusiasm of the people of Bahr el-Ghazal about this project further eased my task. Local officials were quick to turn over copies of their reports on slavery, lists of names of people in captivity, and other relevant material. I also appreciated the willingness of many people in northern Bahr el-Ghazal to tolerate my questions, which to them sometimes sounded absurd coming from a native of the area. Because I am a Dinka myself, it was difficult for some to comprehend why I was asking questions I supposedly knew the answers to. Nevertheless, they graciously and eloquently taught me much about the cultural aspects of Sudan's current war, and I owe a special debt of gratitude to all the people of northern Bahr el-Ghazal. Many people in this region helped in numerous ways beyond the specific interviews I had with them. Unfortunately, I cannot mention them all by name; however, I sincerely thank them all.

I am also grateful for the assistance provided by my colleagues John Ryle and Philip Winter, who are both Sudan area specialists and have worked in South Sudan in various fields including humanitarian assistance and research. During my summer 1999 trip to Bahr el-Ghazal, I had the opportunity to be on a consultancy team with Ryle and Winter; the discussions I had with them on this project have sharpened my thinking.

I gratefully express my appreciation to the Harry Frank Guggenheim Foundation for a joint grant to my colleague Sharon Hutchinson and I, which covered a significant part of my expenses for fieldwork and writing this book. I thank the foundation for its long-standing interest in research on violence and aggression in general, and its interest in our Sudan project.

Loyola Marymount University provided support for this project, including a faculty research grant for the summer of 1998. I appreciate this support and also thank Kenyon Chan, Dean of the College of Liberal Arts, for providing formal letters of introduction to foreign consulates in order to obtain visas for travel to East Africa on my way to Sudan. I also thank Joseph Jabbra, the Academic Vice President at LMU, for his enthusiastic encouragement of this project. Among many LMU colleagues who provided useful comments were Lawrence Tritle and Lisa Marovitch.

I feel especially fortunate to have had the enthusiastic commitment and encouragement of able editors Patricia Smith and Noreen O'Connor. I also acknowledge with gratitude comments made on the manuscript by two anonymous reviewers, whose suggestions for revision of the book were most helpful.

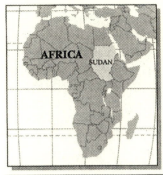

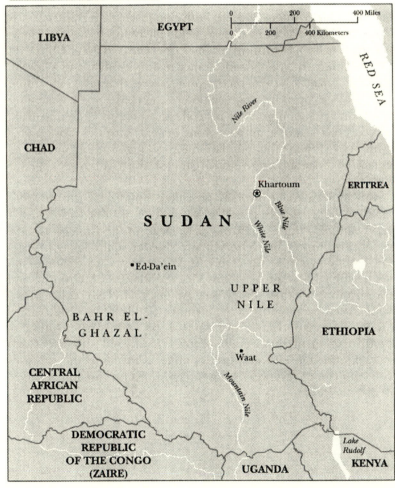

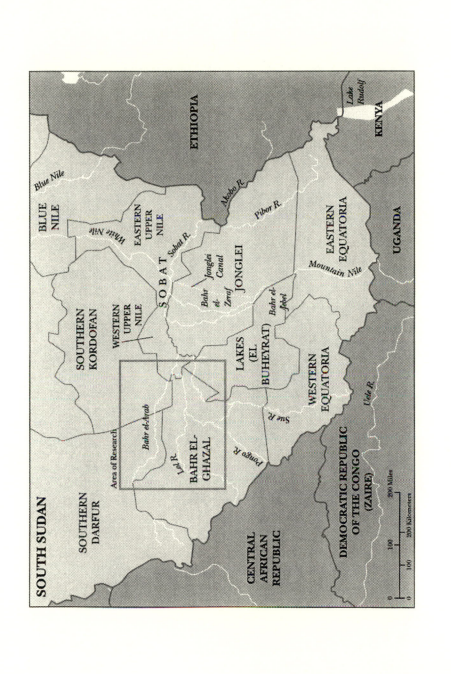

Slavery in Sudan: Definitions and Outlines

Many decades after independence from Britain in 1956, Sudan, the largest country in Africa, continues to make news headlines for calamities such as its war-ravaged lands, bankrupt economy, violent Islamic militancy, cultural and religious conflicts, and killer droughts and famines. But the disaster that has most engaged the attention of the Western world has been the revival of slavery and the slave trade, aided by the indifference and complicity of the Sudanese government. The successive Khartoum regimes since the start of the current civil war between the North and the South in 1983 have been notorious for encouraging enslavement of southern blacks, and increasingly Christian Sudanese, by northern Arab Muslims. Armed by the government as low-cost counterinsurgency militias, the Arab cattle-herding tribes of Darfur and Kordofan provinces, known as the Baggara, targeted in particular the Dinka of northern Bahr el-Ghazal and Abyei. The main reason for these atrocious assaults is that the Dinka are accused of supporting the Sudan Peoples' Liberation Army (SPLA), the southern opposition army confronting the North in the longest war of the twentieth century.[1] Khartoum governments have reasoned that if the SPLA's support base were destabilized, the rebel army would be easy to defeat.

The capture and sale of Dinka women and children from South Sudan into slavery in the North has been going on since 1983. The total number of captives at a given time is estimated at 10,000–15,000. I say at a given time because much of the slavery in Kordofan and Darfur could best be described as temporary. Some abducted slaves are released after they become regarded as unfit. Others escape. Others are redeemed through the assistance of Arab middlemen, or freed by legal recourse. This transitory character of slavery does not mean that while in captivity, the victims are any better off than those who are in bondage permanently. It simply means that some people become free as suddenly as they became slaves. In addition to people abducted for the sole purpose of enslavement, there are hundreds of thousands of South Sudanese displaced to the North by the raiding, the civil war, and the consequential famines that have plagued the southern region since the start of the war. Many of these displaced Southerners have also experienced enslavement. The impermanent nature of slavery does not bother the slavers, for they can always obtain more slaves. They have no fear of any legal measures since the government and the authority of the state stand behind them.[2]

This situation has generated many puzzling questions about how slavery could be happening in this century. How can the government of a modern country encourage such a horrendous practice against its own subjects, simply because they are Africans and non-Muslim? How is it possible that the southern guerrilla force, the Sudan Peoples' Liberation Army, allows people in the areas under its control to be constantly raided and taken into slavery? Why is the world standing by, despite such misery, and not putting the necessary pressure on the government of Sudan to halt this practice?

Some of the nagging questions surrounding the issue of slavery in Sudan have to do with its scale and volume. How many slaves are we talking about? How badly are they being treated in the North? How do we know about their conditions in captivity in the North?

When I returned to Bahr el-Ghazal in 1993, ten years after the start of the war, the local authorities estimated that at least 14,000 Dinka men, women, and children had been abducted and driven to the North. Nobody knew anything about the fate of these captives. Many families had already started to venture into the North, particularly Kordofan and Darfur, in a tireless effort to find their enslaved relatives. Some have found their relatives and helped them out of slavery. Others have only recognized their cattle in cattle auctions in the North, and are still searching for their people. It is worth noting that many young boys were captured while grazing their herds and trying to prevent the raiders from looting the cattle. Therefore, when a man recognized his cows in the North, his hopes were raised that he might also find his child in the vicinity of cattle auction.

The slaves are almost constantly in transit between capture, sale, release, redemption, escape, dumping, and capture again. No one has any idea how many slaves there are exactly. In 1987, human rights groups, including the Anti-Slavery Society, estimated that there were 7,000 children and women being enslaved in Darfur and Kordofan.[3] Other reports put the number much higher based on the fluctuating market price of slaves. Between 1987 and 1988 the price of a slave boy went down from $90 to $10 (note that the price of a cow in northern Sudan was over $100).[4] It is hard to determine the cause of the fall in price for slaves, but going by the usual determinants of market prices—supply and demand—falling slave prices in North Sudan may be attributable to an oversupply of slaves, which in turn could mean that Baggara raids have increased. Robert Collins asserts that the falling prices may have been due to the abduction of children from the camps of displaced Dinka in western Sudan. It is also suggested that, in the face of desperation, Dinka parents may have been pawning their children to Arabs who might feed the children.[5] The SPLA authorities in the South, working closely with their own sources in the North, have estimated that 25,000 slaves are held in Darfur and Kordofan in a given year. They are victims of a devastating government retaliatory campaign. This campaign is compounded by the deteriorating climate in Darfur and Kordofan, which has pushed the Baggara to seek greater access to the grazing lands of the Dinka, as will be made clear in the following chapters.

Slavery or Slander: Defining Slavery in Sudan

Defining what constitutes slavery in the Sudanese contexts has been the persistent concern and subject of tense debate among human rights investigators and activists, government officials, social scientists, and other scholars since the first claims of slavery were made in the mid-1980s. Many have questioned the use of the term *slavery* as an accurate description of what has been happening in the border area between the Dinka and Baggara that has now become known as the "transition zone." The government of Sudan continues to deny that the phenomenon of abducting women and children is slavery and insists that the whole matter is no more than traditional Dinka-Baggara tribal feuding over resources. I will show, however, that the practice is indeed slavery by any definition.

The Slavery Convention of 1926 defines slavery as the status of a person over whom any or all of the powers attaching to the right of ownership are exercised. *Slave* means a person in the condition or status of being owned. *Slave trade* is defined as all acts involved in the capture and acquisition of a person with the intent to sell, exchange, or dispose of him or her.[6] The use of the term *slave trade* to describe the phenomenon in Sudan has been much debated. Some journalists have argued that *slave trade* does not apply in Sudan's context since the term attempts to equate Sudan's case with historical practices such as the trans-Atlantic slave trade. The government of Sudan, especially Hassan al-Turabi, the head of the ruling National Islamic Front, for example, has deliberately widened the definition of slavery to include all forms of exploitation. In this way, the government reduces the practice to a benign sort of aberration common in all societies, rather than the horrific case of chattel slavery practiced now in Sudan. Many people, however, have argued that evidence justifies the use of the term *slave trade* to describe the practice in Sudan, including the practice whereby South Sudanese children or young persons under eighteen are forcibly taken away from their parents or guardians and exchanged for favors or material goods in the North. There is also evidence that these children are put to work by Arab households without remuneration. All this could not be described by any term other than slave trade.[7]

In more recent times, the emergence of the notion of "the new slavery" has provided other definitions that fit the Sudanese phenomenon. Kevin Bales argues that the special characteristic of slavery is that slaves were property of the master; they are also coerced, and the labor of the slave is at the complete disposal of the slaveholder. Bales also notes that while slavery is fundamentally tied to labor, slavery differs from other types of labor such as wage labor, serfdom, and clientage. Many people doing these other types of labor are also subject to gross exploitation, a practice that disguises slavery as so-called wage labor. In countries as varied as India, Mauritania, Thailand, Brazil, and France, as Bales reports, slaves do not have the right to their own sexuality and to their reproductive capacities. In most cases, they do not have a choice to walk away from their desolate conditions, whether because of physical coercion or economic desperation. They are punished by flogging, confinement, deprivation of food, increasing the amount of work, or sale. As cheap commodities, slaves are bought and sold in ways so subtle that no legal measures can be taken against the slaveholder. New slaveholders or masters, according to Bales, are not concerned with the slaves' physical and psychological well-being because slaves are easy to obtain, and in fact, slaveholders find it cost-effective to dispose of slaves in order to acquire new ones.[8] Nearly all the practices in Sudan fit the definitions. Slavery in Sudan is initiated through violent raiding, which reduces the status of an abducted person from a condition of freedom and citizenship to one of slavery, cheap laborer, and a liability when physically unfit. Most important is that citizenship and entitlement to legal protection are undermined, whether through lack of laws or violation of existing laws, leaving the state unable to protect individual rights. Difficult as it may be to provide a succinct definition of slavery, the organized raiding and kidnapping of Dinka children and women from their communities and their subsequent exploitation in the North indicate that slavery is practiced in Sudan.

The ways Southerners are displaced by raids, civil war, and subsequent famines, exploited as cheap labor, and used by the government as magnets for foreign aid in the North, equally amount to slavery. The raids of Dinka villages force people to seek government protection and therefore migrate to the North. The government classifies them as refugees as a way to solicit foreign disaster relief. When such assistance arrives, the government assumes the responsibility of distributing it, gaining several advantages. Foreign aid gets taxed, and the food is used to coerce people into religious conversion. In this regard, Mark Duffield recently wrote:

Aid policy has furnished a complementary form of desocialization through propagation of the IDP [internally displaced persons] identity and predominance of economistic forms of analysis. What has been the impact of food aid on the role of displaced Dinka as cheap labour? . . . Since 1989, government of Sudan has consistently pressed to limit food aid to displaced Southerners, arguing that it creates dependency, demeans both the beneficiary and the image of Sudan, and conflicts with the government of Sudan's plans to integrate them into the national labor force. It was not until 1992, three years after OLS [Operation Life-line Sudan] began and following strong lobbying from the aid community, that displaced Southerners settled around Khartoum were allowed to come under OLS.[9] However, this only applied to those displaced people who were settled in formally recognized "peace camps" around the capital; those outside these designated areas received no official aid.[10]

The degree of suffering inflicted on Southerners by raiding and by the living conditions for captives and the displaced in the North has led many observers and commentators to conclude that the institution of slavery has been resurrected in Sudan.[11] The practice in Sudan includes all the realities and images that the word *slavery* evokes. The focus of this book is not to "prove" the existence of slavery in Sudan, but rather to document, describe, and expose the flagrant abuses of human rights in Sudan since 1983. This book attempts to place the issue of slavery and slavery-like practices in the context of the North-South conflict.

Factors Underlying the Persistence of Slavery

Sudan is a country where old habits die hard. When Samuel Baker, the British explorer of the White Nile, arrived in Khartoum in 1862, almost six decades after England had declared slave trade illegal, he noted that it was the slave trade that kept Khartoum going as a bustling town. Baker observed that a slave trader would sail to the South from Khartoum in the dry season with armed men and find a convenient village. The slavers would surround the village in the night, then just before dawn fall upon the village, burning the huts and shooting to frighten the people. Having caused disarray and turmoil in the village, the slavers would take mostly women and young adults, place forked poles on their shoulders, tie their hands to the pole in front, and bind children to their mothers. Everything the village lived on would be looted—cattle, grain, ivory—and what was of less value to the slavers was destroyed in attempts to render the village so poor that its surviving inhabitants would be forced to collaborate with the slavers on their next excursion against neighboring villages. Probably nothing more monstrous and cruel than this traffic had been experienced in South Sudan. These were indeed painful days that the survivors would have wished to forget. But they have to be recalled by those who wish to understand the recurrent indignities South Sudanese experienced then and continue to experience. By the beginning of the twentieth century, the British had reduced the scale and volume of the slave trade, especially the export of slaves. Yet the physical and moral damage had already been done, and this has continued to cast a dark shadow on the country. Very little has changed, as slavery and its strong foundations in Sudanese society remained critical issues during the twentieth century. These foundations have made it possible for slavery to recur every time the conditions are ripe for it. War, displacement, and poverty function now as triggers for twenty-first-century slavery.

The factors that fueled the practice in the old days persist in Sudan because of the racial setup, religious ideological conflict, poverty, labor exploitation, and political instability. When such conditions escalate in any society, one might add, they almost always trigger slavery or slavery-like practices. The reemergence and increase in slave-raiding expeditions and the sale of victims in Sudan are build upon the racial construction of the country and the cultural ideologies that make up the identity of the Sudanese people. After all, the raiders of the new slavery are radical Muslims, self-perceived as racially superior, and they usually arrive in Nilotic (Nuer and Dinka) areas with no compunctions about killing non-Muslims and non-Arabs, if killing is what it takes in order for them to achieve their desired goals. However, race, religion, ethnicity, and economics could not have brought about the current resurgence of slavery without a strong catalyst. This factor was the second round of the unresolved civil war between the South and the North. The war became the driving force for slavery as well as the shadow that concealed the practices of slavery from the outside world. The war gave government interlocutors the opportunity to explain away the new forms of slavery, or justify the capture of slaves as the inevitable consequence of war. But the point to be made in this book is that the war alone is not a sufficient explanation. Without the strong notions of racial, religious, and cultural superiority held in the North, the war alone would not have caused the resurgence of slavery in Sudan.

Since 1983 northern Arab cattle herdsmen (the Baggara) have carried out government-sponsored systematic attacks against the Dinka of Bahr el-Ghazal to pillage for cattle, to loot grain, and to capture scores of Dinka women and children and sell them into slavery in the North. In the face of all the war-provoked misery in South Sudan, the outside world could not see beyond famine to notice that slavery had become part of the government's war machine. When the news of slave taking first came to the attention of the outside world, quick statements were made about slavery being exclusively a product of war, not to mention that most people in the West could not really conceive of chattel slavery in this day and age. Later careful examination revealed that it was not just because of war that the Baggara were persuaded to act as executors of northern ambitions. Moreover, longer-term survival issues energized the slave raids. Under these circumstances, we need a better understanding of the forces sparking and sustaining slavery and the slave trade in Sudan. Five broad approaches to analyzing Sudan's slavery and the slave trade stand out; I will outline them here.

The Racial Structure of Sudanese Society

Although race in Sudan is a very slippery subject in terms of its biological expression in the population, it matters a great deal in the way people relate to one another. In terms of skin color, which is perhaps one of the most obvious characteristics for lay classification of races, an outsider may regard all Sudanese as black. But as far as the social construction of race is concerned, North Sudanese regard themselves as Arabs, whereas South Sudanese identify themselves as predominantly African, or rather call themselves by the specific ethnic groups to which they belong. These defined racial identities, the history and evolution of which will be explained below, do not stop at that. They evoke emotions of superiority of one group over the other. Sudanese society has become terribly polarized along these perceived racial lines as each group is engaged in either proving the superiority of its culture or disproving the allegations of inferiority made against it. The violent enslavement of Southerners is a result of enslaving communities having developed a racist ideology which ascribes subhuman status to the enslaved communities. The perpetrators of slavery in Sudan, the Baggara Arab herdsmen, use this racial ideology to generate enthusiasm among the young: when a call for raiding is made, they race to the front to prove their assumed superiority. One of the notions used to promote slavery has been the alleged natural inability of the Dinka to confront the more intelligent and militarily agile Baggara. The two main sections of the Baggara, the Rezeigat in Darfur and the Misseria in Kordofan, have both attempted to assert their assumed superior cultural capacities to justify slave raiding. These two Baggara tribes are Arabic-speaking Muslims. The victims of Sudan's slavery are black Africans, mainly from the Dinka sections of Malwal, Ngok, and Tuic, who are non-Muslim and speak a Nilotic language, using Arabic only as a second language, if at all.

In a cover story in the South African *Mail and Guardian*, the respected journalist Cameron Duodo characterized Sudan's tragic years as follows:

"The conflict is both of a racial nature and a religious one, between the Arabised black-skinned north and the negroid-Africans, Christians and animists, called by the Muslims the 'abids', which means 'slaves.'"[12] A mention of Islam or imposition of Arab culture as important factors in the North-South strife in Sudan frequently arouses discord with non-Sudanese Muslims and Arabs. They often express unease about this supposedly unfair characterization of Islam and Arabs as violent and intolerant. In this fashion, Muslim writer Khadija Magardie responded to Duodo's article with anger for having suggested that culture and religion have a hand in the Sudan's war. She demonstrated such utter ignorance about Sudan that her readers must have wondered whether she has ever seen a Baggara person. She suggested "the 'Arab versus blacks' framework [used by Duodo], is questionable since anyone who has visited Sudan and knows Sudanese history will know that the Baggara tribal militias, to whom slave-raiding is attributed, are physically identical to the Black southerners."[13] Well, obviously, if we go by the biological classification of races, the distinction between Baggara and Dinka may be somewhat blurred, given that the Baggara carry African blood and no longer look like the Arabs of Arabia or North Africa. But if race is socially constructed as it is in Sudan and elsewhere, Magardie could not be more wrong. Dinka and Baggara see each other as unequal and make no apologies for maintaining such views about one another. When a Dinka person sees a Baggara attacker on horseback, he/she knows the attacker is an Arab. For Sudanese, race is as plain as the different shades of blackness. If outsiders want to ignore the characteristics that the Sudanese themselves see as suggestive of racial differences, so much the better for the future of Sudan. However, race in Sudan is not necessarily based on appearance alone, but also on people's own racial categorization of themselves. The North Sudanese provide a strong example for the social and cultural construction of race. Now the distinction between Arabs and non-Arabs in Sudan, whether culturally determined or biologically expressed, is as obvious as the colors on the Sudan's flag.[14]

The Baggara and the Dinka, therefore, have significant ideological and cultural differences. The differences are at the levels of race, language, religion, and other cultural patterns. But despite these differences, the two people have similarities in their economic activities. Both groups are cattle-herding people, and share borders where they graze and seek water for their livestock. The main resource they share is the grazing plains of a river called the Kiir by the Dinka and Bahr al-'Arab by the Baggara. Recurrent scarcity of pastures due to droughts has historically led to disputes over pastures and land. For example, northern Darfur and northern Kordofan in the 1970s experienced a period of drought and famine which drove Rezeigat and Misseria cattle keepers farther south in search of grazing areas. When the Dinka resisted them, hostilities ensued and the Khartoum government was quick to back the Baggara using the ideology of racial superiority.

Nioltics' and Arabs' Views of One Another

Perhaps the most common view held by the Baggara, about Southerners in general and Nilotics in particular, is that the latter are naturally slaves. In the summer of 1999, Baggara chiefs and militia leaders stated that their strife with the Dinka was a result of the bad nature of the Dinka. The statement explained that Dinka insistence on controlling the grazing plains of the Kiir River was due to the cultural problems among the Dinka which prohibit progress. This statement also suggested possible ways to deal with the Dinka, including raiding them as usual. They also demanded that the government train and arm the Baggara if efforts at Arabicizing the Dinka were to succeed.

In their colloquial language, Arabic groups in the North always use the word *abd* (slave) to refer to a person of a certain low social class. It is also used to describe the obscene, a person lacking in moral stature, and even the physical appearance of a filthy person. Over time this term has become associated with poverty and only with certain groups within Sudan. At present, it is hurled principally at South Sudanese and the Nuba, particularly because the majority of migrants from the South and the Nuba Mountains now living in the North are comparatively poor. They are less educated, perform demeaning jobs, and adhere to non-Muslim faiths, all of which are reflected in the term *abd*. These varied uses of the word suggest that they go hand in hand with the roles and status of slaves, and since Southerners and the Nuba have historically been the slaves, the phrase has stuck with them.

This is why slavery in Sudan is not a mere accident of war, but rather a practice deeply embedded in North Sudan. The war has provided only a stimulus and a pretext for something the North has long desired. Conversely, slavery in Sudan could be perceived as cumulative in its effect. Even if one were to make an argument that Sudanese slavery is a product of war, the war itself is a result of degrading views that Northerners hold of Southerners, and these views are responsible for slavery. I do not want to reduce the tragic experience of slavery to the mere use of a word, but the Arab notion that Southerners are people who are naturally slaves goes beyond demeaning terms. Many North Sudanese government officials and lay persons act out their beliefs in many areas of life such as allocation of jobs, distribution of public services, and the language used in their daily interaction with Southerners.

The reverse is also true to a certain degree: the Dinka do not hold favorable views of Northerners. The difference, however, is that southern views of Northerners do not emanate from the perspective of superiority. Most people in the South acknowledge that their cultures are different and that is the end of it. There is no indication that Southerners at any point in history have tried to change the North on account of southern cultures being superior. The South has always been on the defensive against Northerners' efforts to become overlords in the whole country. The two wars between North and South speak for the southern rejection of Northern culture. The Dinka have cited their notions about Arab culture and Islam as one of the reasons for their vigorous opposition to the encroachment of northern cultures in the South. For example, in an interview in Nyamlel in 1998, one Dinka spiritual leader and community elder was asked to explain from the Dinka vantage point why the Arabs attack them. He characterized the Baggara as follows:

No amount of things, hard work, courtesy, or generosity of heart could one ever give the Baggara that can please them. We allow them to graze in our areas during the dry season, but when the rains begin, they do not just take their herds and go. Instead, they would look for a pretext to fight with us in hope of seizing our cattle. They do not take a moment to think about the next year. The following year, they would send peace messages begging us to allow them back. They have the right to think of us as dumb, but we are not. We simply think that we have too many mutual economic interests to be in a constant strife with them. The Baggara are shortsighted, unfortunately. You can offer your wife to a Baggara in exchange for peace, and he will turn around before reaching home to come and demand your mother. They are people who cannot have enough of another's property. Their way of worship is strange, they pray in a strange way, they claim to be God's people and yet commit things of which God as we know of him would not approve.[15]

Two events are commonly cited by the Dinka as examples of why they think the Baggara are bent on aggression for no good reason. One was the truce that the two groups had reached in 1989 over cattle vaccination against the bovine virus Rinderpest. The government veterinary services were not reaching the Baggara from the North, while the Dinka were being served by the International Committee of the Red Cross. The Dinka invited the Baggara to bring their cattle for vaccination, fearing that if Baggara cattle were not vaccinated, they could reintroduce the disease into Dinka herds in the future since the herds sometimes meet in the grazing valleys of the Kiir River. The Baggara were welcomed into Dinka territory, and after they had their herds vaccinated, instead of returning peacefully, they attacked Dinka villages and cattle camps and the truce broke down.

The other event followed the truce signed in 1990 to enable the Baggara to conduct trade at three major Dinka markets: Warawar, Abin Dau, and Manyiel. The Baggara were allowed to enter Dinka territory and trade for the whole dry season, but at the end of the season when they were going back, they killed people, took slaves, and burned the markets to the ground. Some markets, such as the one in Abin Dau, have not been revived since, and the people in this area have had to travel much longer distances to other trading towns.

Both truces were renewed in 1991, and every year thereafter until 1998, when the Dinka decided they had had enough of peace agreements with the Arabs. The truces failed because the government conspired to undermine them. Peaceful coexistence between the Baggara and Dinka means the government cannot recruit anti-SPLA militia among the Baggara and thus failure of the Islamic project, of which the Baggara were to be the implementers. The government sent security agents to Dinka areas disguised as traders or cattle herders along with all the other Arabs. These agents were to get as much information as possible on the SPLA military hardware and movements and inform the army. They were also charged with creating mistrust between the leaders of the two groups. For example, some of these agents would cause havoc in the market by picking a fight with a Dinka person, which sometimes escalated, resulting in a bigger Dinka-Baggara fight. On other occasions, the security agents entered the market with guns. When the Dinka realized this and became suspicious of all the Arabs, the situation resulted in expulsion of the Arabs and shooting and retreat of the Baggara back to their areas on the borders. Once peace was destroyed in this manner, the Baggara had a pretext to carry out raids. For this reason, Simon Wol Mawien, the civilian commissioner of Aweil West County, told me in an interview at Nyamlel in June 1999 that he will not allow another peace treaty between the members of his county and the Baggara. "We cannot have another truce with these people, they do not keep their word, and they are being used against us by the government; so until they come to their senses about our common good, we will cooperate no more."

Labor Exchange Between Groups

Slavery in Sudan occurs within a historical context of southern labor migration, especially agricultural labor, to the North. The interaction between wealthy merchant farmers in the North and southern laborers who are comparatively poor has produced asymmetrical relations that are not necessarily restricted to economic power. Racial prejudice, cultural bias, and religious intolerance have also led to exploitation of the weak as the norm. Laborers' demands for higher pay or unpaid dues have been met with both physical and verbal violence. Over time, violence has escalated even at high levels of authority, supported by dominant ideologies that view southern workers as disposable. This was particularly true in the late 1970s and early 1980s when the North witnessed an expansion of commercial agriculture in southern Darfur and western Kordofan, for which Dinka migrants provided—and continue to provide—much of the labor. When the civil war started, the ordinary flow of migrant laborers to the North could be increased by violence inflicted on southern villages. This also makes the desperate Southerners easy to exploit. One of the factors that incited Baggara raids on the Dinka was the Baggara need to form a pool of labor for this agricultural expansion, supported by the government and Islamic banks. "There was nothing we could offer the Baggara that was equivalent to the value of seizing our cattle, fishing our pools, hunting our animals to the finish, abducting our people, and occupying our grazing land," a Dinka elder declared in an interview in June 1999 in Nyamlel.[16]

Recent research in Baggara territory indicates that militia raids are motivated by a combination of Baggara need for cheap labor to compete with expanding mechanized farming and the government's "peace from within" and "peace camps" concepts. These are programs similar to the South Korean strategy during the Vietnam War, when farmers were forced at gunpoint into special areas, enclosed with barbed wire in order to put the locals out of the reach of the Vietcong, which the Koreans euphemistically called New Life Villages. "Peace camps" in Sudan are camps set up by the government to relocate the rural people in an attempt to bring all the possible supporters of the SPLA into government-controlled areas. To attract people into these camps, the government distributes propaganda among the villagers that those who move into these camps would be taken good care of by the government. Those who do not believe the propaganda are forced to go. These camps, however, have been described as no less than "concentration camps."[17] As more South Sudanese are displaced to the North, the government can undermine the SPLA administration more easily. The displaced also become hostages who attract foreign aid, which the government then taxes heavily. Because they are the "host" communities, the Baggara also demand part of the aid intended for the displaced Southerners. Displaced persons' camps are attacked periodically to seize foreign relief, and the Baggara then use these relief items to pay for southern labor.[18]

Religious and Cultural Ideologies and Notions of Superiority

Slavery existed in nineteenth-century Sudanese society only because certain elements were present. First, the slaver had to create an atmosphere of enmity to justify the violence which was institutionalized in the *razzia*—the slave raids of the period of Turco-Egyptian rule (the Turkiyya, 1821–

81) and the Mahdi's Islamic revolution (the Mahdiyya, 1881–98). Second, the society to be enslaved was regarded as inferior and its humanity denied to justify the kinds of treatment characteristic of slavery. This subhuman status could be given on the basis of religion, race, ethnicity, or regional identification. Third, the exploitation of the enslaved communities followed the exploitation of natural resources in their territory, which were used to strengthen the slaving forces against any resistance by the enslaved communities. Current slavery is also built upon these practices.

Indications that the North assumes superiority to justify slavery are omnipresent in the intellectual discourse of North Sudanese. Note how Sadiq al-Mahdi explains the genesis of the superiority of Arab culture, which is inseparable from Islamic culture. "The word Arab is used in the cultural sense. Arab refers to those who use Arabic as their mother tongue. Since Arabic was the language of Islam, and since the Arabs played a major role in the establishment of Islam, there is a close affinity between Muslim and Arab. . . . The people of the world of Islam were culturally Arabized and acquired the Islamic outlook. . . . Arabic, the language of a handful of desert people, became the universal language of an international community."[19] It has been the opinion of virtually all the leaders in Khartoum that the influence of British colonialism prevented Islam from spreading south, beginning first with South Sudan and hopefully into the rest of black Africa. As the foregoing statement suggests, North Sudanese hold an eclectic view of Islam that combines Arabism, Arabic language, and Arab culture in general, a sense of Arab nationalism deeply integrated with their religious identity as Muslims. They have dreamed of the day when this notion will run through black Africa, but believe that South Sudan, due to colonial influence in the area, has interrupted the mission to spread Islam in Africa. This is why the policies of assimilation and Arabization in the South have been so vigorous and bloody, turning South Sudan into a graveyard over the years. The objective has been to find areas in Uganda and Kenya where Muslims reside and then export not only Islam, but also the Sudanese politicized version of Islam, to these areas. Unfortunately, South Sudan has functioned as a stumbling block; thus the onslaught.

Although Dinka-Baggara relations have historically ranged from peace to sporadic skirmishes through frequent hostilities to full-blown war, the period beginning in September 1983 was a turning point. This was the year that Islamic *shari'a* laws were imposed by then-president Nimeiri. These laws undermined the religious diversity of the country, and the South bitterly opposed them. The southern objection to these laws and to a host of other policies imposed by Khartoum was perceived in the North as anti-Arab and anti-Islam. As a result, the Nimeiri government encouraged the Baggara to attack the Dinka of Bahr el-Ghazal, who were considered sympathizers and members of the SPLA. This policy was continued at a more organized scale by the government of Sadiq al-Madhi after the fall of Nimeiri. When the current National Islamic Front government came to power in 1989, the government support for the Baggara assumed a new ideology, the determined commitment of President al-Bashir and his junta to escalate Khartoum's jihad. Al-Bashir called on young Muslims to proceed to training camps. Islam in Sudan was quickly converted from its supposedly historic principles of decency that Sadiq al-Mahdi often spoke of into ideals that justify slavery and murder. One Dinka man asked, "What happened to the benevolence and peace of Islam that we always hear about? Could the Sudanese Islam be different from the rest of Islam?"[20] One can hardly fail to sympathize with the Dinka. They were a merry lot, but they are a people fighting for what they believe to be their birthright, their pride, and their survival, both physical and cultural. They have never given up because of the belief that the suffering they face during the resistance would not equal what they could experience under Arab domination.

Historical Factors

In 1994, Ahmad Sikainga wrote that "The contemporary history of the Bahr al-'Arab region [the Kiir River to the Africans] has been a panorama of raids and counter-raids, ethnic conflicts, and competition over water and pasture principally between the Dinka and Baggara Arabs."[21] Although there is much truth in this appraisal of Dinka-Baggara relationships, the assertion that their conflict is that of recurrent raiding and counterraiding is slightly misleading. What has happened over the past two decades could be more justly described as the government-assisted Baggara assault on the Dinka. As the Baggara are those in need of pasture south of the Kiir River—a Dinka territory—the Dinka have not had a reason to invade the northern Kiir River region. What the Dinka did was simply to attempt to stem the influx of Baggara herders and livestock into the grazing plains south of the Kiir River. Fearing overgrazing and depletion of wildlife resources and fisheries, the Dinka tried in the late 1970s to regulate and limit the Baggara influx. Any Dinka attack on the Baggara who happened to be grazing in the Dinka territory during this period was to avenge previous Baggara raids. Large Baggara cattle herds were commandeered in this manner without a Dinka raiding force ever setting foot in Baggara territory. Historically, especially in colonial times, the cross-border hostility was dealt with through government actions to restrain Baggara movements. The postcolonial governments, however, decided to use the border strife to their advantage by strengthening the Baggara position, to push them against the Dinka as a way to impose rule over them.

During the colonial period, environmental damage caused by over-grazing was avoided in areas along the borders by demarcating grazing territories between the Dinka and the Baggara Arab pastoralists. This was done by involving the traditional chiefs on both sides to negotiate new administrative borders between Bahr el-Ghazal, Darfur, and Kordofan Provinces in an attempt to resolve the border conflict and reach winter grazing, fishing, and hunting agreements. To enforce the resolution of the ethnic conflict, the British drew a line that ran through the middle of the Kiir River from the west to the east, demarcating pastoral and fishing borders as it had been before the British colonization of Sudan. Police patrols on both sides of the borders then maintained the peace between African and Arab ethnic groups on the borders. After Sudan's independence, however, the Arab and Muslim rulers in Khartoum viewed the border demarcation as a colonial design to keep the Arabs and Africans apart. The Arab officials were quick to change every policy set during colonial times regarding North-South relations. One of the significant changes they made was the abolition of border demarcations, giving the Baggara Arab pastoralists the freedom to cross the Kiir River to graze and water their livestock, and fish and hunt without regard for the environmental integrity of the grazing plains of the borderlands.[22] Dinka claims to the territory were dismissed as tribalism.

During the struggle for independence in the North, Southerners were aware of the possibility that they would fall under Arab domination when the colonial period ended, and to express this concern, they objected to the northern drive for independence in the 1940s and 1950s. They complained to the British authorities because various historical experiences in North-South relations prior to the British colonial period were extremely painful for the South, and were still fresh in the South's collective memory. Despite all the resistance against colonial labor and economic policies, especially in Bahr el-Ghazal, the British had won southern support for themselves by the abolition of slavery. They were also comparatively popular in the South for administering the two parts of the country as separate entities. Now that the independence was supported in the North, the South was reminded that as soon as the British left, there was nothing to prevent the North from reverting to its old ways. The South feared that the North might resume the practice of treating the South as a mere source of slaves, natural resources, and land to be taken.

When Sudan was about to become independent, South Sudanese had two main opinions about independence: either the South should become a separate state, or the whole country should remain under colonial rule

until such time as the South could prepare educationally and develop-
mentally to the same level as the North. These opinions were expressed in
various forums and in so many ways that today there is much confusion.
For example, historians now assert that the South had no concrete position over the issue of independence.[23] But careful examination of archival
material shows that South Sudanese were definitely opposed to independence if their fate was going to be left in the hands of the Arab North. In
1952, the chiefs of the Bari people of Equatoria made this statement to
G. W. Bell, a colonial governor, on his visit to Juba from Khartoum:

We have the following [to] put before you: (1) we are all Sudanese, and we do not
fully understand why the northern Sudanese are in hurry for self-government.
While we in the South are still far backward in civilization, we see no reason why
the northern Sudanese are so hurriedly in the self-government status. (2) The
northern Sudanese got education before us, this education was introduced to
Sudan by English government and even now the northern Sudanese are being
sent to the UK for higher studies while the South is still longing for it. (3) We want
education to be expanded first of all to southern Sudan to enable it to choose its
own future wisely, and if this is being pressed by the northern Sudanese, it is for
them and not for the South, and if this is approved by the English government,
we beg that a visit by a politician be carried out in southern Sudan to obtain a full
idea of the southern Sudanese. (4) A lame man cannot win a race with a man who
is not lame. A blind man does not know what is beauty in the world. If my elder
brother wants that our father should die, so that we may inherit the position of
our father, we should say that it is not time for our father to die because we are
still too young. We want the English people to carry out the administration of this
country until we shall be able to choose our right. We the Bari wish that you will
be on our side.[24]

This opinion is presently regarded in South Sudan as the sentiment of
the whole region regarding independence. The people of the South were
aware of the role that the colonial government had played both in keeping their region behind in terms of development in favor of the North,
and in creating the polity itself. Few South Sudanese can say that Sudan's
independence had a positive meaning for them.

One particular colonial policy, however, that caused South Sudanese
to have mixed feelings about the colonial administration was the Closed
Districts Ordinance. This policy, also known as the Southern Policy,
barred North Sudanese from entering or living in the South. Through
this action, the colonial government was able to speed up the abolition of
the slave trade and the northern Arab and Muslim encroachment in the
South. For these two reasons, the policy was applauded in the South.[25]
But at the same time, the policy kept the South from developing economically, and for this reason, South Sudanese were completely confused
about the British stand in the North-South conflict. South Sudanese dealt
with the colonial government from a distance and were unable to gauge

colonial intentions. Their immediate contact with colonial administration was through the linchpin of the colonial system, the district commissioner, who had very little influence on events regarding the future of the colonies. Southerners, therefore, did not know whose side the British were on. If the overwhelming discontent in the South following independence is anything to go by, one could safely assert that the South did not wish to remain in a united Sudan.[26] If they had their wish, the people of South Sudan would have liked the colonial government to maintain the closed districts policy while it promoted education and economic development in the South at the same rate as it did in the North.

Contrary to all that the South had hoped for, the British decided in favor of the North. In 1946, a decade before independence, this policy was reversed under the pressure of a growing Sudanese nationalist movement against colonialism in the North. Movement between the two regions was allowed. The Arab traders and Muslim missionaries were able to enter the South. The British then consolidated the polity of Sudan, forcing Southerners to be joined with the North.

When independence came in January 1956, the British transferred the administration to Northerners. Southerners had only insignificant roles in the newly "Sudanized" government. Northerners hurried to resume all the activities that the Southern Policy had interdicted. Arabic was established as the only official language of administration and education, more Muslim preachers flocked into the South, and northern merchants who also acted as missionaries poured in to exploit southern resources. Two Islamic missionary concepts prevailed. First, if Southerners were left alone, they would go on living as before, and that would mean living in the moral degradation of the unbeliever or the pagan. Second, the period of the Southern Policy had damaged North-South relationships and a quick effort to repair them was warranted. The way to do this was to integrate the South into a national polity via commercialization and commodification of the southern means of livelihood. Large numbers of Arabs, who were better educated under colonial rule, overwhelmed the region, monopolizing all the institutions in the South. The Arabs soon controlled the civil service, finance and banking, education, and the secret police. The South had no say in the formation and the shaping of the country's identity. From the privileged position inherited from the colonial administration, the North resumed everything the colonial government had attempted to inhibit. Efforts of Islamization, Arabicization, labor exploitation, and extraction of southern resources were the crux of the Khartoum governments' policies. The future of a nation was utterly diminished. Very little, if anything, went to the South in return. The South realized that the government had much more to take than to give.

The result was two devastating civil wars. The first war took place from

1955 to 1972; the second, which began in 1983 and is still going on, led to the revival of slavery and the slave trade. The slave trade this time erupted with intensity and violence that reminds us of all the horrors of the nineteenth-century slave raiding and trading that explorers like Samuel Baker wrote about. Since the recorded history of Sudan shows the presence of these factors throughout its history, one may ask why slavery occurred during some periods and not others. In other words, is history simply repeating itself or are the circumstances different this time around? Could it be that slavery has never ceased in Sudan, and that it existed at all times in different forms? The following chapters will address these questions.

Part I

The New Slavery in Sudan

A typical Dinka homestead in peaceful times. Cattle and plenty of farmland are the pillars of the Dinka economy.

After a Baggara raid, a Dinka homestead is destroyed and its inhabitants displaced. A child orphaned by the slave raiders sits in the middle of the ravaged compound.

Chapter One

The Revival of Slavery During the Civil War: Facts and Testimonies

The roots of Sudan's unresolved civil war have a long history, but the modern context relating to the current wave of slavery was set in times of alien intrusion, starting with Turco-Egyptian rule in the nineteenth century (1821–81) through Anglo-Egyptian colonial rule (1898–1956).[1] By providing an overview of the current Sudanese conflict, I will analyze the causes and consequences of the ongoing slave raiding. There is concrete evidence that slavery is not buried in the past, especially since one still finds today the conditions that allowed it to flourish in the nineteenth century. For example, those Dinka areas that have witnessed the resurgence of slavery since the early 1980s were the same areas that had formed the slavery zone in historical times. The present slave-catching communities of Darfur and Kordofan were part of the slave frontier in the nineteenth century. The same Arab groups currently engaged in slavery were slave raiders during both the Turkiyya and the Mahdiyya. Long after Sudan joined the world community in ratifying antislavery conventions and formulated legal provisions that prohibited slavery, the practice persisted among the slaving communities in the North, as its ideology has been coded into the Baggara Arabic language, folklore, daily humor, and poetry. South Sudanese continue to be referred to as *abeed* (slaves) by North Sudanese, whose privileged position today has much to do with their history as slave masters in the past. It is this long tradition of an ideology of dominance that Arab governments in Khartoum have always used to treat the South as a mere source of material resources, and its inhabitants as cheap laborers who can be useful only when they are stripped of their freedom. This long-standing racial/ethnic prejudice has partly prompted the current wave of slavery.

During the first civil war, which took place between the North and the South from 1955 to 1972, the Baggara did not play a significant role. They continued to use Dinka grazing plains and fishing waters. Hostilities between the two groups were occasional. The Baggara even carried on with their traditional barter trade with the Dinka as well as with the southern rebel forces, the Anyanya. There were also extended periods of peace established by the traditional chiefs of the two groups on the basis of mutual interests, especially between the Misseria and the Ngok Dinka. At times, the two groups engaged in social relations that involved interethnic marriages, especially between the Rezeigat and the Malwal Dinka. They also established mechanisms for defusing individual conflicts between subtribes, most notably the truces signed by the leaders of both sides. Many accords were reached during the 1960s and the 1970s, including the 1976 Babanusa accord between chief Deng Majok of the Ngok Dinka of Abyei and Nazir Babu Nimr of the Misseria and the 1976 accord reached in Safaha between the Rezeigat and the Malwal Dinka of Aweil, brokered by the then-commissioner of Bahr el-Ghazal, Isaiha Kulang Mabor, and Sudan's vice president, Abdel Majid Hamid Khalil. These agreements, although breached on many occasions by the Baggara, brought relative peace to the borderland between the Baggara and the Dinka for many years.

But when the second civil conflict broke out in 1983, the agreements disintegrated and Dinka-Baggara relations turned into almost irreconcilable hostilities. The hostilities were caused in part by the massive influx of Baggara pastoralists into Dinka and Ju-Luo territories to graze their livestock during the drought in Darfur and Kordofan. In addition, these pastoralists became hunters, killing small and big game in the nearby forests, and thereby provoking Dinka attempts to deny the Baggara access to their grazing areas and fishing zones. The Baggara started arriving in Dinka areas prepared to use military force to make their way south of the Kiir River if they met with resistance. Intense conflict ensued.

These hostilities would have remained sporadic and manageable, as they had been for many generations, had the government of Sudan not decided to manipulate them for its political designs as a cheap way to bring the South under control. The government tolerated the illegal acquisition of guns by the Arab pastoralists. The Baggara were often better armed than the Dinka because of their access to guns coming into Sudan from neighboring Chad, which was embroiled in its own civil war in the early 1980s. The war in Chad had serious security implications for western Sudan, but in the government's view, the benefits of destabilizing the Dinka far outweighed the security problems.[2] Some Baggara individuals were also known for enlisting in the army and then deserting with the arms. It was also a matter of common knowledge that many western Sudanese who retired from the armed forces were allowed to keep a number of guns for themselves, which they either sold to others in Darfur and Kordofan or gave to family members. Such arms are locally used for protection against cattle rustlers from other herding societies within the

North. By means of these arms, the Arab herders forced their way into the Dinka grazing lands. They also hunted game with impunity, and when the Dinka tried to stop them, the result was often a declaration of war on the Dinka.

These hostilities became more intense when the SPLA deployed forces in northern Bahr el-Ghazal, partly to restore the old colonial borders and partly to protect the Dinka people as well as the environment. The SPLA encountered Baggara Arab raiding forces in 1984–87 on the borders between Bahr el-Ghazal and southern Darfur and southern Kordofan. The SPLA defeated the Baggara Arab pastoralists and drove them away from the southern borders. The SPLA forces then turned to the escalation of the struggle against the Sudan army, following their victory over the Arab pastoralists and hunters. The SPLA forces established their military bases on the borders, extending guerrilla activities to non-Arab ethnic territories of the Nuba Mountains and Ingessana hills in southern Kordofan and southern Blue Nile, respectively.

Like Christian and non-Arab ethnic groups in South Sudan, the Nuba and the Ingessana people had also suffered from the oppressive and unjust rule of the Arabs in Sudan. Although their regions belonged to north Sudan, which was comparatively more developed than South Sudan, they had been as neglected in development as the South. When SPLA forces penetrated the Nuba Mountains and southern Blue Nile for recruitment and spread revolutionary feelings against the Arab and Muslim domination in Sudan, many young men and women from the Nuba and Ingessana joined the ranks of southern guerrilla fighters. Such unity among non-Arabs in Sudan, which had never happened before, sent a wave of fear through the Arab and Muslim rulers in Khartoum. In addition, the Khartoum governments traditionally relied on these non-Arab groups for army recruits under the command of Arab officers. During the second round of the civil war, the government found it difficult to recruit troops from the Nuba and the Ingessana ethnic groups. The Arab governments in Khartoum, therefore, turned to recruit most of their troops from Arab groups.

The Slave-Taking Armies and Their Mission

Two types of forces emerged out of this recruitment policy, and these were meant to be the "final solution"[3] to the "Southern Problem." The first type of force was the tribal militias called Murahileen.[4] The Arab rulers in Khartoum resorted to the Baggara in particular to form a militia force to carry out what amounted to ethnic cleansing against the Dinka and the Nuba. The government saw the militias as an opportunity to assert Arab and Muslim domination in Sudan, and the Baggara pastoralists and peasants viewed their militia forces as the only way to gain their economic goals in northern Bahr el-Ghazal, southern Kordofan, and southern Blue Nile. The militias executed a policy of raiding and looting, capturing slaves, and expelling others from their territories, and settling "pacified" Nuba and Ingessana lands by force. The plan of the militia, as the victims explained it, was not only to collect booty and slaves but also to destabilize Dinka areas. The desperate Dinka would then have to move into the North, where they would be subject to economic exploitation and enslavement.

The second and most insidious forces comprised part of the Sudanese army and were the Popular Defense Forces (PDF). These also included paramilitary tribal groups affiliated with the Sudanese army. Their work took many forms. They were primarily a jihadic force that sprang out of the growing politicization of Islam and Islamic militancy most associated with the government of National Islamic Front (NIF), which came to power on June 30, 1989. One writer described the PDF as follows: "They consisted of existing Arab militias, the infamous Murahileen, student and professional 'volunteers' who rushed to the call of the jihad and adults dragooned into six weeks of compulsory military training whose curriculum consisted of calisthenics and religious indoctrination."[5] Because of this, these forces have also been called Mujahideen, meaning holy warriors. They were supplied with weapons, some money, and army badges. They were also armed with a complete ideology the Islamists had introduced to indoctrinate, shape, and thereby control the Sudanese in all aspects of life. The force was intended to fight the SPLA on the basis that the latter was the enemy of Islam and the Arabs, and that one way to defeat the SPLA was to hit at its support base among the Dinka. The recruits were constantly instructed that their mission was not only to defend the homeland from the "infidels paid by the U.S. and the Zionist State" but also to extend their faith to unbelievers in the South and beyond.

The NIF's other mission was to guard the military trains between Babanusa and Wau, which run through Dinka territory. There were usually several trains going one behind the other carrying supplies and reinforcements to government garrison towns along the railway line up to Wau, the regional capital of Bahr el-Ghazal. To prevent the trains from being attacked or taken over by the SPLA, the government instructed the PDF to ride on them until the trains reached Dinka territory, after which they got off and moved on foot, forming a shield along the sides of the train. These trains moved at a walking speed. All three types of forces—the Murahileen, the Mujahideen/PDF, and the government of Sudan regular army—worked together, each assigned a particular role. The Baggara tribal militias "go on horseback forming an outer circle protecting the train, the army, and the other forces from possible SPLA attacks."[6] They move at an outer distance of approximately five miles but sometimes as far as sixteen miles away from the force on foot along the train. During their movement on horseback they pass through Dinka villages and cattle camps, which they attack, stealing cattle and taking slaves. They then return to the train with their booty, and as the train nears its destination, the horseback militia forces return back to the North as the trains enter Wau. To return to Babanusa, the PDF guards the train, and similar atrocities in Dinkaland recur.

My investigations indicate that the capture and movement of slaves to the North has been predominantly the work of the Murahileen. It has also been established that some of the regular soldiers and members of the other forces guarding the train have kidnapped women and children, whom they took to their barracks. Some of them have reportedly taken this human booty with them to their hometowns and villages when they went home on holidays or when they were transferred. Many children currently working as domestic servants in the towns and villages in northern Sudan were taken in this manner, under the pretext that they were being rescued from the ravages of the civil war in the South and were going to places of care rather than to enslavement. Some of them have been taken to Islamic schools in Khartoum to be trained as future Mujahideen to be used against their own people. Contrary to the stated goal of the army in establishing militias to boost its military situation, the government granted the soldiers free rein in the South to supplement their meager salaries with whatever loot they could come by.[7]

The Raids that Marked the Beginning of the Tragedy

The militias had been active since 1985 taking slaves from the Dinka. The first and most destructive attack on the Dinka communities of Aweil, Abyei, and Tuic occurred in February 1986. Jointly, the Rezeigat raided the Malwal Dinka of Aweil West County of the Bahr el-Ghazal region and the Misseria Humr raided the Abiem Dinka of Aweil East County. The Misseria Humr also attacked the Ngok Dinka of Abyei and Tuic during the same operations. During these violent attacks, many Dinka were killed, including the son of a Dinka paramount chief, Riiny Lual, in the village of Marial Baai. The Rezeigat and the Misseria Humr occupied a large area of Malwal Dinka for nearly two months. During this period, they conducted daily raiding and looting from their new bases within the Dinka territory, and some went back and forth between their homeland and the Dinka area to move their booty. They took two thousand women and children and thousands of cattle. The Dinka in the area were scattered, and large numbers were displaced to the North across the Kiir River into Baggaraland, where they hoped the government might protect them and provide them with shelter and food. The displaced also thought that their kin who had moved there in earlier years might help them. As will be shown later, they were soon disillusioned. Successive governments deliberately decided on a policy of exploitation of the displaced that amounted to slavery.[8] Other Dinka communities in the vicinity of the border with the Baggara withdrew from their villages and cattle camps and moved to Dinka areas farther south and east of the region. The Dinka of Abiem in Aweil East County, Abyei, and Tuic were also displaced in massive numbers as a result of Misseria Humr raiding. Large numbers of children and women were captured and driven off to be sold into slavery or disposed of once they were determined to be unfit for the tasks for which they were taken. People found unsuitable for slavery were left to linger until they were able to find money for bus fare to other northern cities like Khartoum. These individuals have become an important source of information on the conditions of those who remain in bondage.[9]

The second raid took place in January 1987. Baggara raids take place almost exclusively in the winter because it is the dry season in Sudan. During the autumn, the rivers overflow their banks, making it difficult for the horseback raiding bands to cross into South Sudan. Horses also suffer from constant exposure to water, mud, and mosquitoes. Due to the difficulties experienced by their horses during the wet season, the Murahileen attack the Dinka only between January and April. Occasionally, they have raided up until May if the rainy season is delayed. The January 1987 raid targeted the area of Gong Machar in Aweil West County. The raid continued through February, and the Rezeigat took away almost all the cattle that remained in the area, killed many people, and captured about a thousand children and women.[10] They took them across the Kiir River to "store"[11] them in the *zaribas*[12] (fenced enclosures normally used for cattle) while they conducted more raiding. After that, when the raiding bands were satisfied with their destruction and had accumulated enough booty, the captives were taken farther to such Baggara towns as ed-Da'ein and Abu Matariq, where they were distributed among the raiders and their families. The slave raids have taken place every year since 1985. In some years, multiple raids occurred in the same villages in one single dry season. For example, between January and April 1998, there were twenty-four raids in Aweil and Tuic Counties. There were approximately the same number of raids during the dry season of 1999.

By the time the second raid took place in 1987, the SPLA had increased its deployment of forces from the Tiger Battalion on the border areas of Aweil and southern Darfur under the command of George Kuac to protect Dinka civilians. The Baggara militias became aware that they could not do much damage to the forces of the SPLA, whom they were supposed to be fighting. In fact, they made a conscious decision to avoid

SPLA forces by all means and instead attack civilian villages. Since the SPLA force in the area at this time consisted of only 4,000 men, it was not possible for them to completely block the marauding forces of the Baggara. The SPLA spent the whole dry season of 1987 trying to flush out the militias, running from one area to another whenever news came in about a raid. It became so difficult to deny the Baggara forces access to northern Bahr el-Ghazal that the SPLA resorted to a tactic of allowing them to enter and then locking them inside the South to retrieve the abducted people and the looted cattle. In one incident, the Baggara learned of SPLA forces trying to block them from returning to the North. They withdrew into a thickly forested area about forty miles west of Dinkaland, but the SPLA penetrated the forest and attacked them and recouped most of the stolen cattle. Despite the defeat and numerous casualties, the Baggara had found raiding too lucrative to give up. There have been many incidents where the Baggara were defeated and experienced heavy losses, yet they have continued to return to the South.

With increasing SPLA ability to rebuff militia raids, the government army advised the Murahileen to use the town of Safaha inside the Southern Region's border as its base to quickly retreat to when cornered by the SPLA. At this base, the army would be able to provide the militia with needed supplies and reinforcements. There was a small 600-man-strong government army contingent in Safaha, and the thousands of Rezeigat armed men were only too happy to receive such a strong backing by the government of Sudan. Safaha became a strong militia and army base from which the assault on northern Bahr el-Ghazal was launched in 1987. The SPLA, however, continued to attack Safaha and retrieved stolen cattle and took over the town, killing two well-known army officers, Ahmed Musa and Omar Gadim, who were staunch supporters of the militia system. There were constant skirmishes, in which the Baggara were attacking the Dinka villages and withdrawing as fast as possible into pockets of forests before the SPLA could reach them. But the Rezeigat attacks became more and more successful in avoiding head-on clashes with the SPLA because they were guided by Dinka collaborators. Some Dinka reside among the Baggara and show the Baggara where SPLA positions, Dinka dry season cattle camps, and other population concentration areas are located. This is a puzzling phenomenon that cuts across cultures and historical periods and has occurred among blacks in the fight against the apartheid regime in South Africa, in the American West, where native Americans gave each other away, and during the Holocaust, where some Jews worked for the Nazis.[13] It is common knowledge that the Baggara often have difficulties with the terrain and the geography of the Dinka territory and with knowing about the SPLA positions, and benefit from the help of some Dinka.

The Acquisition of Slaves and the
Involvement of the Government of Sudan

The history of current slavery resembles the history of contact between Bahr el-Ghazal and alien intruders in the nineteenth and twentieth centuries. This contact, which began in the middle of nineteenth century, was characterized by violence. The contact began with the influx of ivory and slave traders, followed by the Turco-Egyptians, the Mahdists, and the Europeans, all of whom entered the province in pursuit of either colonial or Islamic interests.[14] When the slave traders first penetrated northern Bahr el-Ghazal, they tried to bring most of its territory under their domination in order to exploit its wealth of ivory and slaves. Firearms enabled the slave traders to impose their rule. The classic means by which slaves were acquired in historical times in Sudan was the *razzia* (Arabic, raid), most associated with Turco-Egyptian slave hunting (during the Turkiyya, 1821–81) and with the Mahdi's anti-Turk Islamic revolution (the Mahdiyya, 1881–98).[15] The Rezeigat and Misseria (Baggara) tribal militia attacks on the villages of northern Bahr el-Ghazal have become the principal means for the acquisition of slaves, and the violence involved is reminiscent of the earlier *razzia*. The current system was organized and sustained by a strategic interest shared between the government of Sudan and the Baggara—the government wants fighters to confront the SPLA and the Baggara want grazing lands and free laborers.

The planning and organization of the slave-raiding expeditions are evidence that the practice is not a mere "tribal feud over grazing areas and water sources," as the government of Sudan has claimed. The degree and time of planning depends on whether the force that is being put together is the Murahileen, that is, the tribal militias of the Baggara, or the Popular Defense Forces, the Mujahideen that guard the military trains. In the case of the tribal militia, before the raid is actually carried out, the slave-catching communities of the Baggara spend several weeks putting together the raiding force. Preparations begin with a message from the local authorities to the chiefs in some of the slaving communities that there will be free arms and some money offered to those who volunteer for the militia. They are also promised that they will keep whatever loot they will bring back from Dinkaland. The preparations also involve native administrators such as the *nazir*, the *umda*, and the sheikh,[16] the army, and the government officials who work in the slave-taking communities such as the police, the judges, and security officers. The Baggara also make an important electoral support base for the Umma Party of Sadiq al-Mahdi, and the party has therefore been involved in organizing the slave raids as well, at least during al-Mahdi's premiership in the 1980s.

The native administrators then make clan-based lists of all the people who are interested in the adventure. The lists enable them to collect taxes from the raiders' booty and to distribute the loot fairly. They also allow the government to keep track of the arms given away, for the government is at times unsure about the consequences of proliferating assault weapons to an undisciplined militia force. Recent interviews with South Sudanese returning from the North and with former slaves who were freed or who escaped have provided information on the planning of slave raids.

One informant was Ali, who was interviewed in Nyamlel (Aweil West) in the summer of 1999. He is half Dinka and half Baggara and has lived with the Dinka all his life. When a joint government army and militia force attacked and occupied Nyamlel for two weeks in 1998, Ali was captured and taken to the North along with 380 others. Because of his light complexion and other Baggara features, he was not enslaved. Instead he was released and told never to return to Dinkaland. Ali stayed in ed-Da'ein only to look for ways to sneak back to Bahr el-Ghazal. He eventually managed to travel to el-Fasher and got on a train that took him to el-Meiram. He then walked back to Nyamlel. His account, and information from SPLA local officials and other former slaves, explain the planning of a slave expedition as follows: "The Baggara usually form a slave-raid 'committee.' Each willing subtribal group brings its representative to participate in the committee. The representative mobilizes men and youth to join the raiding force. The committee determines the date of the raid. And the participants gather in a previously designated location that has water resources. The militia leaders, in collaboration with the *umdas* and sheikhs, would prepare food supplies for the raid. Then they would go to the *hukuuma* (the government) for weapons and ammunition. The government has to be informed about the departure of a raiding force to northern Bahr el-Ghazal so that reinforcements could be sent just in case the SPLA attacks them."

This structured system is strong evidence that the government has made slavery an important institution once again, just as it was more than a century ago in the same area involving the same peoples. The preparations involve plans for the journey south, the attack on Dinka villages, the destruction of homes, the burning of food stores, the looting of cattle, the killing of men who resist, and the abduction of children and women. Also of important consideration during the preparation phase is the journey back to the North, how to deal with a possible SPLA ambush, the division of the loot at some point along the way, the dispersion of the militia to their villages, and the scattering of the slaves. The distribution and scattering of slaves has to be done as quickly as possible so as to avoid accumulation of slaves in one place where they might be found and the practice exposed. Upon the return of the attackers, the slaving communities normally celebrate the successful and safe return of the militias. Bulls are slaughtered to mark the occasion. People sing, beat drums, and make joyous cries. A game of horse riding-skills is played.

In the case of the Popular Defense Forces, slave raiding is a corollary of a jihadic war against the SPLA. As mentioned earlier, their main task was to guard the train between Babanusa and Wau. It took weeks, sometimes months, to get the train ready in terms of supplies and men to take the trip to Wau. The forces were conscripted and given rudimentary training in operating the AK-47 assault rifles. They were inducted into the mentality of martyrdom in the name of Islam. A word was then sent to Baggara umdas in el-Meiram, Babanusa, and Muglad that the government was recruiting Muslim youth to escort the train south. The government paid a varying amount of money to the participating youth in addition to arms, which they kept after the train had reached its final destination. Once a Baggara subgroup or clan received the arms, these arms became the property of the group. The chiefs can collect the weapons at the end of the mission or keep the list of recipients to be called upon the next time the government makes another request. Because they went through Dinka territory, sometimes in collaboration with the Murahileen and the regular army, the paramilitary forces raided Dinka villages along the railway line. Slaves captured in the process of the train movement became the property of individual Mujahideen as payment for their venture. Although material reward was minimal for this group, compared to the Murahileen proper, they seemed to believe that the demolition of the SPLA, the suppression of southern calls for freedom, and possible extension of Islam was the ostensible reward climax of their endeavor.

In sum, the line between the slave-raiding armies of the different subtribal groups in Darfur and Kordofan, the PDF, and the Sudanese army was blurry, as far as slavery was concerned. Often the army undertook a joint operation with these militias to attack SPLA positions or villages suspected of sympathizing with the SPLA. One such operation was the 1998 occupation of Nyamlel mentioned above. It involved not only the collaboration of tribal militias and the Sudanese army, but also the top administration of ed-Da'ein Province. The commissioner of the province, the commander of the armed forces, the nazir and other local administrators were all involved in the organization of the raid, the thirteen-day occupation of the town, and the town's destruction. This occupation, which resulted in the taking of hundreds of slaves, was filmed and broadcast on an army program on Sudan national television. Although Nyamlel is not an SPLA military base, the broadcast portrayed the occupation force as a glorious army capturing a town from the rebels.

The following is an account of the occupation of Nyamlel in May 1998. It is a summary of many statements from the survivors of the raid as well as from escaped slaves. The Nyamlel occupation was a part of an offensive by the ruling National Islamic Front. The attackers were on foot, horseback and in armored vehicles. There were about twelve cars in all. They took cattle, goats, young women, and children. Houses were burned and people were thrown into the flames. Anyang Ngong, a young woman in her twenties, was among the captives. She was from a small village between Nyamlel and Marial Baai. She explained the whole ordeal in the following words:

They beat me and tore off my clothes. They tied the hands of small boys to the horses, and took us to Nyamlel. There, we had to stay at the old rest house.[17] We were guarded by security men belonging to the Popular Defense Forces [PDF]. The commander in charge of the force was named Jenet Hassan. Almost all the strong people in my village were captured and taken to Nyamlel. But there were so many people from other villages. It was difficult to know how many were there. The town, Nyamlel, was crammed with abducted people. Most people were made naked. Women and men were all in one place. The Arabs have no decency. We were kept in Nyamlel for many days. People were being beaten, yelled at, and nobody could move anywhere. Nobody ate anything throughout the whole time that we were kept in Nyamlel. At night, some soldiers would take women from the crowd, take them to the river, and [sleep] with them. Sometimes their commander would stop them from doing this. The commissioner of ed-Da'ein [Abdelrahman Kidder] arrived in Nyamlel with more cars, I think it was three days after the occupation. We were [filmed] and we felt so bad about this, for we were naked. When the time came that they were leaving, it became immediately evident that they were taking us with them. They filled up the cars with people, but there were still more people left, including me. We were divided into small groups. Many people were made to carry things on their heads. Some carried jerry cans of water, others carried bullets, and others carried the Arabs' food supplies. And worst of all, we had to walk in the hot sun, without food. After several days on foot, we reached the Kiir River and we stayed there for two days. Then we were divided up again and put in lorries. People were packed so tightly into these cars. Children were crushed and I thought they were going to die before the last destination. Anybody who complained about being sat upon was beaten. One woman complained that someone had sat on her child, and the guards beat her and her child was thrown off the moving vehicle. We were first taken to Abu Matariq and we spent one night there. Then we went to ed-Da'ein. We were taken to the Commissioner's house for distribution. The most fit were given to various Arabs. The weak ones were sent to the displaced persons' camps. I was taken to Khor Omer camp. At the camp I found most of the people were from my area of Malwal Dinka. There were those from Nyamlel, Gok Machar, Marial Baai, Manyiel, and Achana [all in Aweil West County]. The camp was guarded by security men from the government. We were told that the governor of southern Darfur and the commissioner of ed-Da'ein would send some people to help us, to give us food. There was an organization run by Arabs called Da'wa Islamiyya.[18] This organization is in charge of the camp. The staff of Da'wa Islamiyya are security agents, but they masquerade as relief workers so that foreign aid workers do not know their actual role. Disguised as aid workers these Arabs watch the activities of expatriate workers and report them to the government. The Da'wa Islamiyya people do not allow displaced Southerners to talk with foreigners. They pay money for captured children, and they bring these children to the camp saying that they were orphans. Children kidnapped from the South and brought to the camp with their mothers were ripped from their mothers and taken to the *khalwa* [Koranic school]. The women were taken to farms to work in the field, or to homes to cook, clean, and wash clothes. Some women told us that others were killed when they tried to escape. I was made to be a cook for Arab guests who came to visit the people of Da'wa Islamiyya. Some relief food was brought to the camp by different aid agencies, but the security men would take most of it and sell in town. People were treated very badly in the camp. For example, one time, a woman from the UN came to give us ration cards, and we were beaten later for talking to her. People were also often beaten for visiting and mingling with each other. Every now and then, the commissioner of ed-Da'ein and other big officials would come to the camp to hold big meetings with all the captives. During one of these visits we were told to not resist conversion to Islam or any requests to be "married" to the Arabs. They told us that we could avoid falling in sin by accepting an Arab for a "man." I had to get out of that place. I told myself that it would be better to die running away than be forced into Islam and marriage to another man. One day, when I was sent to the market, I just started walking past the market and I escaped. When I arrived back here, I found that we had lost everything, but I am much better off free and poor than to eat and be abused.

Other incidents in which the army's central role in the resurrection of slavery have been reported by several sources including Dinka labor migrants returning from the North, former slaves, and those who were once stationed in Baggara towns as part of the Sudanese army. One strong case implicating the army was the report of many witnesses that a military helicopter was frequently seen landing in Safaha between January and March 1987. This helicopter reportedly brought ammunition for the militias that raided Aweil West throughout the season. Also reported were cases where supplies were transported by trucks from the Baggara town of Abu Matariq to Safaha, where both the army and the militias were stationed. In more recent times, the Murahileen have been seen carrying radio communication systems and heavy artillery, indicating that these tribal militias were no longer traditional cattle rustlers, as claimed by the government, but rather a well-organized force involving the army. Yet the government of Sudan continued to deny the organized role of the army in slave taking, and dismissed slave capturing simply as "usual tribal abduction."

The linchpin of the government's attempts to deflect world attention from slavery and other human rights issues in Sudan were the statements of Hassan al-Turabi, the staunch Islamist and chief ideologue of the ruling National Islamic Front. He has been seen as the real power in the government since a military coup brought al-Bashir to power in 1989. In response to reports accusing the Sudanese government of complicity in slavery, al-Turabi has constantly suggested that he found it impossible for slavery to exist in Sudan. He has repeatedly cited Sudanese law, which prohibits slavery, saying that "these allegations were no more than a malicious propaganda initiated by the United States because of the American hate for the Islamic cultural project in Sudan."[19] Judging by the scant attention the world has given to the suffering of South Sudanese, one must say that the efforts of al-Turabi may have been successful in persuading the world community that slavery is not practiced in Sudan. But while he is right about the fact that the Sudanese constitution prohibits slavery and other forms of exploitation, what matters in Sudan is the daily application of the constitution. South Sudanese, due to their race or religion, do not enjoy the protection provided by the constitution, since the laws are applied preferentially.

Another means by which slaves are acquired is through the exploitation of the displaced from the South. A large proportion of the thousands of slaves and hundreds of thousands of the displaced South Sudanese driven into the North by the war in the 1980s were Dinka from northern Bahr el-Ghazal. During the 1987 and 1988 war- and drought-provoked famines in northern Bahr el-Ghazal, which prompted the Dinka to flee to the North through Baggara territory, the Arabs exploited this tragedy to acquire Dinka children by means of deceitful contracts. These were bogus arrangements that the Baggara designed to take children from their poverty-stricken parents and guardians under the pretext that they were being offered light labor roles in exchange for food for the family and money for transport. Some estimates put the number of children acquired in this manner at over 2,000.[20]

Testimonies of Former Slaves

Many people in Bahr el-Ghazal who witnessed the slave raids and survived them or who escaped from slavery were interviewed between 1997 and 1999. The stories they narrated about their experiences during the raiding and the march to the North provide a tragic account of the slave raids' impact on the Dinka. The attacks, the burning of villages, the chasing and killing, the looting and destruction of property, and the capture of slaves were described as the most horrific events they had ever witnessed.

Garang Deng Akot is now twenty years old. He had been purchased from his original captor by a cattle-herding and small-scale agricultural Baggara family. He spent eight years working for them grazing cattle and moving with the entire family during the dry season as far as the Sudanese border with Chad. Realizing that his chances of escaping were limited or nonexistent, Garang pretended to have accepted his status as a slave. Within one year after he was acquired, he had earned the trust of his master so much that he was occasionally allowed to take the cattle to grazing areas far away from the village on his own. In March 1999 he found himself alone, and with the help of the changing vegetation, he noticed that he seemed close to the Dinka area, so he decided to escape. He drove the entire herd all day and all night until he found himself in Dinka territory after three days. He informed the Dinka that he had come from across the Kiir River with over two hundred head of Baggara cattle. He told the Dinka that he expected the Arabs to come looking for him and that a raiding party visit might be imminent. He was right. A force of horseback tribesmen had been looking for him all over the grazing plains and stumbled upon tracks which led them to the escaped slave. When they arrived, they clashed with SPLA forces and were beaten off. The young man now lives a comfortable life in Dinka territory after many years of captivity and enslavement. He described the raid in which he was captured as follows:

I do not recall what I was doing at that moment but I remember hearing the sound of gunfire, people running in different directions, and shouting: "Murahileen have come, Murahileen have come." Within a short while, the Arabs on horseback were all upon our village of Majak Baai. The people scattered everywhere. All my immediate family ran toward the railway line, but I ran with my other relatives in the direction of the SPLA base. We were running as fast as we could, but the Arabs on their horses were behind us and shooting at us. They killed several people including two of my uncles, Akot Akot and Garang Akot. I stopped for a moment to look at them and the sight of the bullet passing through someone's head terrified me so much that I ran really fast. But the horses were racing toward me from all directions and I stopped. One of them stopped his horse, got down and came toward me. When I tried to run in the other direction he caught me from behind. The other Arabs arrived and one of them tied my hands with a rope. I was lifted on top of a horse and my legs were tied to the lower end of the saddle. Then they took me through my village, which was set on fire, to meet with the rest of the Arabs who were loading the looted grain on the back of the horses. They tied the rest of the captives to the horses. Then we were marched toward the Kiir River to a location where they had left their livestock. This location, the name of which I cannot recall, had been established as the base from which to stage attacks on various Dinka villages. When we got to this location, there were at least fifty camels carrying ammunition and other supplies. The different groups that had gone to attack the villages regrouped here. It was a good place for them since it had a well for water and the Dinka inhabitants had deserted it long before because of the raids. From here we were taken to Baggara villages north of the Kiir River. The man who caught me, whose name I later came to know as Muhammad Abeid, one day told me that I had to go live with another family and I should regard them as my family from now on. For the next several years, I had no idea about the fate of my family and I was just working for Ibrahim Kheir and his family. He told me that I was to become his son, but I was not treated like a son. I was so upset and sometimes when they treated me like a dog, I wished I had a gun to kill all of them, but I knew in my heart that I would be free some day.[21]

A local official in Tuic County, Thongjang Awaak, also recalled a horrific incident he had witnessed during the raid in Wunrok in May 1997. An Arab man on horseback had caught a young girl and a calf, tied both of them to the back of the horse and dragged them while being pursued by the SPLA. It was difficult for the horse to speed away, but the man would not let go of the girl and the calf. The SPLA soldiers were unable to shoot at him for fear of striking the girl. He was blocked off from rejoining the rest of the raiding force. His horse was struck from the side and he was eventually killed and the girl was rescued, but the determination shown by this man to kidnap and loot at all cost baffled the SPLA.

Some of the most gruesome stories told by slaves who escaped or gained their freedom in the North and returned to Bahr el-Ghazal have also provided an understanding of the nature of slave life and are the strongest evidence of enslavement. The stories of maltreatment involve hard labor such as herding livestock, agricultural work, domestic service, and even sexual and reproductive coercion. They also include verbal abuse. This exploitation of the slaves occurs extensively throughout the country. The provinces of southern Darfur and western Kordofan, in both rural and urban areas, are the principal areas of widespread enslavement, but other urban centers of slavery include el-Fasher, Nyala, Muglad, and Khartoum.

There are numerous accounts, provided by slaves who have run away and by human rights reports, about the way slaves in northern Sudan are treated. These accounts are reminiscent of the way slaves have always been exploited throughout history. The Dinka girls and women held by Arab families become sexual slaves as well as household domestics and farm workers. Consider the following accounts.

When they raided our village, captured me with my children, and marched us to ed-Da'ein, we were quickly distributed to the relatives of the man who had captured us, and I ended up with another man who had several adult sons. I was told of my daily chores right away and I was made to do everything from milking the cows to cleaning the house, cooking, and washing. What I was not told was that I was to become somebody's woman. I was not even given to one specific man. Whenever any of them wanted to be with me, he just showed up at night and there was nothing I could do. When I expressed my objection to their advances toward me, I was threatened with gruesome violence. I was told I could have my breast cut off, my children could be killed, or I could die. One man was coming to me so often that I think his wives became outraged. After some time, when I did not know anymore what had happened to my children, I found a way to escape so I could search for them. Now I have heard from others that two of them are in el-Fasher.[22]

Another woman made the following observations: "During cultivation times, the grown-up Dinka is sent to the farm to cut the weeds from morn-

ing to evening, and if a Rizeigi has a son, he will not send him for er-
rands anymore. Only the Dinka child is sent to do these things. Old Dinka
women are made to work in the house and on the farm. They wash the
dishes and do many household chores. These enslaved Dinkas are given
nothing. If they are barefoot they remain so. The Dinka girls who grow
up there are made their 'women' and the virgin girl who is brought to you
is also made a 'woman.' "[23]

A young woman I interviewed in Turalei in the summer of 1999 provided further illustration. When Teresa Amou Arou was abducted from
Bulal in Abyei County at age twelve, her father was killed and her captor, Bakhur Ahmed from the Misseria clan of Awlad Kamil, took her to
Chiteb, a Misseria town between Abyei and Muglad, and her name was
changed to Zahra. When she was in captivity, she worked on the farm and
went to fetch water. Every morning, she took the millet and pounded it in
the mortar or ground it on the grinding stone. She went to fetch firewood
and cooked the meals every day. She also worked in cutting *karkade* or hibiscus, drying it and packing it in bags.[24] Fearing that she might escape,
her captors would not let her go far without the company of her master's
boys. She slept on plastic sheeting in a makeshift hut where she cooked
the meals for the family. Her master and his sons abused her sexually,
and fearing further physical harm she obeyed their commands. One season, the family moved close to the Kiir River with their cattle, and there,
Teresa found an opportunity to escape in 1998. She now lives in Turalei at
a boarding school set up by the local community for all the former slave
children and supported by the diocese of el-Obeid.[25]

Sexual exploitation could be regarded as another form of slavery that
may have gone unexposed under the pretext of ordinary domestic service. At present, such practices against southern slave women is common.
In many instances, the slave master not only demands sexual services
from his female slaves, which causes an outrage among his wives,[26] but
also instructs his female slaves to give sexual lessons to his young sons.
This is a practice long reported by Dinka women who worked as domestic
servants in Arab Muslim households throughout the 1960s and 1970s.[27]
The explanation given by some of the women who have experienced this
was that, given the Islamic strict separation between boys and girls in public places and between households, the fathers have often found themselves in a dilemma: they want to instill proper Islamic behavior in their
sons, such as maintaining a distance from women, while they worry that
their sons might become homosexuals if they have no exposure to members of the opposite sex. It is granted that slave women have no right to
object to any sexual advances by the master and his sons. But the female
slaves of modern-day Sudan are forced not only to tolerate sexual advances by the masters' sons, but also to arouse the boy's sexual urges

toward females. Many testimonies provided by freed slave women attest to a myriad of sexual abuses by slaveholders and their young sons. One young former slave woman, whom I interviewed in Warawar in the summer of 1998, said that given the horrible atrocities that the Arabs have often committed during the raiding, she could expect sexual coercion. "But to be [gang-raped] by an old man and his children is just not human. Where else on earth do members of one family force themselves on one woman. Even cattle know their sexual boundaries." [28]

Sexual abuse of slaves is not limited to women. Many boys have told adult slaves, with a great sense of humiliation, that they were raped repeatedly by their masters. Upon returning home, one escaped slave boy from Gok Machar was said to have told his mother that the forced sexual contact between him and his captor had happened so often that he had sometimes wondered whether this was a natural occurrence for all men, and he almost believed it was so. When I heard of this boy and went to interview him in 1998, he told me that his only indication that this was unnatural was the pain he had experienced, the dreadful anticipation of his master's visit upon him night after night, and the shame he had felt the day following the molestation. He said that he could not stand the look on people's faces when he considered the possibility that other people knew what this man was doing to him. He still recalled the faces of other boys and girls still in captivity, and the possibility of similar things happening to them made him nauseous.

Another escaped slave provided a further insight about slave experiences. Angong Chan, a mother of three children, was captured in Warawar market during the May 1998 joint PDF-Murahileen attack. She was captured together with her children. The slaver Babikr Salah took her to al-Nuhud and renamed her Zeinab. He was from the Misseria branch that had once reached a truce with the Dinka and he had worked at the Warawar market. He sold two of Angong's children. Her other children were kept away from her because the slaver thought she would not run away leaving her children behind. In the interview, Angong said:

There was no point for me to be there since I was not with my children anyway. Every day, I was made to carry big water plastic containers from the borehole five to seven times a day. I brought water for bathing, washing cloths, and cooking. I would bathe the children. When they wanted me to go to the borehole after dark a male adult had to go with me as a guard. I was also grinding and pounding grain and cooking. For the whole time that I was staying in al-Nuhud, I was made to do all kinds of chores including things that were not traditionally women's activities in Dinkaland such as going with the cattle to distant pastures.[29]

Some of the most horrifying examples of abuse came from freed slaves, those who managed to escape, those who were allowed to leave by their compassionate masters, or those whose freedom was purchased through the various slave redemption programs.[30]

One woman, Abuk Akot Akot, was captured during a raid on Marial Baai in February 1999 and was taken to the North. She had a very young child left behind, and she kept begging her captors to release her for the sake of her infant. The captors thought that she definitely acted like someone who was going to attempt to escape, and they chained her arms together at the elbow. Because her arms were tied so hard, there was no circulation and they started to rot/Yet she was determined to run away. She said, "I refused to be a slave of the Arabs. I was ready to do anything to prompt them to kill me instead, and I told myself that running away would either get me killed or get me home. I managed to escape only to come and find out that my husband had been killed during the raid and my property was totally destroyed, and my arm is rotting. . . . I will not accept to be disabled by this. I will do everything possible to regain the use of my arms. It is the only thing I have got now."[31]

Garang Anei, a forty-year-old man from Aweil West, had lived in western Sudan before returning to Dinkaland. He had witnessed the slave trade and explained that "Many Dinka women who were abducted by the Rezeigat were 'married' by Arab men for years and after giving birth to a child or two, the women were told to go back to Dinkaland. Some went back upon the realization that the children they had given birth to were not going to be their children anyway, and others decided that they could not leave their children behind. They now linger in limbo. No children, no going home, no job, so they sometimes accept enslavement."[32]

Another former slave whose freedom was obtained by his relatives provided an insight to the lives of slaves. Arop Ajing is a fifteen-year-old boy from the Tuic Dinka who was captured while grazing south of the Kiir River near Abyei. He had been a slave in a place called Chiteb in Kordofan. His aunt who was living in the North purchased his freedom. He explained why many slaves got killed in the North instead of being used as laborers. "When the Misseria hear that some Arabs have been killed by the Dinka in the South, revenge is carried out against the slaves. After all, it is easy to go back to Dinkaland for more during the next raid. The life of a Dinka person does not count for much in the eyes of the Baggara."[33]

The southern captives were sold and distributed, and those unfit for anything were left to die or to live in limbo between Arab villages, for they did not know their way back or were too weak to travel back to the South without adequate food. Some of them managed to make their way into one of the northern cities after a year or two. By this time their captors would have forgotten that their arrival in Khartoum, for example, might expose the practice of slavery to expatriates or human rights activists residing in the capital city. Many of the stories of slave's lives became known in Khartoum through the narratives of the few captives who were deemed unfit for enslavement and were let go. Other narratives came from children who were very young at the time of capture and were taken to Islamic schools in the northern cities, and managed to sneak out of such schools.

One concern that investigators of slavery in Sudan have had is whether or not slave markets exist and what the going rate for slaves might be. Officially the slave trade is illegal, but the only effect of this has been that the slaves are not sold openly in any known markets. For fear of being found, the slavers have made sure that there were no slave markets that lasted for more than a few hours following the arrival of slaves from the South. The longest the slaves were allowed to stay in the *zariba* was one day. Only in rare cases did the newly abducted slaves congregate in one place for as long as two days.

But what the slavers fear is not legal redress from the government, but rather outsiders learning about their activities and reporting them to the world. What became the tradition with the slave raids was that after the slave raiding forces had crossed the Kiir River on their way back to the North and felt safe in their territory, they would stop at some established points of rendezvous on the outskirts of the towns. Here, the slavers would divide the slaves and the booty taken among themselves, thus scattering the slaves in the slaving communities, leaving behind very little trace of their activities. The division of the loot is based on several factors: the taxes to be given leaders back home; the individual firepower of those carrying weapons; and the decision that each militiaman may keep the slaves he individually captured. Any remaining slaves that could not be sold quickly were sometimes offered as presents to local government officials. These local officials have quickly learned the language of the central government of categorically denying the existence of slavery in Sudan while becoming prime movers of this practice. One escaped slave boy from the Tuic Dinka, Achuil Deng, testified to this point.

The government does not question the Arabs about their activities against Southerners. In Angreb near Muglad, one Dinka slave boy held by somebody called Khojli Muhamed one day refused to herd cattle. He told the Arab that he wanted to leave and the Arab took him to the police station of Angreb. The police officer in charge ordered the boy to return to work and warned him against attempting to run away. He told him, "if you try to escape they will kill you." The police are usually Misseria, and they help their brothers to retain their slaves. An Arab killing a Dinka slave boy is very easy. If he suspects that you are being disloyal you get a bullet without warning.[34]

The absence of slave markets has been held by the government of Sudan as the main argument against allegations of slavery, and has discouraged researchers trying to investigate reports of slavery. In addition, the area that has become the slavery zone is extremely difficult to enter. Educated South Sudanese and foreigners are heavily scrutinized in the area. Because foreign aid is needed, however, expatriate relief workers are allowed to go to the area but are not permitted to make any contacts with displaced Southerners without permission of government intelligence. The international nongovernmental organizations (NGOs) operating in the transitional zone are required to employ only the local staff recommended by the government, so the NGO local staff are actually security agents who monitor the movement of expatriate staff. Expatriate aid workers cannot visit the camps unless they are with local staff. Any displaced persons seeking to talk to the foreign aid workers during visits are secretly taken and tortured. Displaced Southerners in the North, therefore, are unable to report their experiences to foreign investigators.

Children and women slaves, however, who had changed hands from one slaver to another, some many times over, related terrifying experiences with the slave trade. They talked about transactions involving the sale of children by their original abductors soon after they arrived in Baggaraland. These former slave children have also talked about the forced Islamization of slave children by their masters. As my interviews with former slave children indicate, almost every child or woman who has been captured and sold into slavery was subsequently forcibly converted to Islam. Conversion to Islam means being forced to drop their Dinka names, learn some Koranic verses, pray five times a day, fast during the month of Ramadan, and undergo certain North Sudanese rituals including female genital mutilation. I spoke with one woman who had been "circumcised" and three men whose wives had also been forced to undergo the procedure. Those resisting these practices were beaten, verbally rebuked, or killed.

In response to reports of slavery, the Sudan government has angrily issued statements denying that slavery and slave trade are practiced in northern Sudan. In fact, the government of Sadiq el-Mahdi reacted to such reports by arresting Ushari Mahmud and Suleiman Baldo, the two university professors who were the first and only northern Sudanese to report on slavery in writing. They were accused of wrongfully defaming the nation. Various Khartoum governments have since obstructed efforts by human rights groups and aid agencies to investigate these reports. In response to the large number of western media reports, especially from the United States, the National Islamic Front government has claimed over the years that what is happening in southern Kordofan and Darfur is a part of the traditional tribal abduction that has been practiced by the Dinka and Baggara throughout history. It also said that the constitution of the country prohibits slavery and that if it were taking place, the culprits would have been punished. More recently the government responded to the increasing evidence of slavery by forming a committee to investigate the issue. But what is certain is that there is already evidence implicating the government in the practice of slavery, and that the committee is merely a part of a campaign to disinform the world. Otherwise, the government should have invited journalists, members of nongovernmental organizations, diplomats, human rights groups, and members of the civil society including Southerners to participate in such an investigation in order to end these accusations, if they are false, once and for all.

Slavery in the Shadow of the Civil War: Problems in the Study of Sudanese Slavery

Studies of human rights in Sudan since 1983 have blamed the resurgence of slavery in Sudan solely on the civil war. From raids in 1986 to the famine of 1998 in Bahr el-Ghazal, an estimated two million died in the South and four million were displaced.[1] These deaths, unprecedented in number in Africa and the most since World War II, were caused by both famines and genocidal practices of the government of Sudan. As a result the UN and nongovernmental organizations (NGOs) established Operation Life-line Sudan (OLS) in 1989 to provide humanitarian assistance.

This war has blighted the central as well as the regional economies, and has caused the political landscape between North and South to crumble. The war caused more destruction in each succeeding year than the year before, most of rural Sudan became increasingly impoverished, and political animosities were enlarged by the Sudanese regime's plans to fight the war using militia forces. The conflict became beneficial to some,[2] and competition intensified among the Sudanese army, regime-sponsored militias, and northern merchants. Slavery and slave trade have provided some of the benefits to these groups.

Large numbers of publications have appeared on the subject of slavery being one of the unavoidable indignities of the civil war. The slave raiding by war-sponsored militias has resulted in the greatest forced movement of people of Dinka sections of Malwal, Tuic, and Ngok from their districts to seek refuge in other districts to the south or through the "enemy" lines into northern Sudan. The routes of slave raiding and the patterns of destruction and displacement are all too familiar. But the fate of the captives has been the subject of a controversy similar to the debate in nineteenth-century America on what constitutes slavery and what should be done about the slaves. The controversy that has arisen today over Sudan's slavery is between those who doubt the credibility of the reports out of Sudan that chattel slavery could ever exist anywhere at the beginning of twenty-first century, and those who believe that the racial,

A group of children, most of whom were freed from slavery, are housed at a camp in Panlit, near Turalei in Tuic County. The Catholic diocese provides school materials for them and the community donates food for their sustenance.

economic, and cultural complexity of Sudanese society could easily cause a resurgence of slavery. Major newspapers and television networks in the United States have covered this issue since 1995. Schoolchildren in the United States who have learned about how "cheap" human beings are in Sudan collected their allowances to enable Christian groups and anti-slavery activists to purchase the freedom of Dinka slaves from the Arabs of northern Sudan.

Virtually no scholarly research and writing has been conducted on this facet of the war. Although the number of Dinka children and women who have fallen and continue to fall victim to the Muslim northern Sudanese raiders and slave dealers can never be determined, there is no doubt that the traffic was carried on and that it continues today on a large scale. People of South Sudan started reporting the reemergence of slavery in 1983. The English language newspaper the *Sudan Times*, edited by Bona Malwal and published in Khartoum, carried articles about slavery from 1986 to 1988. Ushari Mahmud and Suleiman Baldo also reported on slavery in a booklet in 1987.[3] In 1995, a report issued by Human Rights Watch described the conditions of displaced children in northern cities.[4] So during the period from 1983 to 1994, much became known about the traffic across the Kiir River. After 1995, the international community became aware when Christian organizations from the Western world started a campaign to purchase the freedom of slave children and women and return them to their villages in the South.

An estimated 50,000 South Sudanese have changed hands in Darfur and Kordofan since 1983. Some of them had been slaves for as little as two weeks before they escaped, but many more remain in bondage. Slightly more than 5 percent of all the slaves were taken to Sudan's borders with Chad to be enslaved to work with grazing animals, with the rest accounted for by the proliferating demand for free farm labor and domestic service in southern Darfur and western Kordofan. The need by the Baggara to clear brush from the vast territories of this region, and the curtailment by war of the traditional migrant farm labor from Bahr el-Ghazal and Abyei in the 1980s transformed Dinka-Baggara relations into a major area of conflict. As the traditional relationships between southern migrant labor and Baggara farm owners ceased due to war or decreased wages, slavery and continued raiding for slaves assumed an even greater importance as a source of labor. Vast territories belonging to Aweil and Ngok Dinka have been so frequently raided by Arab slavers that whole villages have been either depopulated by a combination of raiding and war-induced famines, or have been deserted. The population of Gok Machar, for example, has been tremendously reduced since 1985.

Southern Darfur and western Kordofan also took advantage of the war and met their labor needs through other war-related means. The population of Dinka, finding itself engulfed by war and famines, the worst famines being those of 1988 and 1998, has moved into the North in the hope of finding jobs or relief. The raids and war-provoked displacement of the Dinka are intertwined. Dinka territories were losing their population in uncounted thousands through displacement to the North. The following statement by a Dinka man who had been in Darfur before returning to Dinkaland illustrates some of the calculations made by Southerners seeking livelihoods in the North: "One had to choose between a possibility of starving here in the South or trying your luck in the North to seek employment. Others who have relatives already living in the North decided to join them hoping [the relatives] might assist them with jobs or access to relief. There is a Dinka saying, *cath ee nguot*—traveling is female. It means that it is better to move about—because you might run into something better—than to sit still."

Many more Dinka among those displaced by the famine of 1988 had moved to the North thinking that the government would come to their rescue. But displaced Southerners in the North do not get any government assistance as a result of efforts to undermine their citizenship. Southerners lack political status in the North for three main reasons.

First, they are not Muslims in a country where elite politics is increasingly Islamicized and secularism is declining.[5] Second, they are excluded from public services as a result of widespread and virulent racial prejudice. Indeed, one report to a humanitarian donor agency noted that the Arab-African racial hierarchy that exists in Northern Sudan is in some ways comparable with that of apartheid in South Africa.[6] Third, displaced Southerners lack legal redress against the gross exploitation because they have been readily stigmatized as supporters of the rebellion in the South and therefore undeserving of the protection of the law.

Two thousand of these South Sudanese became victims of an attack by the Baggara in what became known as the ed-Da'ein massacre. One afternoon in 1987, fearing that they were going to be attacked by the Baggara, displaced Dinka congregated in front of a police station in the town of ed-Da'ein, requesting and hoping for police protection. The police told them to spend the night in railroad freight cars. But the Arabs armed themselves and attacked the Dinka who were packed into the railroad cars, and the police watched as thousands of them were being slaughtered and burned inside the rail wagons.[7]

The massive movement of Dinka into the North, and the government's tolerance of incidents like this, have given the Baggara the chance to explain away the labor exploitation and justify slavery. People who were put to work as slaves could easily be called wage laborers if anyone asked. Displacement of so many also means that they do not have to be paid, or paid enough, because there are so many of them that they are "disposable," to use Kevin Bales's term.[8] Displacement is also used either to deny the existence of slavery or to justify it. In other words, the slaveholder congratulates himself for providing a job and feeding these "people who would otherwise starve to death,"[9] as some slave masters have said. Former slaves reported that whenever they complained to their masters about being overworked or underfed, the Arab slaver often replied by saying that he has done them a favor by enslaving and feeding them. In an effort to deny that slavery exists, many government officials, including the Sudanese ambassador to the UN, Mahdi Ibrahim, have issued rhetorical statements over the years. For example, in 1998 Ibrahim asked why anyone in Sudan would want slaves when there are thousands of displaced people living in the North who would work for minimum wage. This was a veiled admission that indeed displaced South Sudanese were treated as slaves in the North, because what the ambassador described is in fact what happens to the displaced. When the displaced are denied relief services or forced to convert to Islam in exchange for food aid, many of them have resorted to taking menial jobs in Arab households, construction, or cleaning where they have been underpaid and treated like slaves in every way.

International Corporate Interests in Sudan and Slavery

Foreign governments directly or indirectly supporting Sudan's war on the South have incessantly argued that all of Sudan's problems, including the mounting death toll, can be addressed and resolved only when the war has stopped. For example, in November 1999, the UN Human Rights Special Rapporteur Leonardo Franco reported that the exploitation of Sudan's vast oil reserves has "seriously compounded and exacerbated" the atrocities committed in the country's sixteen-year-old civil war. Franco's report found that the Sudanese government has forcibly removed thousands of civilians from the region in order to protect the oil-producing areas, burning several villages to the ground and using bombers and artillery to clear a 100-kilometer area around the southern oil fields. Since the oil exploitation is being implemented in partnership between Talisman Energy of Canada and the government of Sudan, the Canadian government came under heavy criticism, especially from the U.S. Congress and State Department, for allowing Talisman to continue its 25 percent partnership with Sudan in the Greater Nile Oil Project.[10] In response to this criticism, Canadian Foreign Affairs Minister Lloyd Axworthy declared, "We have to provide sufficient [corroboration]. I really want to see the hard evidence. We will weigh that evidence according to our own judgment."[11] While Canada and other countries with similar views were trying to find the "hard evidence," nothing was halting the raiding, killing, and enslavement of the South Sudanese.

The Canadian government indeed went forward with an investigation of whether or not Talisman's ventures in Sudan were promoting the war and fueling slave raids. A government envoy, John Harker, was dispatched to Sudan to probe into the controversial Sudan operations of Talisman and the claims that human rights abuses are indirectly assisted by the company. Harker came back with evidence that Canada was inadvertently promoting the suffering of South Sudanese. He also reported on the government of Sudan's complicity in the slave trade. The report says that the government of Sudan uses Talisman's airfield to stage attacks on the SPLA in the South and the Nuba Mountains. Harker recommended that his government find a mechanism to ensure that Talisman is cognizant of the rights of South Sudan to oil revenues. He recommended that the substantial revenues and royalties paid to the government of Sudan by Talisman be held in a trust fund until the country's civil war ends to ensure that the South benefits from oil revenues.[12]

But Axworthy ignored the report and declared that Talisman would be encouraged to work toward peace instead. He claimed that the main problem was the war, which could not be resolved by forcing Talisman to vacate Sudan. He said that the suffering of the people of South Sudan could be mitigated only when the war ended. Since the oil started flowing in 1999, many more international giants in the field of oil prospecting (such as China and Malaysia) have moved into Sudan to stake their shares against pleas from human rights organizations and at the expense of the human security of South Sudanese. More militia raids, the government army's aerial bombing, and infantry launching artillery on civilian villages have all intensified in western Upper Nile since late 1999. Massive death and displacement have since occurred on an unparalleled scale. This is clearly a case of history repeating itself. The international claims that the war has to stop before anyone can do anything about forced movements of population and slavery were the same words used in response to the Nazi atrocities in Europe in World War II, and to the pleas by the people of Rwanda on the eve of genocide in 1994.

Sudan's Slavery as Seen by Researchers

In light of this, it is puzzling that the Arab capture and enslavement of Southerners has been almost written off by academics, politicians, and UN agencies as exclusively war-provoked, and that its full scale can be grasped only after the war has ended. It has been relegated to an obscure corner like many other crimes against humanity that plague Africa. It has also been treated as only a recent phenomenon, an understanding of which can only be achieved when the whole North-South conflict has been resolved and disentangled. This reemergence of slavery, it is worth noting, is not unique in the relative neglect it has suffered at the hands of researchers and international agencies. There has been a similar tendency to gloss over the role of the government of Sudan in the extensive raiding and the arming of the militias.

The reluctance of researchers, especially Western researchers, to probe into these two aspects of the Sudanese new forms of slavery may be the result of skepticism about the existence of the practice. Some have suggested that horrifying atrocities against Southerners are taking place, but that it is difficult to document this as slavery. For humanitarian agencies, especially the UN Commission on Human Rights, the reticence could be explained in terms of fear of offending the government of a UN member state, which might prompt it to expel expatriate workers, and ignorance of Baggara-Dinka relations which make the practice of slavery possible. UN agencies flatly refused to call the situation in Sudan slavery. The exception was Special Rapporteur Gaspar Biro, who reported extensively on slavery during his many trips to Sudan from 1994 to 1998.

Overall, academics shy away from calling it slavery. One possible explanation for the fear of using the word *slavery* is that it has a racial basis. Therefore, to make Sudanese slavery the object of close scrutiny might be construed by the government and by the Arab countries as an artful attempt by Southerners and other antigovernment critics to draw attention to their political cause. Researchers fear that the issue of slavery is being inflated as a way to draw attention to southern suffering in general. The government of Khartoum has repeatedly accused some African countries and the United States of trying to disunite Sudan, and of using accusations of slavery to stir up anti-Sudan sentiment around the world. The government views it as a campaign to defame Sudan, Muslims, and Arabs. This has already caused investigators to fear that the government of Sudan might accuse them of trying to deflect attention from the role that Western countries have played in magnifying the North-South divide.

"We Do Not Have Slaves Here, We Just Have Dinka"

This reasoning is somewhat far-fetched in regard to the new forms of slavery in Sudan. Southerners, to be sure, do have numerous grievances, which they could use as campaign tools against the government. Such things as religious persecution, economic exploitation, cultural extinction, and physical abuse of southern civilians in the North, could all be viable reasons to generate international attention to the southern cause. Southerners did not pick slavery as a weapon of propaganda. The institution of slavery in Sudan has a long history and has been an established feature of life long before the modern Sudanese polity ever existed, and long before the Dinka had any reason to desire shaming northern Arabs and Muslims. The northern claims that the question of slavery is now used to defame Arabs and Muslims are oblivious to the fact that slavery was known to have existed on the Dinka-Baggara border since the sixteenth century.[13] Slavery, however, as practiced now by the Baggara and other northern Muslims is far more complicated and nuanced than the notion of slaves as mere beasts of burden. Southern slaves in Darfur and Kordofan are, to a great extent, despised, verbally humiliated, physically abused, and are constantly told that they are "just *jengai*"[14] and can expect only a harsh treatment commensurate with their subhuman status. Any opportunities of winning the sympathy of any family member, which might give the slave a chance to think that he or she is an equal, are discouraged by the head of the family who owns them.

Dinka slaves, whether enslaved by Baggara or sold on to other northern Sudanese, by and large do not enjoy any civic or personal rights. The Baggara, in particular, easily ignore such rights. Furthermore, they even fight among themselves when one Baggara person treats a slave with some degree of mercy. Some slave owners get annoyed at others who are kind to their slaves, because they may fear that their slaves might demand similar treatment. The owners believe that when slaves see other slaves being allowed certain personal rights, then they might protest their status. In parts of the Baggara territory, slavery bears strong similarities to the institution of slavery in the American South in the nineteenth century. What is different, however, is the incessant denial by the Baggara that what they practice is slavery. Some slave owners are said to have told their slaves that they were like slaves because the Dinka should be and are slaves by nature, but not because of the amount of work they are forced to do. "We do not have slaves here, we just have Dinka. They work for us in order to escape poverty in their homeland," one slave owner stated. "We have never known of slavery. . . . Even more, our raids have nothing to do with slavery; we want cattle, we want the Dinka grazing land; if they stand in the way, capturing is the way to frighten them," another Arab reportedly boasted.

Inevitably, there are harsher aspects of exploitative labor relations between Northerners and Southerners that amount to slavery. It is not uncommon to find slaves in Darfur and Kordofan working alongside wage laborers. Some Dinka clans had moved into the Baggara territory and allied themselves with the Arabs. Members of these Dinka groups living in Arab territory can be hired as wage laborers. Their function is to translate between the slaves and masters, to perform as foremen, and to be put forth as willing workers by the Arab landowner if he is confronted about slavery. It is therefore not uncommon to find that most of the Baggara raids into Dinkaland are guided by members of these Dinka clans who have knowledge of Dinka territory, patterns of cattle movements, and population centers. Growing numbers of aid workers who have traveled in Darfur since 1985 have reported witnessing or hearing about two famous Dinka, Akech Ja'ali and Abdel Bagi Ayii, the former of whom has become a Rezeigi. They reportedly meted out the inhuman treatment that was commonly inflicted on Dinka captives by the Arabs.

The Dinka like Akech Ja'ali and Abdel Bagi Ayii are not strangers to the slave trade. They are known to have provided valuable information to the Baggara, which proved instrumental in manipulating national and international opinion about the institution of slavery. "The Dinka in the Baggara territory," observed one aid consultant, "are being perpetually exploited by the Arabs through the help of other Dinka, who act as interpreters or mediators between Arabs and the displaced Dinka."[15] Back in Bahr el-Ghazal, where these two men come from, people speak of them as the ultimate traitors. Abdel Bagi Ayii has tried to justify his behavior in the following words: "If you cannot defeat your enemy, join his ranks and work against him from within. Since our people were moving into the North anyway, somebody had to be here to help them find means of subsistence in the foreign land. But for the Arabs to accept a Dinka as genuinely pro-Arab, one has to act like a total sell-out. This is why whenever I recommend people for jobs, relief, or release from bondage, the Arabs respect me and they respond accordingly."[16]

When I visited Warawar in the summers of 1998 and 1999, people spoke about Abdel Bagi with mixed sentiments. Some said that his presence in the North is good for the Dinka because he keeps track of Baggara movements and on the eve of a raid, he sends one of his men to inform the Dinka so that preparations can be made against the raiding force. Other people, although acknowledging his positive role, said that his residence with the Arabs has blurred the whole image of the southern struggle because the Arabs use him as an example of Arab-African coexistence, even though he is only a figurehead. One Dinka man asked me during my 1998 trip to Bahr el-Ghazal if I was familiar with the Arab adage, "kill a slave by using another slave." When I responded that I was, he told me that Abdel Bagi had proven the Arabs right. "He is the symbol of mental slavery, and the pinnacle of Arab exploitation of Southerners," a Dinka chief from Warawar asserted.

In early times, such exploitation did not involve large numbers of Dinka. The victims were often labor migrants who had the options of seeking jobs elsewhere, or simply returning home. There was a real shortage of laborers. This was to change with the present war and the massive raiding. There is considerable evidence that the current traffic in slaves, notably from the Dinka of Aweil, is more the consequence of Baggara need for Dinka grazing areas and government arms, than the direct result of the war itself or of some Dinka aiding the Baggara. There were three factors that were fundamental to the slave trade. First was the pressures that the government was putting on the rural Dinka population as a strategy to undermine SPLA support in the Dinka area. Second, the Baggara need for grazing coupled with the government's effort to resurrect and fuel the historical Dinka-Baggara animosity had increased the raids against the Dinka. The Baggara launched devastating raids into Bahr el-Ghazal, and with the sophisticated arms provided by the government, they annihilated whole villages, killing the men and seizing the women, children, and cattle. Third, the movement of the Dinka to the North to escape the raids and in the hope of finding food and the means of subsistence there exacerbated animosity. The Baggara felt that the migration of thousands of Dinka into their area would increase interethnic competition over resources and services, and the result was general strife and an increased anti-Dinka sentiment within Baggaraland (Collins, 1992).[17]

Calling attention to the war could not have the effect, even if intended, of obscuring from view the northern Arab drive to question the African identity of the South through slavery. Both are inextricably linked to one another. The war implicates the government, which uses the slave raids as a weapon against the southern insurgency; similarly, the traditional loathing for the Dinka among the Baggara means that in exchange for the government offers of arms, they showed no scruples when they enslaved the Dinka.

By contrast, focusing on the Baggara want for Dinka slaves would do very little to portray the government war machine in a bad light. Except on certain occasions, as when the commander of the government of Sudan army, the commissioner in ed-Da'ein, and a large force joined with the Baggara militia to raid and take over Nyamlel in 1998, the usual Baggara raids had little to do with the war. The Baggara raids and the enslavement of Dinka are carried out within fairly well-established networks and belief systems, which were oriented mainly toward supplying cheap labor for Darfur and Kordofan and to assert Baggara presence in Dinka grazing valleys of the Kiir River. There was also the Baggara desire for Dinka boys to indoctrinate into their warrior ranks in order to create more effective Baggara raids in the future. These three factors have always provided the impetus for the slave raids and the slave trade in Sudan. The raiding for the purpose of clearing grazing areas, stealing cattle, and abducting Dinka boys and girls has been the norm in the Baggara-Dinka relationship, especially in the 1970s, although the scale has often been small, only to be increased many times by the current civil war.[18]

Government Rhetoric on Slavery

Beginning in 1986, three years into the war, the successive governments of Sudan, including the Transitional Military Council, the era of Sadiq al-Mahdi's premiership, and the National Islamic Front (NIF), used their influence on the Baggara to turn the long-existing system of raiding into a weapon of war. This objective, which merged in the 1990s with the narrow northern ambitious drive to ram "national unity" down the throat of South Sudan, prompted the various Khartoum governments to increase the magnitude of slave raiding in South Sudan. The NIF manipulation of the policy of proxy war, often backed by the use of the Popular Defense Forces, contributed much to getting the Baggara chiefs in Darfur and Kordofan to step up their assault on the Dinka and increase the magnitude of destruction in Dinka territories. As shall be seen, it took the NIF government the better part of the 1990s to turn what it terms "tribal abductions" into a large-scale system of subjugation of an entire people into slavery. The Khartoum governments have pursued this campaign of terror mostly in the Dinka regions because of the assumption that the SPLA is a Dinka organization. Other areas have also been the targets of government attacks, including the Nuba Mountains of central Sudan, the Equatoria region where aerial bombardment is a daily practice, and western Upper Nile, especially areas adjacent to the oil fields where oil production started in September 1999. The policy regarding the oil area is to clear the region of its civilian population to eliminate any threats the southern people might pose to oil production.

The governments of Khartoum practiced this policy under the guise of suppressing the rebellion in the South, and did it so far into the South and so fast that it meshed with the larger northern strategy of ensuring northern religious and cultural primacy over the entire country. Supporting slavery and the trading of Dinka slaves was subordinated to the political imperative of unifying the country at the expense of the southern religious, cultural, and political identity and freedom.

The government rhetoric on slavery, when pressured about the human rights situation, explains slavery as part of "usual" tribal raiding. The government has tried to portray the Baggara-Dinka conflict as one in which there is raiding and counterraiding, a situation the war has made difficult for any government to control. But it has claimed that such raiding between two hostile "tribes" is beyond its control, and that if slavery occurs, it should not be blamed on the government, nor can the government be expected to subdue it. The role of these government policies has for the most part been glossed over in publications addressing the issue of slavery, which portray Baggara raids and slavery as mere corollaries of the actual confrontation between the SPLA and the government of Sudan. In other words, many researchers and humanitarian organizations have bought the government's line that slavery is not its responsibility. Indeed, the government has gone as far as suggesting that the government-sponsored militia force, which accompanies the train to Wau and captures slaves along the way, acts in response to the SPLA threats to the train. "If the SPLA can refrain from attacking the train, we will have no reason to use the militia," the late vice president, Zubeir Muhammad Salah, stated in 1995.[19]

In light of this, writing about the role of the war in Sudan's slavery could scarcely evoke bad memories about a northern Arab tie to this practice. The practice of slavery in Sudan was essentially a northern Arab enterprise. Northerners, whether the Turks in Khartoum and Cairo, the Mahdists, or the successive governments that followed independence from Britain in 1956, hunted for slaves in the vast southern territory or acquired them from displaced persons' camps to sell in the discreet markets of northern Sudan. The existence of slavery in northern Sudan and, by implication, slave raiding found sanction in the Sudanese interpretation of the Koran and laws deriving from it. As Robert Collins writes, the present NIF government was not the first in Sudan to drum for a holy war. "In 1881, Muhammad Ahmad al-Mahdi proclaimed his determination to rid the Sudan of corruption, specifically the theological corruption of Islam by the Turks. . . . The message of the Mahdi to return Islam to its purity came from the reforming zeal and example of the Muslim holy men in Arabia."[20] Many rural people in the North, including the Baggara, absorbed the message. The appeal for a new religious orthodoxy by the NIF, an orthodoxy that desires to build a theocratic and territorial state with no ethnic frontiers or geographic boundaries, is a replication of the nineteenth-century religious reform, and the Baggara have enthusiastically responded to it again this time around. In both periods, the government tried to justify the slave-raiding expeditions to the Islamic militants as an Islamizing mission. These militants are told that this is a mission to purify the Sudanese society according to the wishes of their ancestors, who had not been able to achieve it due to forces of corruption that have evolved out of religious and ethnic heterogeneity. In sum, the focus on the SPLA–government of Sudan war as the only way to understand how and why slavery happens falls short of providing a comprehensive view of current slavery.

Looking at the History of Slavery in Sudan

The limited interest shown in addressing the historical, racial, and ideological foundations of the present slave trade has to be explained by reasons other than the lack of an obvious connection. In part, this lack of interest in relating slavery to the history of Sudan's own coming to existence as a country has to do with the very nature of the subject, whose origins are obscured by the complexity of the racial origins of the country. The relationship of most South Sudanese with the foreigners from the North was based on the military-commercial nexus of the *zariba* system. The exploitative system introduced by the Turco-Egyptian regime into non-Muslim Sudan gave the idea to the later Sudanese Muslims. Although all Sudanese subjects were exposed to exploitation of one sort or another, those who were Muslims had the option of collaborating with their colonial masters and benefiting from the new commercial opportunities that the Turkiyya opened up in the South. The Turkiyya just wanted slaves from Sudan, but the nomad Arabs, as Muslims, did not have to give their own people to the government when called upon to pay their tribute in slaves.[21] They went on government-sponsored slave raids to take slaves from the non-Muslim areas along the Kiir River. It was these slave raids during the Turkiyya that later took on a jihadic nature during the Mahdist state, when South Sudanese were classed as infidels or unbelievers. The time frame of the northern enslavement of Southerners, unlike that of most other African regions (which only lasted for approximately three hundred years, from the sixteenth through the nineteenth centuries), has been going on ever since the early civilizations of the Upper Nile valley were overturned by marauders from the North (eighth to twelfth centuries). The enslavement of the Nilotic people of Sudan, moreover, involved many types of governments that have ruled the region, a good number of which have used slavery as the backbone of their economies and military strength.[22]

The history of slavery in this distant past is complex and more intricate than the map of the current wave of slavery. The latter brings forth only a short list of people involved in slavery such as Sadiq al-Mahdi's elected government of the 1980s, and the NIF government. But the former conjures up the names of Muhammad Ali, Zubeir Pasha, the Mahdi, Khalifa Abdallahi, and the Ansar of the Mahdi, to mention but a few, whose authority, wealth, and status were built upon the ill-gotten gains of the slave trade.[23] These are familiar people who have ruled Sudan and whose roles in the enslavement of the Nilotic people are still remembered through the writings of Western historians. The injustices of the past and the continuing burden of their legacy are manifested in the current slavery. They may have faded from the memory of the Nilotic people themselves but the recurrence of these practices in the same manner keeps them alive in peoples' myths and stories. The people involved have been the same in the eyes of Southerners, the direction where the raiders came from has always been the same, and the destruction has always been horrifying. They have all invoked holy jihad in different ways and under different names. What seems to be different with each attacker is the reason for their aggression. The government now does it for the sole purpose of suppressing dissent and homogenizing the country. The raiders accept the government's call for jihad because of their political and economic calculations. And the slave buyers prefer slaves coming from the South for the moral comfort that they find in enslaving non-Muslims and non-Arabs rather than having to enslave coreligionists.

Very few stories and myths of the Nilotic people of Sudan concern the Turco-Egyptian or the Mahdist slave-raiding expeditions. That these various governments practiced slavery and the slave trade would scarcely arouse the indignation of Nilotic people today if these practices had ended then. Such practices would have been relegated to the pages of history had they been stopped by modern governments, and treated as deplorable periods, which should not be repeated in the history of a nation searching for an identity shared by all.

Understanding the reality of the current slave trade becomes far less complicated for researchers when their focus is the war as the single cause. It is easier to blame it on the war because the connection is quite obvious. But to establish a connection between current slavery and the past practices requires more careful examination of the evidence, and many researchers have opted for the short cut, and settled for the notion that the civil war in Sudan explains all the current practices of slavery. Nevertheless, reports by human rights activists, NGO workers, UN Special Rapporteurs, and official documents of the SPLA and testimonies of former slaves provide indications of the nature of the trade and numbers of Dinka abducted and taken to slave markets in northern Sudan. Reports by human rights agencies such as the widely respected Human Rights Watch, the UN Special Rapporteurs for the Commission on Human Rights in Sudan, Gaspar Biro and Leonardo Franco, have heightened international attention and infuriated and saddened many people around the world. These reports offer detailed accounts of the slave abductions and the mournful experiences of the Dinka slaves in Darfur, Kordofan, and as far north as Khartoum. These reports say that slavery had historically been a feature of ethnic rivalry in Sudan, but that the war has revived and increased the practice. In more recent times, Christian organizations from the Western world have added more reports to the volume of documentary evidence. Their writings painted a clearer picture of the workings of this practice and provided indications of its scale.

The Lack of Documentary Evidence on Slavery

Other factors of a more methodological nature have discouraged researchers from inquiring into the historical connections between nineteenth-century slavery and the current slavery and slave trade. Foremost among these is the lack of concrete documentary evidence that the current wave of slavery is built upon the same foundations as in the past. It is difficult for outsiders to argue about race and religion as the foundations of Sudanese slavery because the racial lines are not that clear-cut for a Western researcher. It is also argued that "The Turco-Egyptian regime in the Sudan was neither theocratic nor self-consciously based on the principles of religion. . . . Turco-Egyptian slave-raiding expeditions were not jihads."[24] Although this indicates that slave raiding into South Sudan dates back to the nineteenth century, there is a general resistance among academics to attribute the persistence of slavery in Sudan to racial and religious factors that made it possible in the past. The little that is known about the relationship between the slave trade during the Mahdiyya, for example, and the current forms of slavery, comes from the official communication between the North Sudanese and the British colonial officials regarding slavery. When one compares these documents to what the current slave takers say, one finds definite similarities, but for the researcher to do the comparison, one needs to have a clear perception of the racial, religious, and ideological foundations of the Sudanese society. With few exceptions, most researchers, although well-intentioned, do not believe in this approach because they do not realize that race and religion are factors in the formation of Sudanese slavery. Instead, they have focused on the obvious: without the war, there would be no slavery in Sudan. The approach taken in this study is that war is a mere trigger and an amplifier of a system well established in the history of Sudan since it came into existence as a nation-state.

Baggara traders who believe in maintaining good relations with the Nilotic peoples, and who have established discreet truces with the Dinka so that they can have a trading network, are an important source of information about Baggara intentions regarding slave raids. They report that race, religion, culture, and history of contact between Dinka and Baggara, in which the Baggara assume their superior position, are all invoked in Darfur and Kordofan as a way to justify the slave-raiding expeditions. This means that even without the war, the Baggara could still be pushed by their hostile climate to use their assumed cultural primacy to attack the Dinka. The accounts provided by individual Baggara and by some Dinka who switch sides from time to time provide useful information as well. However, these facts are not always unbiased and are necessarily limited in coverage. One has to use them with extreme caution. What records that may come from the officials about why the Baggara insist on slave raids, about the numbers of slaves in bondage and on their conditions, are fragmented and may be unreliable. Documents issued by the Baggara radicals explaining their hostility toward the Dinka, and reports by relief officials from Darfur and Kordofan, which provide the basis for some of the estimates of the volume of the practice in the area, are incomplete. They have also been criticized as only reflecting an antigovernment stance, of magnifying the scale of slavery in order to arouse and justify a stronger local and international pressure on the government as the force behind slave taking.

As for the sources within South Sudan, the problems are no less formidable. As a nation at war, the South simply does not have a system of keeping track of slaves taken, slaves redeemed or escaped, or a general description of what the situation is like for the slaves in the North. There are no written accounts describing the condition of villages following the raid, what people do to rebuild their lives, or any estimates of what the people have lost. In Turalei, Mayen Abun, Nyamlel, Warawar, and Marial Baai, some of the Dinka towns where slaves are captured or where most of the redeemed slaves are returned, no records are kept of former slaves. The redemption program has been criticized for having no conception of what happens to the children and women who are rescued from bondage and returned to the villages that had been ransacked. This criticism is amplified by the lack of records on the freed slaves, how their families treat them, whether they indeed have families to go back to, and whether they are still exposed to a possibility of being recaptured.

As for the northern slave takers, most are not really aiming for huge profits to be made from the sale of Dinka boys and girls. The traders use their human commodity as favors to family, friends, and government officials. Up until 1999, the number of persons each slave taker retains after the distribution of the human war booty ranged from three to six and rarely exceeded ten per slave raider. In fact, many Baggara raiders are said to not care much for slaves, and they dispose of their captives upon arrival in Baggaraland. Therefore, there are many Baggara who have never participated in the slave-raiding expeditions, but operate as brokers to convert the war captives into slaves, although none is of the order of those who were involved in nineteenth-century Nilotic slavery. The brokers sell their human merchandise at scattered points throughout western Sudan, and sometimes as far north as Khartoum. Since this trade is done so discreetly, and is kept to the minimal level in order to avoid exposure, the evidence for it is very difficult to obtain. Much like during the early years of the Anglo-Egyptian rule in Sudan when slavery was made illegal but the officials of the colonial government were tolerant of slavery, the present situation in Sudan is that nobody knows who among the Baggara is a slaveholder and who is not. Slave owners simply deny that southern children working for them are slaves, and without the government's unequivocal stance against the practice, charges of slave taking cannot be brought to bear. Until such time the central government and its local organs in Baggaraland genuinely decide to stamp it out and allow neutral investigators to examine the situation, no one will ever be able to find the real culprits.

Whatever inclination some of these traders may have to maintain records of their transactions are curtailed by the fear that the government may punish such documentation of slavery. The government of course fears that the word might get around and foreign journalists and other expatriates may catch wind of it. Therefore, with the support from the Save the Children Fund (UK) and from UNICEF, the government—which continues to deny the existence of slavery—agreed in May 1999 to establish what it called the Committee for the Eradication of Abduction of Women and Children under the auspices of the Ministry of Justice. The function of this committee has been the training of local people in tracing, retrieving, and reunifying "abductees" with their families. The establishment of this committee allows the government to masquerade as genuinely working to end slave raiding. It has also caused some slave traders who have no access to the "inside story" to think that the government is truly against slavery. The result is that only very few slave traders have made even verbal remarks about their illicit business. The written word is almost forbidden and it is scarcely used. Thus, lack of records has caused researchers to turn away from describing the horrific situation of the southern war captives in the North as slavery. Many researchers and aid workers have followed suit with the government rhetoric of calling slaves many names but slaves. The government refers to slave raids as "tribal abductions," the victims are described as "abductees," the children are labeled as "orphans" and then sold into slavery, and such international organizations as UNICEF have been duped into condoning the government's policy and language.

Another factor contributing to the lack of documentary evidence is the inability of the victims of this great human tragedy to write down their own experiences and observation. Since the raids take place in rural areas, most of the victims have been either illiterate or too young at the time of capture. Because South Sudan has been neglected in the field of education by all the governments that have ruled the country, the Dinka areas especially have more than 90 percent illiteracy rates. The situation was exacerbated by the current war, which has caused schools to shut down since 1983. Most, if not all the information on Dinka slavery came from interviews with former slaves, officials in the South, and the wounded or the old that survived the raids. They described the events leading to capture and the march to the North through rough terrain. They provided graphic accounts about many of those who died along the long journey. They painted the scene during the distribution of the human war booty within the North, and finally, the conditions they were forced to live under in northern Muslim households, the agricultural fields, or while grazing cattle under the vigilant eyes of the Arab masters.

How, then, can one reconstruct a story that conveys an unbiased picture of the Sudan's slavery and how the slaves fared in the northern environment that is utterly foreign to them? How does one do this without inviting criticism if there is no written testimony from the culprit and the victims of this inhuman practice? How does one produce an accurate and professional work under the burden of inadequate knowledge of a practice that stretches back for centuries?

Of necessity, anyone investigating the Sudan's current slavery and its roots in history must make use of firsthand information that is suspect. These are the accounts of aid agencies and UN officials whose precarious status in Sudan forces them to seek neutrality at the expense of describing the real situation. One also uses information provided by the government acting as an apologist for a system from which it has gained political and military ground. The opposing information to the above is that which is furnished by SPLA officials, Western journalists, church organizations that are sympathetic with the South, and antislavery groups.[25] Their accounts, despite their commitment to the well-being of southern slaves, have been criticized, especially by UNICEF, as biased and self-serving, and it has been claimed that their activities are aggravating the situation by pouring foreign currencies into an area ridden with poverty.[26]

Writers who have borrowed excessively from the government's rhetoric about the civil war and "ancient tribal animosities" being the cause of current slavery have done so on the basis of an alleged lack of firsthand information, and have therefore fostered a distorted view, a caricature of the truth. Others, as a reaction against such blurring of reality, proceed by reconstructing the experience of the slaves through interpreting the testimonies of the few that have escaped or been redeemed. In this regard, however, it is worth noting that the actual experiences of the slaves may vary on the basis of slaveholders, the area where they were enslaved, and the demeanor of the slaves during their bondage. Others have focused on the war and famine as the causes of slavery, to the extent of almost accusing the Dinka of selling their children when faced with circumstances of desperation.[27] Yet, more have even suggested a possibility that the SPLA may be staging the whole thing as a way to provoke western intervention.[28] Lack of reliable information has caused some writers and policymakers to treat the subject as a mere intellectual exercise, thereby stripping it of its human dimensions.

Because the raiding and enslavement of the Nilotic people are being obscured in the shadow of the conflict, much about the northern Baggara culture that has driven slavery for centuries remains unknown. The focus on war and famine as the only causes of slavery leaves the researcher without the fervor to explore the long and important history of Dinka-Baggara strife that has driven slavery. Not surprisingly, there are not many studies that reveal the trail of the present forms of slavery into historical times. We know that raiding and abduction of Southerners by the Baggara has never stopped since the Sudan polity was created, but there are no baseline figures of the actual number of Dinka or Nuer that have been taken and absorbed into the Baggara populace through enslavement. Nor do we have records of why or how it was carried out and maintained. Despite the fact that all observers attest to the activities of the slave traders, few have attempted to estimate the total number of South Sudanese sent into slavery in the North.[29] The historian from Aweil Dinka, the late Damazo Dut Majak, who was an authority on alien encroachment in Bahr el-Ghazal, argued that tens of thousands of Dinka were taken from the region into various forms of exploitation. These included forced reproduction of children for the Baggara, resulting in large number of Baggara who are part Dinka by blood and remain fully Baggara by culture. This concurs with Collins's assertion that "the low reproductive rate of the Baggara, especially, was an important dynamic for them to seize the more fertile Dinka women and their children . . ."[30] This system, Majak observed, existed throughout the years of subsequent alien rule in Sudan until our day.[31]

According to Ahmad Sikainga, a northern Sudanese historian with extensive research experience and knowledge of relations between Bahr el-Ghazal and Darfur, the relationship between Northerners and the people of Bahr el-Ghazal has always been that of masters and servants. Even the ordinary northern traders known as the Jallaba used to rely on the people of western Bahr el-Ghazal for porters and builders of *zaribas* in the nineteenth century. The Jallaba had often facilitated the slave raids as a mechanism to force the local people to settle around the Northerners' *zaribas* where they were not able to grow much of their own food and therefore were forced to work for the Jallaba.[32] The present practice by both the Baggara and the government of creating havoc in the South so that as many people as possible are forced to flee their homes is a bizarre recrudescence, if not continuance, of the old system.

The Majak thesis about the "continuous strife" between Dinka and Baggara and the Baggara's constant interest in taking Dinka children and women, is part of a widespread oral tradition in Bahr el-Ghazal, especially among the Aweil Dinka. It is repeated in standard oral transmission of the history and culture of the Malwal Dinka. But there are few, if any, records documenting it, and supporters of the thesis could easily be criticized as biased since most writers on the topic who are critical of the government come from the area. Recent reports, for example, have argued that the intensification of Baggara raiding on the Dinka has more to do with the current war than with an insatiable Baggara appetite for Dinka slaves that dates back centuries. These recent writers argue that only after the drought became more serious in western Sudan, especially in the late 1970s and early 1980s, did the Baggara intensify their slave taking. Even then, it is argued, the raiding was more likely about grazing areas and free government arms than about taking slaves. The taking of slaves, it is argued, was only a means of terrifying the Dinka into vacating their homeland. Destabilizing the Dinka is what the government wants for political and military purposes, and it is what the Baggara want for economic and survival purposes.

Carrying this critique even further are journalists, who condemn Southerners' assertions that the current wave of slavery and the slave trade had begun with the first contacts between all the foreigners from the North and the Nilotics, and that the practice has never stopped since. These writers contend that to the extent that there is slavery going on now, it is a mere consequence of the war. In line with this assertion, one writer, although in not so categorical terms, states that "the PDF militia specialize in bloody raids against southern civilians, and in some areas they have helped reintroduce that old staple of North-South relations

in Sudan: slavery."[33] Contrary to all the oral tradition and some historical writing, this statement suggests that the practice had stopped until
the war triggered it again. These varying opinions result, to some extent,
from the lacunae in existing documentary material. Although these journalists acknowledge that the situation is tragic for the Dinka, trying to
address the issue divorced from its historical roots is bound to be a little
more than just looking at the symptoms. Lack of documents to allow the
establishment of the historical connection is not evidence that there is
no connection.

Problems of Definition

More scholarly research on Sudan's current slavery is undoubtedly discouraged by the ambiguity that surrounds the meaning of slavery: What
is meant by the use of the word *slave?* The general consensus in studies
of slavery from ancient to modern times is that to be a slave is to have
all the attributes of chattel. With minor variations from place to place,
the slave is the absolute property of the master, to be used or disposed
of according to the whims of the master. In other words, the slave-master
relationship means that some societies have a well-established law that
distinguishes between free person and slave.

In Sudan, there has never been such a law. The constitution of the country prohibits slavery and any other slavery-like exploitation, but the application of this constitution is practiced preferentially on the basis of
religion and race. Non-Muslims and non-Arabs have very limited protection under the Sudan criminal code of 1991. What exists is lay interpretation of the Koran, Islam's holy book, from which most of Sudan's laws are
derived. Both Koran and Hadith allow Muslims under conditions of war
to force their war captives to work for them, a clear indication that the
government is guilty of not enforcing its own laws against kidnapping, assault, and forced labor. In addition, the feeling of racial superiority that
the Arabs assume over Africans has also been held up as justification for
labor exploitation of the Africans. What makes the situation complicated
in Sudan is the presence of large number of Southerners impoverished by
war and drought and displaced to the North. Under these circumstances,
many of them accept petty and marginal jobs, which they regard to be degrading but find themselves without much choice. This situation, which
has existed since the birth of Sudan as a nation-state, has provided the
Arabs with the justification to enslave the African Sudanese under the
guise of wage labor, and in this way to blur the line between free person
and slave. As a Muslim society, northern Sudanese try to put a human attribute to slavery. All the former slave children that I interviewed for this
study mentioned that when they surrendered their fate to the master and

never questioned their status and appeared submissive, their masters had constantly told them to feel at home. When the slave remained loyal, the owner felt bound by his faith to maintain certain prescriptive rights that he believed the slave had as part person and part property. For example, numerous former slave children have indicated that their master used to tell them that they were not separate from his children. "I make you work so that you can eat. . . . When you work, you should consider it working for your own future," as one boy explained what his master had told him repeatedly. If these remarks can be believed as reflecting a genuine concern by northern slaveholders for the welfare of their slaves—a rare event in any case—they could make a stark contrast with the experience of Nilotic slaves in the past. Then, the master enjoyed the fruits of the slave's toil without regard for his or her well-being.

Slaves in present-day Sudan, moreover, have different functions than their brothers and sisters in the nineteenth century. Some roles overlap during the two periods, but additional roles have been added this time around. In the past, slaves were used to build strong armies of conquest, particularly during the Turco-Egyptian and the Mahdiyya eras. During the colonial period slaves were used in agricultural production. Currently, although still performing some of these roles, they have quite different functions to fulfill. Southern slaves are much sought after in northern Sudan to perform household chores, to make up for the low birthrate among the Baggara, to cause political instability in the South, and to reconfigure the genetic and cultural identity of the South. All this comes in an effort to ensure achievement of a grand future goal—the goal of national unity. The more Southerners they can move into the North to be subjected to humiliation and exploitation, the more Southerners begin to integrate in the hope of becoming equal. Through slavery, the North hopes to demilitarize, in the long run, the clash of cultures between Arabs and Africans. Slavery speeds up the process of imbuing the African with Arab culture, leading to gradual immersion. In other words, Sudan's current slavery is not solely an issue of servitude and economic production, but a question of a government bend on shifting whole identities and boundaries in favor of some ethnicities to the disadvantage of others.

Within this order of things, enslavement of Southerners, and by implication the slave raiding in Bahr el-Ghazal, are seen as integral parts of the struggle to keep Sudan united at all cost. Northerners, government workers or laypersons, never address the moral issue of slavery. This is because slavery is sanctioned by religion, fueled by political ambition, armed with a cultural project, and built upon racial superiority. As a result, Northerners view the ending of slavery as resting with the South: if the South could just be a little less obstinate about its identity and allow

Sudan to be monocultural, that would end the strife. This is why the question of slavery within northern Sudan will never become the object of political or social concern among the leading politicians, whether religious or secular. Given this situation, many Northerners will speak out on many issues of social, economic, and political injustice, but will have no crises of conscience over the question of slavery. And unlike slavery in the nineteenth century, which was ultimately adjudged by economic criteria, current Sudanese slavery is not subject to scrutiny in terms of its economic significance. Slaves are not used in the North for large agricultural or other large productive activities but are made to perform household tasks or absorbed in what Hassan el-Turabi calls the "cultural determination" for Sudan to be Arab and Muslim.

What southern slaves accomplish in the North in terms of economic utility and return for the slaveholders can be compared to work performed by wage laborers. By putting southern slaves to work alongside a few wage laborers, no matter how minimal the pay, the outrage over slavery is preempted. It is easy for an Arab slave owner to avoid criticism as well as free his conscience if he can create a situation for the Southerners displaced to the North where they have no choice but to accept the exploitation of their labor. The slaveholders have attempted to justify keeping slaves by claiming it to be an act of mercy. They can tell their critics that the people they have put to work are laborers rather than slaves. In the eyes of the slavers, what outsiders call slavery is actually an act of benevolence because they are providing jobs for the otherwise impoverished and starving Southerners. The slavers are often convinced that they are doing a favor for the captives; they regard the Dinka culture as inferior and believe that these Southerners are fortunate to have been incorporated into a superior culture. This is the kind of explanation that has caused some historians to describe early slavery in the Muslim world as benign. Some writers are doing the same regarding present-day slavery in Sudan.[34]

A courteous treatment of slaves, undoubtedly, makes slavery more acceptable to the northern society and sometimes to the slaves who were caught at a very young age and incorporated into northern culture and religion. But this does not make it less than slavery. A slave is a slave. Moreover, the current Sudanese slavery is less an economic practice than a cultural project, because there are many poor Baggara who hold slaves that often live no worse than their master. As the testimony of former slaves indicate, many slaves appear to be accepting of their position, but in fact, this has been a very effective way to avoid punishment, and to earn the trust of the master until such time when there is opportunity to escape. Many slaves also tried to please their masters by working hard and showing obedience, with the hope that he might gather sympathy and reward them with their freedom. Some of the slaves managed to earn enough cash to enable them to escape. They used public transportation that takes them further north where they could divert to the train, and the train takes them to el-Meiram and then they walk the remaining distance toward home. Most slaves from Malwal Dinka that managed to run away took this route. Others fled toward home directly from Darfur or Kordofan, but many have died in the attempt, and this is attempted less often.

There have been no large-scale revolts, however, because it is impossible to access arms where security agents are forever vigilant. Lack of organization among slaves also makes it nearly impossible to put together mass protest. Such organization is lacking because of fear, but mostly because of the fact that slaves are scattered over a wide geographical area with no chance of contact between them. The only Southerners living in large groups are housed by international aid agencies in such places as el-Fardus[35] in the province of ed-Da'ein. But they are surrounded by government security agents, and access to them by expatriate relief workers is so scrutinized that even resident relief workers themselves do not know much about what occurs in these camps. Even during the times when expatriate aid workers were allowed to enter these fenced displaced persons' camps, they were usually prohibited from taking with them educated Dinkas to help with interpretation.

The assertion by some historians that slavery in the Muslim world was more merciful than plantation slavery in the Americas seems to be repeated when people describe the tragic experience of the southern Sudanese in such terms as "slavery-like." The language employed by UNICEF regarding Sudanese slavery is particularly a case in point. Even if one was to document that southern slaves in northern Sudan are not being treated harshly in terms of economic production, one would still be left unable to account for the mental slavery, the cultural humiliation, the political co-option, the forced labor, and the various forms of economic exploitation, not to mention the sexual and verbal abuse that many are subjected to on a daily basis. Are these less slavery-like than plantation work? What about the rigid social stratification based on race and on whether or not one can be called *abd*, slave? What about the possible psychological consequences for those who are coerced to give up their cultural beliefs to seek acceptance among the Arabs out of aspiration to rise above their inferior status? What about those who get indoctrinated into the Muslim jihad carried out against their own people? Are all these people not part of the history of slavery in the Muslim North? Does the submission by the slave to the mercy of his/her master, or even accepting to be absorbed into the society of the slavers, make slavery any less evil? Is the slave not just a slave after all? Even the simple reference to a

Southerner as *abd* in northern Sudan without necessarily forcing him or her to perform slave roles is a form of slavery.

Whether or not these aspects of slavery qualify as slavery is a question that has been debated for generations by historians, philosophers, and social scientists in an effort to either extol the virtues of slavery, or condemn the evil in it. It is this debate that continues to influence the attitudes of many writers towards Sudanese slavery today. Some argue that "a slave is a slave" and that the use of such words as "benign" or "harsh" to determine whether or not slavery exists in Sudan is a futile exercise.[36] But numerous others see Sudan's slavery, past and present, as nothing short of being a blessing for many of the Southerners that are made slaves in the North. The notion that most child slaves are happier in bondage than in the cruel circumstances of the war in the South is not uncommon in popular discourse, including some portion of journalism in the Western world. This pro-slavery attitude is only thinly disguised in the search for definitions of what constitutes slavery. Their question has been whether what is happening in Sudan is really slavery or is only like slavery. The defining characteristics are either that the practice involves harsh economic exploitation or that it is benign. This is obviously an attempt to compare Sudan's slavery to nineteenth-century plantation slavery and transatlantic slavery. This exercise glosses over the current slave raiding itself, whose barbarities are no less shocking than those associated with the slave trade of the old days. The unfortunate consequence of this effort to define Sudan's slavery by making comparisons to the past in other areas of the world as the only way to determine its presence has been obscuring the tragic experience of South Sudanese during the raiding and marching to the North. It has also concealed the desolate conditions in bondage and, as a result, reducing it to merely another form of servitude resulting from the war-provoked economic difficulties of the whole nation.

There is yet another factor behind the lack of scholarly interest in investigating Sudan's current slavery and the slave trade. It is the absence of antislavery activity by Southerners within northern Sudan. Due to the utterly criminal nature of the NIF government, the large and conscious southern population in the North is unable to organize against slavery, which might have forced the government to allow investigators to research the issue. But even the mention by a Sudanese citizen that slavery exists in Sudan is a punishable offense, and people are frightened into silence. Slaves themselves, as already noted, have not had the opportunity to challenge the slaving communities. They are also made apprehensive by the tragic events that have happened in the past, where thousands of Southerners were killed when they protested their status, or when they simply asked for government protection, as was the case in ed-Da'ein.

Chapter Three

The Suffering of the South in the North-South Conflict

"It is unfortunate that you did not arrive here four days ago before the escaped slaves were finally dispersed," remarked Geng Deng, the Aweil West representative of the Sudan Relief and Rehabilitation Association (SRRA), the humanitarian wing of the Sudan Peoples' Liberation Army/ Movement (SPLA/M). As we walked to his compound from the airstrip where I had just landed in a UN plane, Geng Deng explained to me the fate of some Dinka women and children. They had just been freed from enslavement by paying an Arab middleman a fee to locate them and purchase their freedom from the Dinka's northern neighbors, the Baggara Arab herdsmen. The local administrator explained:

If you had come last week you would have seen for yourself the magnitude of the problem of slavery. There were about 380 people who had gathered here to complain to the local authorities for having failed to provide them with protection when they were captured and for not affording them any assistance after having been freed. And since we hear that people around the world doubt the existence of slavery here, it would have been good for your research and for us if you could talk to escaped or redeemed slaves, and photograph the marks of torture on their bodies. It would have been good to provide you with the evidence so that you could go back to tell the world that we are still undergoing a practice that may be outdated in other countries, and perhaps in the whole world except Sudan. Slavery is not outdated here. It is being used by the government of Sudan as a tool of war.[1]

I had no reason to doubt his explanation. All indications on my arrival in Marial Baai in June 1998 were that the land of Malwal Dinka, along with the rest of the Dinka territory bordering the Baggara, had been the subject of large-scale devastation in Sudan's ongoing civil war between the North and South since 1983.

Signs of destruction in the wake of a fresh Baggara raid, which had just taken place one month before my arrival, were also obvious and unmistakable. As we flew over the villages adjacent to Marial Baai, especially

In the aftermath of a slave raid in Gok Machar, two young siblings whose parents perished in the raid and whose property was destroyed sit around a clay pot cooking some leaves for a meal.

closer to the railroad, they were burnt to the ground. In Marial Baai itself, a village of 5,000 inhabitants and considered the central town by 250,000 more, people were talking about a possibility of another attack, since the Baggara were said to be trying to carry out their last attack of the season before the rains come.[2] There were no signs of ongoing life activities. The normal activities of this season for the Dinka would include clearing the planting fields in preparation for the rains, cattle movement from grazing areas called *toc*[3] to the villages, and travel back and forth between markets. All this was at a standstill in anticipation of attacks by slave-raiding parties.

More obvious signs of abnormal circumstances included the alertness in everyone's eyes to the planes passing overhead. There was constant fear that one of these planes might be a government aerial bombing plane. It was particularly ironic to the people of Bahr el-Ghazal that some planes bring life by way of food aid, and others bring death as the government bombs civilian villages. One man described this contradiction in the following words: "Planes are like birds in a way. They both fly. But they are fundamentally different. With birds you can tell the bad ones from the good ones. There are birds of prey against which you have to protect your chickens and there are those which are delightful to the eye as they soar. Planes that fly over South Sudan either bring death or life and we have no way of distinguishing the friendly ones from the enemy until they either land with food, a joyous thing indeed, or drop bombs, a disastrous occurrence." Although the area had not been under such attack in a long time, bombings were taking place in many other areas in South Sudan, and there was no reason to rule it out here. In fact, a few weeks later, Nyamlel, the main center for the county about twenty kilometers from Marial Baai, was hit by six bombs. This bombing did not hit any targets or inflict human casualties because they missed the center of the town and dropped the bombs across the river. The inhabitants of Nyamlel explained the missed targets as a result of pilots having used the old maps of the town, which had placed it on the wrong side of the river.[4]

On the afternoon of my arrival, the SPLA representative Geng Deng had received word that the May 1998 raiding force, part of which had proceeded to the provincial capital of Wau, was on its way back to the North.[5] This time, the train was taking back the war booty captured in the previous raid, and a possibility of attacking the villages again could be foreseen. However, the SPLA was planning to attack them to prevent them from taking to the North the cattle and people they had seized during the earlier attack. Two weeks earlier, this force had sent a reconnaissance along the railway line to ensure that an SPLA attack on the train could be avoided. This had scared the civilian villagers into fleeing the area. The people in Marial Baai had been discussing the raid and every movement of this force since its last raid four weeks earlier. All were convinced that another raid just one month after the last one would amount to even greater disaster, not only in the destruction it might bring upon them now, but also due to its future consequences. A raid occurring in June means displacement from the fields during a planting season and it means that the raiders would find all the cattle herds returned from the distant grazing areas of the dry season. A raid at this time of year could have a destructive impact on Dinka livelihoods far greater than the dry season raiding.

At that time these were all reasons for everyone to be alarmed. Since 1983, anywhere between two and five attacks annually had sent the villagers fleeing their homes every single time, leaving behind their belongings, taking what they could, dragging their children, and losing family members to the raiding force. But with this, the fifth raid in one single dry season, the people decided to act.[6] Congregating in front of the county office located in a grass-roofed house where the local civilian authority merges with the SPLA military command and the SRRA, heads of Dinka groups took advantage of a gathering of local officials to demand an explanation for their suffering. Why did the SPLA and the commissioner seem to know that Arab raids are imminent, and yet the raiders were allowed to devastate the civilians without a swift response from what is supposedly a people's army. "Another raid is about to take place and you are here unable to tell us how you are going to protect the people. We would like to know what the SPLA wants us to do." Chol Malong, a community elder, demanded an explanation. It is important to note that, although the true attitudes toward the SPLA could not be accurately represented, the Dinka civilian population regards the SPLA as the government of the area. The very existence of the SPLA is due to civilian support in terms of feeding the soldiers, housing them, paying taxes to the local administration, and replenishing their ranks with new recruits. However, whether their support of the SPLA is coerced or proof of a genuine belief in its ability as an ally or protector depends on individual commanders, even individual fighters, and always on who is asking. Civilian views of the SPLA throughout South Sudan are highly contingent on the behavior of the soldiers. For example, in some areas where the SPLA soldiers have behaved arrogantly and violently, such as in eastern Equatoria, the rebel movement has not always been terribly popular.[7]

Engrossed in the more immediate matter of UN food drops expected to take place the next day, the local officials did not react at first to the civilian fear.[8] They had just heard of yet another case of mass starvation in nearby villages, one of many reports they had been receiving for two months. Having lost most of their property due to the government-sponsored raiding over the past year, many village heads and clan leaders had began to discuss the limited possibilities available. Should they urge their people to move away from the area? Should they form a force of their own and demand that the SPLA arm them so as to protect themselves? Should they push the SPLA to choose between acting like a government (as it has claimed to be in other matters) by protecting its people, and the possibility of losing civilian support?

The commissioner of the county has constantly assured his people that he would work with the military personnel to tighten security. He also assured them that civilians would be alerted in advance about any imminent Baggara attacks to enable them to flee the area with their herds and bury their crops in the ground. The practice of digging holes inside the homestead and storing the grain inside it has been the only way to ensure that the Baggara raiders do not destroy the grain when they burn the houses. When it is stored this way, the house may burn but the people can recover their assets when the raid is over. Yet, it was clear that the people were losing trust in the ability of the commissioner's authority to protect them. "Perhaps the Dinka chiefs could arrange a truce with the Baggara as they have done in the past to avoid confrontation?" I ventured in an attempt to elicit their opinions about the conflict. This idea was utterly surprising to most of them. Which Dinka person in his right mind can hope that the Arabs will respect the Dinka so as to maintain any agreement with them? People said unanimously. "They don't think we are humans like them," another person suggested. The SPLA officers and the commissioner all seconded the words of the Dinka civilians. Throughout the ages, the Dinka offered the Baggara the chance to be at peace with them, and indeed they tried on many occasions in the past to create an atmosphere of peaceful coexistence, to no avail. "There is nothing we have not tried with these people," declared one of the officers while everyone nodded in agreement, "but we will fight any attack if they come today," he continued.

The fear which the raids have inflicted upon the civilian population could not be easily mitigated. Vivid in their memory is one particular raid in January 1996, when the SPLA forces had been stationed on the North-South border area, in an attempt both to give their people a sense of security and to keep the Arab militia at bay. And despite this force, a well-armed Baggara militia accompanied by a regular government of Sudan military force ransacked the area in a matter of hours. The SPLA managed to drive the raiding force off but only after it had caused a great deal of damage, leaving the villages even more unable to entrust their security and protection to the SPLA. This raid weakened the confidence that the civil population had placed in SPLA. After many such episodes of unmitigated destruction, the civilian chiefs and clan leaders invoked various traditional ways of responding to such situations. "We pray to our gods and ancestors to avert the raiding forces, but we continue to suffer. We are told that the Arabs constantly attack us because they want us to adopt their way of worship; why is it that their gods have answered their prayers while ours have not? Are their gods stronger?" one spiritual leader inquired in Nyamlel in June 1999.[9] Having failed to avert the destruction, many clan leaders began considering what they regard to be the most humiliating thing that could happen to a people—to allow or encourage their people to relocate to other Dinka areas. Even more humiliating would be to move to the government-controlled cities both in the South and North.[10]

During the past ten years, people who have relations in the North, especially in the town of ed-Da'ein, have moved there to join them, only to find that their relatives are unable to sustain everyone.[11] They either try to go back to the South or find work as servants in Arab households, farms, and cattle camps. These options are related but hardly rewarding. To go to the South requires a lot of money to pay for the bus to el-Obeid and then pay for the train to el-Meiram, after which one walks back to Dinkaland. To earn enough money for this journey could take up to a year of intensive labor. Upon failure to generate enough money for transport, a slave may decide to walk back to the South following the same route he or she was taken through when captured. In the case of those who willingly migrated to the North in hope of finding sustenance, they may follow their routes back to Dinkaland when they find that the conditions in the North are not favorable. But walking back to the South means risking one's life. The foot journey takes anywhere between one week to ten days in a rough terrain with no adequate water or food. One could also run into another raiding force coming back from the South, and the fear of being recaptured prevents many people from embarking on this journey. It is a journey many people have taken, but one that someone with children, like most displaced South Sudanese, cannot undertake. Many people, therefore, resign themselves to being servants, hoping that they will break away when the war ends. Many more labor on in the hope of making enough money at some point to enable them to undertake the trip. Others who have connections within the government-held southern towns have also moved back and forth between these towns and their home villages. Some who have tried moving to the government-held towns of Aweil and Wau have found themselves living as refugees on the edges of town with no access to food or the necessary amenities. These are the people the government uses as reason to solicit international humanitarian assistance. When such assistance is provided, as it has been since 1989 following the establishment of Operation Life-line Sudan (OLS),[12] the government diverts the relief supplies for sustenance of its besieged army garrisons.[13] It also uses food aid to coerce the displaced into renouncing their religious beliefs and becoming Muslim.

All of these people who have moved away have become known in the aid world as internally displaced persons (IDPs). They have been the subjects of much of the international relief efforts in both North and South Sudan and in government and SPLA areas. Those who have decided that they could not leave their homelands have become the victims of the government's endless atrocities. Many observers have described Khartoum's conduct of war as "genocide."[14] But after almost a decade of being robbed of their humanity by the government and militia forces allied with it, the Dinka communities of Aweil and Gogrial decided to take their defense into their own hands. Some communities among them have requested that the SPLA provide them with arms to participate in the defense of their territory and assets. Some young men recently displaced from towns or those in the cattle camps have enlisted for military training and have acquired arms. Nevertheless, the suffering continues unabated, partly because of the unbalanced levels of weaponry. The Dinka militia formed in response to the Arab raids in 1995 is called Titweng, cattle guards. Their main objective is to prevent the Arab Murahileen from raiding Dinka villages, to prevent property from being destroyed, cattle from being looted, and women and children from being captured. However, they have a problem of arms supply. They are trained but cannot really contain the better-armed Arab and government militia forces.

The Devastation of Dinka Life and Livelihood

The raids have stripped the Dinka of their main economic resources— cattle and labor. As a result of these raids, the Dinka territory of northern Bahr el-Ghazal, as in many places in South Sudan, exists under conditions of severe food deficits. Food production and local welfare systems have been disrupted everywhere by these raids. There is much more that the raiding has destroyed in Dink life that goes beyond the economic. Although Dinka fish, trade, plant crops, and even hold salaried jobs in the government, cattle herding remains the unrivaled center of their social, economic, and religious life. The raiding and the war in general have disrupted every aspect of Dinka life. The Baggara Arabs have stolen large numbers of cattle, and life has been drained from many Dinka traditions. Given that Dinka cattle culture is the foundation of every aspect of Dinka life, economic and spiritual, the destruction of this base resulting from Baggara raids undermines the very existence of the Dinka as a people.

The direct consequence of asset depletion by the raiding and by the war in general has been mass displacement of Dinka people. The displacement provoked by raiding has undermined countless communities and traditional communal relationships. This situation has been aggravated by hostile climatic changes in the 1990s, when drought alternated with floods, devastating the second pillar of the Dinka economy, agriculture. Insecurity due to war and restriction of mobility between the government-controlled garrison towns and the countryside has caused the loss of another important economic resource, trade. Finding themselves unable to sustain their livelihoods, thousands of Dinka have been forced to move randomly in search of sustenance. Some have gone into government-held towns, others have relocated to relief centers within the SPLA-controlled South, and still others have crossed the hostile borders into northern cities.

The choice of where to relocate was influenced by individual calculations based on either the knowledge that some humanitarian assistance would be available, or the presence of relatives in the area where one wishes to go. Wherever a family chose to go, they could not predict what the circumstances would be like in the new location, and the result was almost invariably a disappointment. In government towns, they were so marginalized that they became refugees in their own country. They were also denied access to international relief supplies, because such relief, although granted to assist the internally displaced, was being diverted to the military. For example, in 1998 in feeding camps around Wau, the death rate rose as high as sixty-three per ten thousand per day.[15]

In relief centers in SPLA-held areas, humanitarian assistance was so limited that more people died of hunger and disease around relief centers than in their original home villages, particularly in 1998. The insufficiency of relief in SPLA areas was often the result of either flight bans by the government in its genocidal mode, insufficient donor funds, inadequacy of the flight system from Kenya, diversion of food for military purposes, insufficient amounts of food delivered, a shrinking overall food base in the South, or a combination of all these factors.

In the North, the displaced were so deprived of both humanitarian aid and government services that people felt they had become second- and third-class citizens. Basic services were unavailable for them since they took up residence on the edges of the cities where there were no facilities. Their makeshift settlements around the city were considered illegal slums. Therefore the government was unwilling to provide such services lest the displaced get the wrong idea that their occupation of these parts of the cities was condoned by the government. Every effort was shown by the government to remind the displaced that they were outsiders and that extending services to them was out of the question.[16]

Even the international relief assistance in Khartoum and other northern cities had been tied to the recipients' religious status and ethnic identity. In 1988, for example, I witnessed that much of the relief assistance was distributed in mosques, while the Southerners who were desperate, sometimes starving, and who asked for food aid were required to declare themselves Muslim before receiving assistance. Up to the present, unless the aid agency can distribute the food directly to the beneficiaries, which is not possible at all times due to government harassment of expatriate aid workers, aid has been largely diverted from the displaced to the market or to feed the army and the militias. Monitoring of relief items by expatriate aid agency staff was so scrutinized that it was rendered impossible. Foreign aid workers cannot move freely. Most of them do not speak local languages, and the displaced Dinka do not speak foreign languages. But when foreign aid workers tried to use Southerners as interpreters, government security agents would not allow this. The result was that information about the displaced that could facilitate effective relief delivery—why they were displaced, where they came from, how they were treated by the government—could not be obtained. The government is aware that it is through such investigation by foreign aid workers that information about human rights abuses such as slavery could be detected and revealed.

The killing, the looting, the destruction of property, and the prevention of people from producing their own food by the Arabs have caused the rural Dinka to have a humiliating and degrading reliance on international relief assistance. A large number of Dinka who are still residing in their home villages now avoid serious food shortages only by a stream of international aid. United Nations World Food Program reports that it has fed at least half a million Dinka every year since 1991.[17] The Dinka find this degrading because it has remade their world into a world that does not make sense to them. Many people and families find themselves forced into a defensive modernity and a frightening connection to a world they had not even imagined. Before now, the Dinka had never considered any connections with the world beyond the grazing grasslands. Connection with anything urban was limited to government officials, occasional trips to town markets, and small-scale labor migration to the North. It was the ultimate humiliation that they found themselves forced to beg for assistance, a position in keeping with what the North has wanted the South to be all along, a mere dependent of the North. It fits into the North's declared policy of psychological submission of the South. The more the South is made to doubt and question its distinct identity and the more Southerners look to the northern government for assistance, the faster they will be politically subjugated.

The Dichotomy of North and South in Sudan

These highly provocative practices by the government have conjured up the historical sensitivities between the North, identifying itself as Arab and Muslim, and the South, whose population identifies itself as African and black. This dichotomy is simplistic on the surface, but it speaks volumes upon a closer scrutiny. It shows the multiple diversities, heterogeneity, and divisions that polarize Sudanese society. The dichotomy of North and South in Sudan provides extra readings in addition to those of geography. North and South in Sudan also define racial structure, religious polarization, culture clash, varied historical experiences, power struggle, and unbalanced development and resource distribution. Because these dichotomies are largely implicated in the reemergence of slavery, they warrant a brief explanation.

Today, Sudan is known to the world as an Arab country, although the majority of its citizens are phenotypically African. But the Africans of the North who are genetically part Arab and part African have decided that they are more Arab than African. If we accept the notion that racial identity can be determined by a communal choice rather than by genealogy, then we must recognize the cleavages that divide Sudan into an Arab North and an African South. Arabism in Sudan is therefore a cultural construction rather than a genetic reality. But it is real inasmuch as it impacts on the daily lives of some of its people and the destiny of the country as a whole.

Regarding religious identity, the Islamization of what is now north-ern Sudan following the defeat of the Christian kingdoms of Nubia in the seventh century ushered in the start of the religious identity con-test that still pervades modern Sudanese society today. Islam entered Sudan through long-distance Arab traders and slave raiders between the seventh and eighth centuries. The Arab colonial forces in Egypt invaded Sudan and after a bloody fight, they imposed on the two Christian king-doms of Maqurra and Allwa certain conditions, which included the pay-ment of annual tribute to the Arab invaders consisting of 350 slaves, gold, iron ore, foodstuff, and animals. During this period slavery was legalized, and the situation worsened after the Arabs finally overran the Nubian kingdoms and started a new era of slave-based colonialism.[18]

This lasted until it was replaced by Turco-Egyptian rule from 1821 to 1881. This period introduced North Sudanese to the South as partners of the Turks and Egyptians in slave raiding, devastation, and plunder. Mo-hammed Ali Pasha, the Ottoman Sultan's viceroy in Egypt, who estab-lished Turco-Egyptian colonial rule in Sudan, increased the export of slaves to 30,000 per year for the sixty years of the Ottoman rule. The experience of the people of the South with slave raids from the North did not allow for a distinction between the Turks (as foreigners) and the Northerners (as fellow Sudanese). They were all slave raiders from the North, in geographic terms.

In 1881, when the Mahdist state overthrew the Turco-Egyptian colonial rule, it did not only expand slavery, but made slavery the mainstay of the northern economy. It also forcibly drove millions of African Sudanese from their villages and made them die of hunger and war-related deaths. At times, the entire Mahdist state relied on revenues from the slave trade and the use of slave labor. By 1898, the population of Sudan under the Mahdist rule and those areas within its proximity was reduced from eight million to two and a half million people. It is this Mahdist state, a source of horror at the time for the African communities where slaves were cap-tured, that became a source of pride to North Sudanese because it repre-sented their victory over foreign (Turkish and Egyptian) occupation and the assertion of Sudanese nationalism. To the Southerners, the era is re-membered as a nightmare because it gave the Arabs a freer hand in their pursuit of black slaves and white ivory in the South. It is this historical experience that is partly the cause of debate over the identity of Sudan today. What was a cause of freedom and national pride for one group was a benchmark of oppression and death for another.

In 1898, the British and the Egyptians recolonized Sudan under a colo-nial system known as the Anglo-Egyptian Condominium rule, which had overthrown the Mahdist state. The North considered this a humiliation while the South embraced it, at least initially, as a welcome intercession. Part of the reason for these opposing viewpoints relates to slavery. The Anglo-Egyptian rule had declared slavery illegal, to the relief of the South and to the outrage of the North. For Northerners, as a tradition sanctioned by Islam, an economic asset, and a matter of racial hierarchy, slavery was not supposed to be meddled with by a foreign rule. For Southerners, the declaration of slavery as illegal was long overdue and a government that would introduce such a policy was indeed "the real government."[19] Although the British colonial administration did not completely abolish the slave trade and slavery, but rather opted for a "modern" form of slavery, at least raiding and export of African Sudanese was greatly reduced.[20]

When the British were ending the imperial era in 1955, there was jubilation in the North. The cause of happiness was as much the coming of freedom as it was about the prospect of finally and effectively bringing the South under northern control. Conversely, the process of colonial disengagement horrified the South. Many southern leaders called upon the outgoing colonial authority to delay independence until the South has gained an equal level of education and economic development with the North. They were aware that the North would automatically try to immerse the South into a dubious polity. Southern fears proved justified even before the British had packed their bags. In the process of handing over power to a Sudanese administration, the South was automatically given a marginal position. The result has been the refusal of the South since the day the country became independent to join with the Sudanese polity, especially since the rules of that polity were imposed by the North to the detriment of southern identity and prosperity. The South earnestly started what was to be known to history as the seventeen-year-long Anyanya war (1955–72), the first round of the unresolved North-South conflict. A movement calling itself the Anyanya spearheaded the grievances of the southern people following independence. Angered by the biased administration, the southern revolt called for secession of the South.[21]

The animosity that has resulted from the first war, combined with various historical experiences as explained above, has continued to set up vicious boundaries between the North and the South.[22] They have created static self-definition and dynamic aspirations. The Northerners consider themselves as descendants, defenders, promoters, and inheritors of the Muslim faith. They yearn to identify with and to develop as an integral part of the greater Arab nationalism. They are so determined to persuade the whole world that Sudan is an Arab country that they seem ready to risk the disintegration of the country to achieve this goal. Muslim figures in the North like Hassan al-Turabi call this drive cultural self-determination.

Northerners' determination to create an Islamic and Arab nation in Sudan is not just to be proud about identifying with Arabs and Muslims. It is also out of a conception that Arabism has a superior rank to Africanism, based on the way they view the racial hierarchy. A problem, however, arises when it comes to those Northerners with physical features such as pigmentation, shape of the nose, and hair texture that are typically African. Most people in the North share these features with Southerners, and yet regard themselves as Arab. When this is the case, they seek other ways to prove themselves Arab and seek acceptance into the greater Arab nation. One of these paths to Arabism has been Islam, for this religion in Sudan and the region of northeastern and eastern Africa is tied to Arabism. To be Muslim in this region is to claim shared roots with Arabia and with the family of the prophet Muhammad. For northern Sudanese, Islam is not just a religious faith, but also a vehicle for their racial promotion. It is this northern insistence on defining, presenting, and recreating the country in terms of an assumed image that ties the nation's genetic identity to its religion, which is the crux of the conflict, and that fans violence, including slavery. This is what makes it impossible to find a basis for a united peaceful state in Sudan. How much are the Northerners willing to pay in order to achieve the unity of Sudan through racial and religious intolerance? How long will it be before the North comes to a realization that the unification of Sudan is impossible if imposing Islam and Arabism on all Sudanese is the only avenue to unity they can see?

The Southerners, on the other hand, have not made any attempts to be other than what they have always been. They have always referred to themselves in terms of their ethnic nationalities and have had no desire to recreate these nationalities. They have viewed themselves as Dinka, Nuer, Bari, Zande, and hundreds of other nationalities. Most rural Southerners have linked themselves to these cultural and ethnic roots and do not even reach the level of the state when talking about their world. They do not identify with a polity called Sudan, nor is there any consciousness or political decision to be part of Africa. The history of the effort to identify with Africa is recent and is confined to the literate. It grew out of the history of unfriendly contact with Northerners. It is a defense mechanism against the encroaching and offending Arab culture. A conscious battle to connect with Africa in opposition to the northern recreation of Sudanese identity was started primarily by the educated, whose world has expanded beyond their ethnic locale. It was the educated who first saw Northerners' pursuit of Arabism not only as an identity crisis in the North, but also as an aggressive attitude bent on eliminating other identities. This feeling was particularly heightened by the application of an Islamic criminal code in 1983 by President Nimeiri. Consequently, the conflict is much more intricate now than it was on the eve of independence in 1956. There were serious disagreements at that time, but the adoption of Islamic laws, national policies regarding the expropriation of natural resources, and the question of autonomy for the South, have all been implicated in the resurgence of the second round of the civil war. The war itself has also developed characteristics that the first war did not have. With the resurgence of slave raiding as part of the current war, it therefore appears that the longer the search for a political solution takes, the more difficult it will become for Sudan to find a solution and remain united.

The effort to maintain what the Khartoum government and its allies call "territorial integrity" has been attempted through several means, but a policy of dominance and violence have been the avenues the government has pursued most vigorously. The country's national identity has been defined as Arab despite the obvious cultural diversity. Islam has been chosen as the creed of the state without tolerance of other faiths. The constitutional and legislative tenets of the country have been derived from Islamic law in defiance of the ethnic-based legal multiplicity. These credos relate only to the dominant group. The rest of the country is to submit or face lethal persecution. Hassan al-Turabi, speaking in March 1999 in Cairo, explained that those who submit would become beneficiaries of Islamic benevolence, but those who resist would face the wrath of Islamic jihad. It is this northern model of imposed unity, a model followed by all the Khartoum governments since the Mahdist regime and always rejected by the South, which has been the recipe for war, enslavement of Southerners, and persecution of non-Muslims who defied this model of governance.

The International Response

During 1987–89, human suffering, especially that of displaced persons, rapidly approached catastrophic proportions.[23] Although the Khartoum government was eventually forced by the deteriorating humanitarian situation and the pressure by the international community to acknowledge the magnitude of suffering its policies had brought upon the southern population, its response to the famine crisis did little to reduce deaths. The formation of a consortium, Operation Life-line Sudan (OLS), to provide food and health relief operations could not deal with the issue of slavery, since the humanitarian program was not designed to deal with the root causes of the crisis. Slave raiding was one of the main causes of famine.[24] Yet it is quite difficult to understand why a huge operation such as OLS, led by the UN Children's Fund (UNICEF), could not decide whether or not these practices amounted to slavery, and how to protect women and children from such policies. Slave raiding continues. Sponsoring of militias by the government of Sudan goes on, and the displacement of Dinka, Nuer, and other South Sudanese continues unabated. Large numbers of South Sudanese continue to be forcefully moved and subjected to a sort of wage slavery and economic exploitation. And the argument that such exploitation cannot necessarily be termed "slavery" is to suggest that forcing happy carefree cattle keepers into a new life as cheap labor—disenfranchised, landless, assetless, and voiceless—is a lesser evil than slavery.

From 1994 to 1998, the crisis continued to be aggravated, particularly by the government's decision to (1) deny aid agencies access to certain locations, and (2) use the militia to escort the military train to Wau, giving them a free hand to raid, loot, and capture. In 1996, Gaspar Biro of Hungary, the UN Special Rapporteur on human rights in Sudan, reported an alarming increase in the number of cases of slavery. He wrote: "The abduction of persons, mainly women and children, belonging to racial, ethnic and religious minorities from southern Sudan, the Nuba Mountains and the Ingessana Hills areas, their subjection to the slave trade, including traffic in and sale of children, women, slavery, servitude, forced labor, and similar practices . . . are carried out by persons acting under the authority and with the tacit approval of the government of Sudan."[25] All these policies were carried out under the nose of UNICEF. And all that this agency could do was bicker about whether or not there really is slavery in Sudan. In 1998 and early 1999, UNICEF spent a lot of time engaging in a debate about the ethics of trying to obtain the freedom of slaves through payment to Arab middlemen, which some Christian organizations from Europe and America were engaged in. There was also a lot of UN and NGO discourse about the importance of working on this issue through the very government of Sudan that condones and promotes the practice. In May 1999, UNICEF wrote a $900,000 proposal to fund efforts to understand and reconcile the Dinka and the Baggara as a response to the incessant claims by the Khartoum government that what human rights groups claim to be slavery is actually a part of the usual tribal conflict. The government had suggested that a grassroots investigation of the allegations would reveal otherwise; UNICEF accepted this and believed that the same government which initiated the hostilities and caused and encouraged slavery was genuinely interested in bringing peace to Dinka-Baggara border.[26]

Imposing a ban on aid agencies from flying to all areas in need of food was a political as well as a military move on the part of the government. Politically, the government wanted to assert to the international community that it had not given up its prerogative in the South by allowing aid to be delivered under the auspices of the SPLA. Militarily, denying people access to aid in their own locations forced them to flee to the locales that receive aid. First, this was convenient for the government because it forced the people to vacate their villages. Those villages then became useless to the SPLA.[27] Second, when large numbers of people were displaced and congregated in particular relief centers, these centers became the target for militia raids. These political and military tactics on the part of the government should have been rejected by OLS as a violation of the tripartite agreement between the government of Sudan, the SPLA, and OLS to deliver aid to all areas without hindrance.[28]

Government Complicity in Slave Raiding

The use of militias against the civilian population of the South is a policy all the successive Khartoum governments—from Nimeiri to the Military Transitional Council, to the democratically elected government of Prime Minister Sadiq al-Mahdi—have pursued vigorously. Nevertheless, it was not until the Mahdi's government was overthrown by the National Islamic Front (NIF) in a military coup in June 1989 that the government's decision to use militia raids, denial of relief, and aerial bombardment provoked more vigorous raids, massive displacement, and the deaths of some 700,000 between 1989 and 1992. The total estimated deaths over the period of the war would later come to two million by 1999, and the count continues.[29] These deaths are a direct consequence of violent confrontations, unprecedented famine, and disease provoked by war. The militia raids have so far caused the capture of thousands of slaves from Dinka, most of them during the reign of the NIF. Displacement to the North makes southern women and children easy prey, and there are accounts of children being abducted at night by the Baggara from the refugee camps in southern Darfur and western Kordofan.

Throughout the critical years leading up to the overthrow of Prime Minister Sadiq al-Mahdi in 1989, the Baggara and the government were secretly negotiating deals to enhance their mutual interests at the expense of the rural Dinka. The government, led by the Umma Party at the time, had two goals. One was to please the Baggara so as to keep and strengthen the support of the western Sudanese, who are the main voters for the Umma Party.[30] The other was to use the same Baggara to weaken the SPLA and its support base among the Dinka through a policy of genocide by extermination of the rural Dinka population, whose men were the troops of the SPLA. However, the Baggara themselves had their own agenda and keeping friendly intercourse with the government in Khartoum enabled them to accomplish this goal. It was the goal of persuading the government to arm them with automatic weapons and ammunition so as to clear the grazing areas south of the Kiir River of its Nilotic inhabitants. This mutual understanding between the Baggara and the Khartoum governments is still maintained today with the present government, and it is this understanding which drives the slave raids.

Northern Sudanese, including the NIF government, the Baggara, the opposition groups, and the ordinary civilians, have all had varying viewpoints on how to deal with the South and the issue of slavery. The government treats all the Southerners, without the exception of those allying with it, as holding an antigovernment attitude, whether they live in Khartoum or in the South. Those who live in Khartoum can easily be accused of forming a fifth column in support of the SPLA when they complain about their conditions in the city. And having been "barred from obtaining identity cards due to their lack of registerable address, they are subject to arbitrary arrests, floggings and forced recruitment into the national army."[31] The Baggara view the South, particularly their neighbors, the Dinka and the Nuer, as a stumbling block to Baggara survival. If the government is willing to aid them, the political divisions within the North become secondary. In this case it does not matter whether the government in Khartoum is NIF or Umma. The opposition groups regard the use of tribal militias to augment government control as a dangerous card, which threatens not only the efforts of the opposition to change the government, but the overall national unity.

Given these views of the South, each has a different approach to the issue of slavery. The government uses it as a mere tool against the SPLA and as a weapon to shake the confidence of the South in maintaining its own identity independent of the Arab and Islamic drive. To achieve this, the government has committed serious atrocities that many people think amount to genocide as a way to plant fear in the Nilotic people of the South. But what the government is doing is not just genocide and ethnic cleansing. It is worse. The government wants large numbers of Southerners, especially Dinka and Nuer, to move to the North in order to absorb them into the northern races and cultures and to use them as cheap labor, and therefore reconfigure the racial and ethnic structure of the country. In fact, the practice of slavery, which is race based, is not to separate the Northerners and Southerners. The policy is to keep the two together while promoting northern cultures through popular media and education, a process which will eliminate all other non-Arab cultures. But to meet its goals, the policy of absorbing the southern cultures into the northern ones can only be beneficial to the North if the absorbed Southerners maintain a subservient position in the North. But in the minds of northern Sudanese, the only way to create a subordinate sector of a society is to eliminate the dignity of that sector. Enslavement and treatment of a people as livestock ensure the creation of masters and servants without leaving room for the servants to question and protest their status. Only after this structure has been accomplished, and slavery is one of the best tools for it, can Sudan, as a united polity, ever enjoy peace and progress.

The Baggara view the slave raiding as accomplishing two goals. One is purely economic and a matter of immediate survival. The other is a matter of long-term assertion of Arab culture. It is an issue of genetic proliferation. The Baggara belief that one of the reasons why the Dinka cannot allow their lush grazing lands to be shared is that they are wicked and bad-natured.[32] This requires the Baggara to do something by way of changing the Dinka culture and mentality, either through cultural invasion or by injecting Baggara genes into the Dinka gene pool. Introducing the Baggara culture into Dinka has proved more difficult over the generations. It is now believed that the genetic alternative might work but requires the use of violence, and hence the raids. The practice is partly meant to move as many Dinka women as possible to the Baggara territory, and force them to beget children, who may continue to claim their Dinka origins but will act in accordance with the Baggara wishes. Robert Collins insists that "the low reproductive rate of the Baggara, especially, was an important dynamic for them to seize the more fertile Dinka women and their children."[33] Such children do not only increase the numbers of the Baggara fighters, but will also increase the efficiency of raids by causing serious divisions among the Dinka people.

Both the government and the Baggara have mutual interests. The government desires to defeat the SPLA through the use of Baggara raids. The Baggara wish to defeat the Dinka through the training and arms supplied by the government, in order to gain access to grazing and water for their herds. They both want cheap labor, genetic mixing, political victory, and consequential pacification of the South. The abduction of Southerners, their subjugation and maltreatment confirms and plants in their minds their subordinate position in the North. The North wants to beat Southerners into subjugation with the expectation that in the end they will choose between continued suffering and submission to subservience and slave status.

The opposition groups in the North view the issue of slavery as a useful tool for antigovernment propaganda. Human rights records of the NIF government are dismal, and the emergence of slavery and slave trade tops it all. The northern opposition groups use it merely as a way to bring international pressure to bear on the government, but not necessarily to criticize it for its barbarity. No northern opposition party has attacked the practice of slavery in an effort to mitigate southern suffering. In fact, one easily notices that in their press releases these northern opposition parties have mixed feelings about the slavery issue. On the one hand, they want to use it in their campaign against the NIF government. On the other, they fear that an international campaign against slavery paints a negative picture about the northern Arabs in general, and therefore, would like it to be resolved locally and quietly. Even the northern opposition parties that have formed an alliance with the SPLA have yet to issue a public condemnation of the practice of slavery.

It is not clear what causes the reticence of the northern opposition at the present. But historically, all the leading northern parties that have ruled Sudan have also been implicated in the abuses of human rights in the South, including slavery itself. For example, it was during the late 1980s, when the Umma Party and the Democratic Unionist Party (DUP) were both in a coalition government led by Sadiq al-Mahdi, that some of the most memorable atrocities against the Southerners in the history of Sudan were meted out.[34] Both the ferocity with which the Baggara raids were pursued and the attacks on displaced Southerners in Darfur and Kordofan during this period were more evident. Police brutality in Khartoum against displaced Southerners and denying them relief supplies were also as inhuman as they became during the reign of the NIF. Now that the Umma Party and DUP are in opposition and very critical of the government's oppressive policies, their attitude toward the NIF government regarding the question of slavery is being watched keenly, especially by Southerners. Of interest to the South is the position of these northern parties in reference to some of the policies that their governments had helped institute, and which the present regime has built upon, like the use of Baggara raids against the South. Their comment on the issue of slavery was particularly eagerly awaited, and none of them has come forward with a firm stance against it.

This position leaves room for wonderment. Could it be that the northern opposition does not understand the exact situation on the North-South border? Or is it that they fear the government might embarrass them by pointing out their role in igniting the practices of militia recruitment and slave raids when they were in power? The latter is more likely because the NIF government has already challenged the opposition to prove that the present crises in the country were a creation of the NIF, rather than inherited from the previous governments. The first possibility is negated by some events over the last few years.

In 1995, during a period of intense raiding activity, one of the leading figures of the Umma Party, Mubarek al-Fadhil al-Mahdi, traveled to Bahr el-Ghazal with the prominent Dinka journalist and politician Bona Malwal. Both men were members of the leadership committee of the opposition group National Democratic Alliance (NDA), which brings together northern and southern opposition groups in a concerted effort to over-

throw the NIF government. The trip was arranged to enable the Umma
leader to acquaint himself with the horrendous conditions that the followers of his party had created for the Dinka. The NDA leadership had
hoped that the Umma Party's influence among the Baggara could be used
to at least turn them away from fighting the Dinka if they could not be
persuaded to fight the NIF government. In a meeting between Dinka and
Baggara elders convened by the two visitors, it was pointed out that the
hostilities between them were only in the interest of the government and
were detrimental to the survival of the two groups. It was hoped that such
trips, if maintained, might reduce the hostilities between the Dinka and
the Baggara. Unfortunately, no northern opposition figure has set foot in
Bahr el-Ghazal since, and whatever hopes of reconciliation the first visit
may have created were dashed before long. Since then, many Southerners claim that the northern opposition had deliberately decided to stay
away from a Dinka-Baggara peace initiative because they may also need
to use these hostilities at a future time when they are in power.

Part II

Underlying Causes of the Revival of Slavery in Sudan

Chapter Four

The Legacy of Race

The relationship between race and the institution of slavery has been ne-glected in the study of slavery within Africa. Historians acknowledge the existence of individual slave traders' racial sentiments but tend to over-look the strong racial foundations upon which the institution of slavery is built, especially the way in which racial ideology was so instrumental in the persistence of the slave trade between North Africa and sub-Saharan Africa. Neglected as well is the way race continues to fuel new forms of slavery. Detailed studies have shown that the Arabs and Muslims were involved for centuries in trading Africans. These studies have also estab-lished the ways African slaves were used in Ottoman North Africa and other parts of the Ottoman Empire in the nineteenth century. The fate of African slaves who were taken to many parts of Arabia, Persia, Egypt, and as far as India have also been studied extensively. Other studies examine slavery as a lucrative economic enterprise which generated huge profits for North Africa and the Arab world. But the study of the racial bases of slavery appears to present non-African scholars with difficulty. There is as yet no general recognition among historians and social scientists of the importance of race relations in the continuity of the institution of slavery within African countries that have populations of mixed races, such as Sudan, Tanzania, and Mauritania, as well as many Indian Ocean island states. Furthermore, an explicit awareness is lacking about the legacy of race in the persistence of slavery in modern-day Sudan, both during the many successive imperial periods (Turco-Egyptian and Anglo-Egyptian) and recently in postcolonial times. Development studies have looked at ethnic warfare and slavery as related to social history and labor migra-tion in contemporary times. These issues may well be related to past pat-terns of the slave trade, kidnapping, and the integration of slave descen-dants and freed people in different regions. Slavery and the slave trade in modern-day Sudan may have taken new forms and systems of trans-action, but they are the direct descendants of the extensive, efficient, and economically lucrative slave trade of the nineteenth century. There has yet to be a study of race relations, ethnic warfare, and slavery combined in the ongoing social and political history of countries with problematic racial structures, such as Sudan.

Slavery in Sudan has taken many varied forms and has a long history. Yet beneath this multitude of practices and actors rests the same institution, and in many cases the same slaves and sometimes the same masters. Slavery was introduced into Sudan by Arab traders. It was then taken over and used by a series of governments (Turco-Egyptian, Anglo-Egyptian, and northern Arab settler governments). In practicing slavery, these governments changed it, but they also adapted themselves to it. The survival and transformation of the racial basis of slavery has had very important consequences for the resurgence of modern forms of slavery, and it has had equally important political consequences for the way the nation of Sudan has fared since independence. Sudan has been struggling to become the nation that it never was and never will be, a nation built on the image of one racial and cultural group and the suppression of the others. There has never been the will to create a nation beyond Arabism and Islamism on the basis of diversity. Because of this history, the post-independence strife has been going on for so long that people cannot think of Sudan without thinking about its civil wars.

The survival, revival, and transformation of the racial foundations of slavery in Sudan have been obscured by the ways in which modern scholarship has described slavery within Africa. The connection between race and slavery is also mystified by the fact that race relations are difficult to study in a nation where the boundaries between "races" and ethnic groups are not so clear cut, at least to the outsider, and where the histories of the many racial groups that have occupied Sudan throughout history are so varied. I attribute this oversight to two factors: first, the academic demarcation between precolonial, colonial, and postcolonial slavery. This divide is artificial because all three periods are connected concerning the practice of slavery. The second factor is the assumption by some historians that slavery within Africa was more benign than transatlantic slavery. I contend that a slave is a slave; a Muslim slaver in Africa is no more humane than the European slave trader or the plantation owner in the Americas.[1]

A proper study of the racial foundations of Sudanese slavery will require a careful search through a variety of sources. The sources include official comments by Sudanese administrators on the issue of slavery, and documents of official communication between the Colonial Services and their home governments. Also of importance are the personal letters and memoirs of former British administrators now in the Sudan Archive at the University of Durham. We also have the analysis of interviews conducted with freed slaves and their communities in Bahr el-Ghazal, and with the officials of nongovernmental organizations (NGOs) providing relief in the war-stricken communities and displaced persons' camps, as well as with those individuals participating in the redemption of slaves. I have conducted these interviews over the past five years. The sources are obscure but can nevertheless increase our knowledge and teach us about the similarities between nineteenth-century and contemporary racial foundations of slavery in Sudan.

The comparison of these two periods is not without justification. The study of the racial foundation of slavery is important within both the social and political history of Sudan, for this is a vast country with two hostile regions, North and South, which have been forced into a polity far too difficult to maintain in harmony. The racist attitudes of some groups toward others were the foundations of the very concept and the institution of slavery. Just as the slave trade became a well-established system in the eighteenth century, it took various forms throughout the history of Sudan. The direct forms preceding British rule included activities of many alien intruders. Three of these events deserve a mention—first, the vigor with which Muhammad Ali, the viceroy of Ottoman Sultan in Egypt, sought to use black Sudanese as slave soldiers; second, the Mahdist state's reliance on slavery and the slave trade for state income; third, the insistence of individual Arab slave traders like Zubeir Pasha[2] on the racial and religious grounds that black Sudanese were legitimately not good for much but to be slaves. However, just as the slave trade was made illegal under British colonialism, it survived in various direct and indirect forms, most of which had to rely on racial ideology to legitimate them and to gain wider acceptance and success among the northern Arab populace.

It was the perception among the Arabs, the Turks, and the British that black Sudanese—Southerners, Nuba, and people of the Ingessana hills— were not only uncivilized and unintelligent, but also barbaric, good only as slaves. The institution of slavery was one of the few means by which to tame these peoples. To demonstrate by evidence and to understand how this came about, we can turn to the official communication between the colonial authorities regarding slavery and to the petitions by northern Arab leaders to the colonial government as a point of comparison. These documents reveal a glaring contradiction in the colonial attitudes between the government's claim to be against the injustice inherent in slavery, in one way, and its secret role in promoting it, in many other ways. Whether this contradiction was caused by colonial fear of the Arab slavers or out of the Sudanese government's own interests is a story we may never fully grasp. The reality will remain in the hearts and minds of the gentlemen who ran the colonial service.

Slavery Under British Colonial Rule

The assumption that the British colonial government ended slavery in Sudan came from three sources—first, the efforts of the Sudan Colonial Service to suppress the transatlantic slave trade; second, the campaigns by abolitionists such as the British Anti-Slavery Society; third, the declared colonial policy to stem the practice from its "roots" in Africa. Recent browsing through archives in England and Egypt, however, tempts me to question these widely held but unfounded assumptions. The British did not end slavery in Sudan. They only changed its forms and produced different definitions of what was classified as slavery. The dominant feature in the British policy against slavery was the effort to stop the export of slaves for sale outside Sudan, and toleration of internal slavery. It was mainly through the propagation of internal slavery that the colonial government conducted the state economy, the military, and local law and order.

Colonial administration made use of the institution of military slavery. After reconquest in 1898, slaves were recruited into the colonial army and were used to obtain more slaves. Recruitment was first confined to ex-slaves and their offspring, and then it became more and more an institution that grew to encourage all others of lower social status to join in. The colonial policy was constantly changing to address public opinion back in Great Britain that was very critical of slavery, and to respond to the plight of black slaves and to the constant plea by the Arab slave owners to be allowed to keep their slaves as retainers. Initially, the British policy was to eliminate slavery, which the Sudan colonial authorities started to do, but the Arab North complained, and the colonial administrators became confused. Some slaves were granted the right to leave their masters and the right to full protection if they were to work for the government. Most southern slaves were unable to return to their families and had to accept the government's slavelike employment, a kind of "wage slavery." The colonial government made it a condition that a freed slave take up some career in order for his/her free status to remain protected, but some of the jobs that they were encouraged and sometimes forced to do amounted to another form of slavery. In fact, some tasks were so strenuous that some slaves preferred slave status, depending, of course, on the character of the Arab master who owned them. The dividing line between freedom and slavery became blurred for southern slaves.

In addition, the government did not fully enforce measures to stop raiding in the South, which the Arabs were carrying out for the sole purpose of capturing slaves. This was partly due to the alleged difficulty of controlling the vast Sudanese terrain, and partly due to the uncooperative relationship between the colonial government officials and the infamous Slavery Supression Department. But it was equally due to the fact that the government had embarked on an unofficial policy which allowed the Arabs to capture Southerners, forced the slavers to release the slaves, and then channeled the freed slaves into the colonial system. This policy sent mixed messages to northern slave owners, given the illegality of slavery on the one hand, and the government's tolerance of some forms of slavery on the other. This policy, one may add, was typical of the British colonial manner of juggling international opinion concerning slavery, especially American public opinion, governing the "savage" South, running a colonial economy, and appeasing the northern populace.[3] Robert Collins captured this state of affairs: "Discretion and caution were to be employed by British administrators, and although all inveighed against the practice of slavery, British officials were quietly told by their superiors not to interfere between slave and master unless there was gross abuse. They were privately willing to tolerate slavery while denouncing it before the British public."[4]

The question remains as to how British these racist colonial policies really were. No doubt the British wanted to suppress slavery. As far back as during the reign of the Turco-Egyptian overlords, the British antislavery position was very clear. The appointment of such strong men as Samuel Baker, Charles Gordon, and Romolo Gessi to champion the fight against slavery, especially in Equatoria and Bahr el-Ghazal, speaks unequivocally about the British intentions to end slavery. By the same measure, during the Anglo-Egyptian Condominium, the British government at home was keen on the suppression of slavery. In addition, many officials appointed to run the colonial service were inducted into the policy and were constantly instructed through official letters to conform to the policy.

The reality on the ground, however, was that a British official in Sudan had to deal with opposing local viewpoints and decide which side to take: the northern Arab side, which held negative racial perceptions toward Southerners and had built the institution of slavery upon these perceptions, or the southern slave side, which might arouse anti-British sentiments among the Arabs, and could possibly cause Muslim rebellions. The relationship between northern Sudanese and the colonial government of Sudan was never an easy one. Because of the very nature of political and economic orientation, the two groups were forced to be antagonistic to one another, and the colonial officials wanted to avoid this near head-on collision. The Arabs wanted to maintain their economically dominant position over the rest of the Sudanese in their own way, and that included the continuance of slavery, while the colonial government was instructed to carry out abolition. The issue became even more heated over the activities of the Slavery Suppression Department, which continued to reveal the horrors that were being committed by the Arab slavers.

The Arabs, who felt somewhat unjustly treated over the claims of harshness of slavery, could reasonably expect some return for their acceptance of abolition. What they got was the colonial design that abolished slavery on paper but gave a blind eye to domestic enslavement. The British antislavery culture became an Arab-British culture, which hated the concept of slavery but could not do without it. In dealing with this awkward situation, colonial officials had to uphold their government's antislavery stance while accommodating the wishes of the Arabs that some form of slavery should be allowed to continue. The colonial views were closer to the views of the Arabs who benefited from slavery than to those of the slaves who were its victims.

The example of the converging views of the northern Arabs and British colonial officials demonstrates how a colonial government was able to create a false impression of the suppression of slavery while redefining and convoluting the ideology of slavery to allow the institution to continue in disguised forms. The idea of conferring a free status upon a slave came to Sudan with the British colonialists creating an army and finding government wage laborers among exslaves, whose free status was only in name because they were government slaves. This group was identifiably southern, and therefore they were *abd* (slave) in the eyes of the northern Arabs. They were held up by the colonial officials to represent the omnipresence of freedom in Sudan whenever the government needed to respond to the inquisitive antislavery movements around the Western world. The colonial government maintained this fragile balance by declaring that slavery was illegal in Sudan, and issuing freedom papers to the slaves, but giving them conditions under which to maintain their free status. When the slaves were not able to uphold the conditions, this gave the northern Arabs enough leeway to argue against abolition and demand that the government should rethink the abolition policy. It reinforced the Arab slavers' views that the black slaves were not suitable for anything else, and that they should be kept in servitude for their own good. The dilemma confronting the colonial government is understandable. As Martin Daly states, the Sudan colonial government was ready to go to the limits in defending slavery while it publicly espoused a slavery suppression policy because of both its own priorities and Sudanese enslaving traditions.

But it must have been clearly recognized that the abolition of the slave trade was impossible so long as domestic slavery was tolerated: a demand for slaves would be supplied just as it had been in the closing years of the Turkiyya. The hypocrisy of the government's policy was partly obscured by semantic niceties: there were no slaves, only "servants", no owners but "masters". It should, however, be recalled that aside from its impact on the over-all labour supply slavery was a matter of little moment to Wingate, Slatin and the central government. It occupied little of their time and became an issue mainly because of outside intervention. The moral side of the matter was not pertinent.[5]

As in the American South during the post–Civil War era, where the plantation owners insisted on racial ideologies to justify continuance of black slavery, the British colonial policy to end slavery in Sudan was viewed by both the northern Arab sectarian leaders and the Baggara as a threat to their system of production and their privileged position over the blacks. Thus, the Arabs resisted the policy, implicitly using racial ideology as a justification. When the black slaves tried to escape, the government did not enforce the policy granting free status. Consequently, when the slaves were recaptured, they were put back into servitude under the nose of the colonial government, so long as they were not sold and exported.

This chain of events—illegality of slavery, the unbearable alternatives that the slaves were presented with, the Arab claims that the slaves were unfit for anything other than slavery and that they were socially irresponsible—all provided the colonial official with a conscience-clearing process. The colonial official abolished the slave trade on paper, made concessions to the Arab slave masters to keep them supportive of the government, lifted the responsibility of caring for freed slaves off his shoulders, and managed to run the country without interruptions. This process became self-perpetuating, facilitated by racist views toward South Sudan, and endured until the use of slaves as soldiers was abolished (about 1945) and wage labor was introduced into northern farming societies. Despite these advances, the northern Arab farming and herding societies retained their taste for free or very cheap labor, and continued to seek to assert the legitimacy of slavery by retaining the notion of *abd* (slave), which equates Southerner with slave. This racist notion continued to serve as a recipe for slavery throughout the subsequent years, awaiting an event, such as the civil war, to trigger the reemergence of full-scale slavery.

When the British colonial government formalized the illegalization of slavery following Kitchener's sweeping victory over the Mahdists, the Arabs and other Muslims of the North had used black slaves for far too long. They had treated them with utter contempt and stripped them of their humanity. Farm labor, the military, and domestic service were largely reliant on slave labor. This suggests that the northern Sudanese resistance to British conquest was directed more toward the British antislavery policy than toward the conquest itself. A letter by Arab community leaders addressed to British officials right after the battle of Omdurman in September 1898 illustrates this point:

We beg most respectfully to state that the best help the government could give to the natives to ameliorate their present state and save them from danger of want and hunger, is to keep to them their black servants, male and female. But what is going on at present by the entrance of soldiers to the house with Dervish blacks, has caused the greatest confusion in the town—many Arabs, because of their black complexion, have also been taken with blacks as blacks—and the Dervish blacks who were the Khalifa's Mulazimin and who now accompany soldiers to search in the houses for blacks are personal annuities leading their soldiers to commit many irregularities. It is evident sir, that all the natives who are now in Omdurman are loyal and friendly to the government, those who are disloyal have either been killed in the fight or have fled away with the Khalifa toward the west. We therefore, take the liberty to submit this on behalf of ourselves and as representatives of the others, to kindly take our humble request into favourable consideration and after the government is settled down and the natives began their different works under the protection of the government, it would not be difficult to the government then, through the Sheikhs of the districts to gather the necessary number of soldiers to its army from districts.[6]

When the British won the war against the Khalifa and he fled to the west, many slave soldiers switched sides and joined the Anglo-Egyptian army. These former slave soldiers, along with other black slave soldiers who had served in Egypt and had come with Kitchener's expedition, were used as the force to clear the city of any remnants of the defeated Khalifa's army. They were also instructed to round up any other slaves throughout the city for recruitment in the new army. The individual British officials involved had suggested that by recruiting them into the army, they were freeing the slaves from the Arab masters who ill-treated them, but this was not a direct official policy. It was rather a corollary to another colonial policy, "the new slavery," to borrow Kevin Bales's expression.[7] The new system was that of forced cheap labor composed exclusively of African Sudanese. Some slaves, a small minority in fact, considered it an empowerment which they enjoyed a great deal. They remained military slaves,[8] for they could not desert to rejoin their families, but they definitely gained an upper hand against their former masters, who had sold some of them to Egypt and kept some for their own military use and labor. The majority of slaves, however, did not feel free.[9]

Despite the British policy to suppress the direct practice of the slave trade, that is, the sale of slaves outside Sudan, indirect forms of slavery remained founded on the enduring racial ideology, with people in northern Sudan referring to retainers and servants as slaves. The governor general of Sudan, Reginald Wingate, had long declared to his officers that domestic slavery was tolerable. Colonel Jackson later announced publicly to the Arab slave owners that "Sudanese slaves will remain with their masters, so long as they are well treated and adequately fed and clothed."[10]

The Sudan Colonial Service headed by Colonel Jackson justified his government's surprising decision in a way that delighted the Arabs. He asserted that although "the slave trade was illegal between many of the Sudanese slaves and their Arab masters, there had developed in the course of years an affectionate attachment like that which often prevailed between the Negroes in the southern states of the USA and their owners, and in such cases the slaves were unwilling to break away."

This was an official affirmation of a widespread view among the Arab Northerners that justified slavery on the basis of the assumption that a "slave mentality" had developed among black Sudanese. This assumption of mental slavery not only gave rights of enslavement to the Arabs, but also made the black Sudanese all too accepting of the role of slaves despite the misery involved in it. Even now, the term *abd* (slave) is used in a pejorative way by some people of Arab identity in northern Sudan toward Southerners. "Slave" has been equated with *janubi*, or "Southerner." The word is also used throughout the Arab world, especially in the oil-rich Gulf countries, which employ Africans as domestic servants. But slavery was neither reduced to mere words of address, nor to domestic enslavement. The Arabs of northern Sudan continued to feel betrayed by the British for taking away their legitimate right, sanctioned by tradition and religion, not only to buy and sell slaves they already had locally, but also to capture more and export them.

Sudan was a large country with uncontrollable borders and with many Arab and Muslim slave traders determined to maintain the institution. This led the colonial officials to argue that the suppression of the slave trade was more difficult than anticipated. They had found a perfect scapegoat and despite the clear ban, many Southerners were smuggled out either through the western border with the French Sudan, or by traders who claimed to be pilgrims to Mecca. The institution of slavery continued for many years under the noses of the British colonial authorities despite their assertion that they had entirely snuffed it out in Sudan. But the failure of the British colonial government to end slavery in Sudan was not due to technical difficulties alone. The British antislavery policy was founded on contradictions embedded in their racial attitudes towards the black Sudanese. The first was the suppression of slavery through the use of a slave army. So long as the government continued to use recently freed slaves and the descendents of slave soldiers to serve in the colonial armies, there was still room for slave traders to continue their practice by channeling their captives through the institution of military slavery. This contradictory behavior also offered opportunities for soldiers of Arab descent in the colonial army to keep retainers, concubines, and servants under the claims of protecting them from reverting to slave status. The Arab slaver deemed it in the best interest of a poor black woman or a young black boy to remain as a servant to an Arab soldier or an Arab farmer. It was alleged that these slaveholding soldiers or farmers were treating their slaves better than they would be if they were recaptured and resold to new masters.

Furthermore, the colonial administration was not in unison with the British home government over the approach to the suppression of slavery. As a matter of fact, the Sudan colonial government deliberately obstructed the activities of the Slavery Suppression Department. Antislavery activities were dealt a blow from which they never recovered—not because the British did not desire to suppress it, but because the staff of the Slavery Suppression Department were nearly helpless witnesses of an old northern Arab way of living that was fighting to survive. While the queen of England was "concerned at rumors she has heard that R. Slatin Pasha[11] favours slavery in the South—and takes the side of the masters, against the slaves" (as a letter said from a British general to Prince Francis of Teck), the officials of the Sudanese administration were not overtly keen on the ending of slavery. Although many of them agreed with the antislavery policy, many more were lukewarm about it due to the alleged difficulty of managing such a vast territory. Governor Wingate tried to deal with the problem of terrain by cutting off the South from government support and banning Northerners from going to the South, even though he did not really put the ban in action by way of border police. Others were openly opposed to the suppression policy.[12] The opponents of the suppression policy wished to appease the northern Sudanese public and also held outright racist sentiments toward the Southerners. Note the following letter, which Slatin Pasha had written earlier to a British army general in response to the queen's concerns regarding slavery in Sudan.

I was surprised to learn from your letter to Prince Francis of Teck . . . that her majesty the Queen of England views with disfavour the position I have taken as regards the slavery question. I am sure that her majesty cannot be ignorant of the inherent bad qualities of those Negro races whom we seek in vain to raise to our own level. These god-forsaken swine do not deserve to be treated like free and independent men. We free them from masters who ill-use them, enroll them in the army, and treat them generally like free men. In return, some desert from their battalions carrying off their rifles, fire upon the escort of their comrades sent after them, and eventually meet with the death they deserve. Others of a more inquisitive nature penetrate into our tents at night, and appropriate the few unconsidered trifles that the poor has in his possession, so that even in the middle of our own camp one has to sleep with his revolver under the pillow.

Some of the slaves that the British had given freedom to leave had no knowledge of their families' whereabouts, and were unable to start a new life without falling back into the hands of Arab slavers. Some women, fearing the possibility of recapture, chose to remain in the vicinity of army barracks, hoping that the army would help in the instance of slavers' attempts to put them back into slavery. Some of them initiated sexual relations with the soldiers, while others were forced into such relations. This did not sit well with people like Slatin, who came to the conclusion that the women chose the army locations purely out of sexual desires.

The black ladies . . . show no inclination to desert us, on the contrary they are only too ready to leave their masters and husbands for the vicinity of our camps hoping no doubt to be better served by the soldiers after long enforced continence. Their expectations of finding in the hearts of the Sudanese soldiers a response to their erotic inclination seems to have been thoroughly justified. Our soldiers bucked up by their long abstinence from amorous joys fall easy victims to these husky charmers, and the result is that close to my camp there is a colossal temple of Venus occupied by several hundreds of dark wenches of every shape and shade, but alas all alike in their unmitigated ugliness. These ladies carry the principle of individual freedom so far as to be ready at any moment to indulge in the freest of love, naturally the enjoyment of these universally coveted pleasures militated against the efficiency of the soldiery and is liable to produce a dangerous weakness in the army. . . . I am convinced that the *Sirdar* Sir H. Kitchener and also major general Rundle, both of whom regard the matter from other than a purely sentimental point of view are quite of my opinion. These officers cannot however, speak their minds freely on this subject because as British officers, they have to reckon with British public opinion.

Antislavery activists back in Europe also received their share of criticism from the Sudan colonial officials for their "uninformed" campaigns against slavery. The Colonial Service often argued that the conditions in Sudan which made it difficult to eradicate slavery could only be understood by those who live through them, and that any criticism against the British officials in Sudan for their stand as regards the slavery issue is unfair. Slatin inquired:

Would it not be a worthy task for Mr. Allen the honoured president of the Anti-Slavery Society to come here and constitute himself the guardian of public morals than to deliver high sounding but empty discourses in comfortable lecture halls in England on universal freedom and brotherly love? It is unfortunately the case that the greater number of English voters and even many honourable members of parliament are incapable of dealing with the Sudan and the conditions existing there. . . . These are the reasons for expressing the opinion that the blacks should be made to remain under the protection of their former masters, who were forced to treat them well on the whole.

Although officials of the British Colonial Service were men of their own generation and time, their unmitigated racist attitudes in dealing with the issue of slavery only made it possible for the "peculiar institution," as Kenneth Stamp calls it, to continue despite the official suppression policy. Their arguments for leniency towards domestic slavery resulted from a dilemma they faced between the illegality of slavery and the consequences of abolition. Both sides of the dilemma were addressed with racial overtones. On the one hand were the effects of abolition on the local economy, which relied exclusively on black slaves, and the impact of free slaves on the morality of the northern Muslim society on the other hand. This was a dilemma which echoed the attitudes of many Euro-Americans toward the freed slaves on the eve of abolition in the United States. Colonel Jackson articulates the dilemma of British colonial officials in Sudan:

The government had to choose between almost equally distasteful alternatives: temporary sanction of slavery or the immediate liberation of the slaves, the latter, a course of action, which might bring economic ruin upon the country. Liberation [of slaves] would have resulted in the abandonment of most of the cultivation along the riverbank. To have freed all the slaves would have meant letting loose upon the society, thousands of men and women with no sense of social responsibility, who would have been a menace to public security and morals. And finally the whole Arab population might have risen against what they regarded as a gross injustice, for after all, they had bought their slaves and paid for them.

The Revival of Slavery After Independence

Many arguments have been made over the nature of modern slavery, whether it has something to do with race relations or is a purely economic institution. These arguments are important to keep in mind because they are the perceptions, the excuses, the attitudes, and the antidotes to this institution. The study of slavery in Sudan has a long history of varied opinions, but in the face of such horrors, one cannot be bogged down by definitions. My undertaking is not to resolve the above contentions, but rather to provide an explication of the revival and renewal of slavery in South Sudan with all its brutalities and tragedy over the course of the current war. This renewal follows almost exactly in the footsteps of the nineteenth- and early twentieth-century slavery described above.

The current revival is not divorced from its past roots. Some colonial officials who served in the South had predicted it on the eve of independence. A colonial communication might capture the nature of abolition and persistence of slavery. Over half a century after the British reconquest of Sudan, Richard Owen, the governor of Bahr el-Ghazal based in Wau, wrote to his superior in Khartoum, B. W. Bell, lamenting the prospect of removal of British control from the region and the fate of southerners under the Arab rule. When the independence of Sudan was no longer a distant possibility, many colonial officials serving in the South and experiencing the brutal injustice that South had to live under had become sympathetic to the southern grievances, and were worried about the future of the South. They could see that handing the power over to northern Sudanese to administer the whole country without some kind of autonomy for the South would practically amount to turning the South over to another colonial power. It would mean that much injustice characteristic of the Turkiyya and the Mahdiyya, especially and most specifically slavery, might return. Owen's letter predicted the current revival of slavery in Sudan.

At this very critical juncture, when American and British public opinion may decide what is to happen here, has the issue of slavery even been raised? Sitting and looking around us, under the present dispensation, it is almost incredible that slave raiding could ever exist again. It is a bad dream we wish to forget; decent northern opinion wants to forget it; it is an ill-omened word and anybody hesitates to name it. And yet no one with knowledge of the country and sense of history can blind himself to the horrid fact that removal of all British control from the country in general but more particularly from the South, will mean the recrudescence of slavery. It will not be on the same scale as in the Mahdiyya, nor will it come at once or in a great wave. For a couple of years there will be no occurrence, partly because everyone in the New Sudan will want the country to shine in the forefront of the civilized world, and partly because it takes a little time for the veneer of 50 years enforced habit to wear off and immemorial habit to reassert itself. And then a Rizeigi, reverting to type, gets away with a Dinka girl on the Bahr . . . Next year there are 2 or 3 more cases. Two years later the Rizeigat make a little raid on a Dinka settlement. The local chief is bribed and silenced. Next year there is another. News reaches the Sudanese D. C. at Aweil. Getting the slave up to the Kababish won't be so very difficult since Sheikhs and people are not likely to give away their co-religionists for doing a thing which tradition sanctions, while the administration, while not countenancing such a thing, will not be all that zealous and active in nosing it out and hunting it down. A Southern MP will hear of it and make a fuss. Reassurances will be given; investigation will be promised; it may even be instituted — but without the British there, how much will happen? And so the business is well away. That is not gilding the lily. It is the true picture. Whether, how, or by what channel it should be intimated to [Her Majesty's government] or get across to the public is not my business. Perhaps it has been. But unless we do get this across I doubt if we shall have done our whole duty. It is a thing which might even influence American opinion. Remove British control, and two and a quarter million people slowly revert through neglect to exploitation and thence to the blessing of barbarism.[13]

Over the past two decades, Sudan has become a pariah state over the issue of slavery, which is occurring almost exactly as the colonial official had predicted it. Given the determined commitment of the government of Sudan to execute its ideology of homogenizing Sudan to become an Arab and Islamic country, the largest African state has been ravaged by war leading to the death of over two million Sudanese. Starving the South, destroying infrastructure in the South, and promoting Islamic militancy have been the elements that characterize the country. But most of all, the NIF government has become the subject of widespread criticism for encouraging enslavement of southern blacks, and increasingly Christian Southerners, by northern Arab Muslims. Exactly as predicted fifty years ago, the recrudescence of slavery has happened on and off throughout the period of independence. In addition to the tyranny of the army and violations of human rights, successive Khartoum governments have promoted or tolerated the subjugation and enslavement of the people of the South—all of which the government of Sudan denies. And the response to international concerns over it has been frustratingly lukewarm.

Some of the arguments against the historicity of claims of the persistence of slavery in Sudan arise from disputes over the definition of the terms *slavery, slave trade,* and *slave.* By looking at the context of the socioeconomic and political establishment in which the North had an upper hand, it is safe to affirm that slavery has never been abolished in Sudan, neither by the Anglo-Egyptian colonial regime nor by the successive minority Arab settler colonial regimes. But using the conventional definition of slavery, which includes capturing, selling, buying, and maltreatment of slaves, one would suggest that pure chattel slavery quietly reemerged as a social institution in the late 1970s. It increased in scale in the early 1980s, around the same time that Sudan's second round of civil war resumed between the Arab North and the African South. For the last seventeen years, government soldiers and government-supported militiamen from the North have been allowed and even encouraged to capture children and women from the South and sell them into slavery in the North. And as a participant in the practice, the government of Sudan has made every attempt to ensure that this remains a secret. Despite the government's denial of slavery, throughout the vast southern region, where the Arab world meets black Africa, the resurgence of systematic slavery is evident in the accounts of freed and escaped slaves. Lashing marks, branding scars, and permanent injuries on their bodies offer vivid corroboration of their testimonies. Numerous reports have documented that many women have served as concubines for the army, some as unpaid domestic servants, and others as farm labor. Children sold into slavery have been used as either farmworkers or to graze cattle in the desert for Arab herdsmen. Many more children have changed hands multiple times and have made their way into the capital city of Khartoum.

While the number of slaves in Sudan is easily in the tens of thousands, more precise statistics are difficult to obtain. The United Nations Special Rapporteur reported in 1994 that in the past several years tens of thousands of black Sudanese had been abducted from South Sudan and the Nuba Mountains and taken to the North. Thousands of young boys are routinely captured in the South during the raids or are rounded up in displaced persons' camps in the North by government agents and taken to Islamic religious schools. They are also taken to what one newspaper called cultural cleansing camps where they are beaten, renamed, forced to convert to Islam, and often compelled to fight on the front lines against their own people in the South. As shown earlier, many writers on Sudanese slavery have suggested that these practices are by-products both of the unresolved civil conflict and of the racial, political, and economic structures and history of the country. The challenge for scholarship and for humanity is to not ignore these factors nor to take them for granted, but to investigate them in order to understand the new forms of slavery.

The government of Sudan could have a number of reasons for promoting slave raiding and trading. The first could be out of a pure religious and racial hatred against the African non-Muslim South. However, an equally important but more practical reason is to suppress the rebellion in the South. The government's assumption is that the Dinka, the largest ethnic group in the South, constitutes the largest support base for the opposition Sudan Peoples' Liberation Army (SPLA), and that arming and sending Arab tribal militias to destabilize the Dinka will weaken the guerrilla army. But to persuade the Arab tribes to do this, the racial card has to be played. This policy has received wide acceptance among the Baggara Arabs, the herding northern tribes that share the border with the Dinka. Some evidence that the unique Dinka-Baggara relationship persuaded the Baggara to become a paramilitary militia for the government may come from recent events on the political scene in Sudan. For example, as mentioned in Chapter 4, in 1994 some northern opposition groups decided to join up with the SPLA against the NIF government. They put together an opposition army, which began fighting the government on the eastern border in 1995, but the Baggara did not agree to go and fight against these armies in the same way that they did in response to the call for jihad against the South. The government and the Baggara have considered the war against the South a natural way to deal with the southern infidels and troublemakers. If two birds can be struck with one stone—suppress the rebellion in the South and get some slaves to work on the farms and herd the cattle—this would be a great achievement on the part of the government. The Baggara are, in their turn, interested in displacing the Dinka from their grazing areas, which have been the subject of constant dispute between the two groups, and the government capitalizes on this border animosity for its slaving interests.

To put the policy in action and attract more Arab slave raiders, the government made announcements to the Arab chiefs that free guns would be distributed to their men, and that when the raid was successful the men could keep the booty, including cattle and war captives. These captives were then sold to the army, to the farmers, and to wealthy herders. Many Arab traders who have been interviewed by NGO workers about their rationale for these inhuman measures and about the fate of these slaves have argued that the slaves are better off with their Arab masters than in poverty-stricken and war-ravaged forests of South Sudan.

Justifications of Slavery, Then and Now

My assertion, then, that modern forms of slavery in Sudan are comparable to past practices is based on two facts. First, it has to do with the claims by the successive colonial regimes that what outsiders view as slavery is actually a practice which benefits both the "slave" and the "master." This notion is always propagated by the dominant sector, that is, the Arab Northerners who serve as the masters and who seemed to have persuaded the colonial authorities to take the same view, and never by the blacks who serve as the slaves. Such variation in views is evident in a letter written in March 1925 by three sectarian Arab leaders, namely Abdel Rahman al-Mahdi, Ali al-Mirghani, and Sherif al-Hindi, to the director of intelligence. The letter was an appeal to the government to reverse an earlier order that had been issued to give the slaves the right to leave their masters if they wished to do so:

We feel that it is our duty to bring to your notice, our opinion on the issue of slavery in Sudan, with hope that, the government will give it due consideration. We have been following the policy of the government regarding this class of slaves, since the reconquest. . . . What concerned us in this matter is that, slavery in Sudan today has nothing to do with what people generally know about it. For the slaves who worked on agricultural land are partners with landowners in actual fact. For they have benefits and rights which enable them to be a class existing by itself, and they can not be classified as slaves, as it is generally known in the real sense. Those Sudanese families who still keep slaves at present, are treating them as if they were members of their families, because of the increasing need for their work. If at all there is an injustice felt by any side now, it is the masters who are under the mercy of their slaves. As you all know very well, that the work under current circumstances is the most important issue in the Sudan, and which its solution requires great attention. The government, companies and individuals who are concerned with agricultural production are in need of every single labour, which can be obtained to participate for making agricultural schemes successful. The government and its officials must have noticed that, during the past few years, the majority of slaves who have been set free, have become unfit to do any work, and that the women have resorted to prostitution and the men have become alcoholic and lazy. For this reason, we urged the government to consider with great attention the logic of issuing freedom papers or documents without distinction, for the people who consider that these papers set them free from any work responsibility, and to relinquish any obligations which keep them under control. Since those slaves are not slaves in the manner known to International Law, there is no need to give them freedom documents, unless there is a need to give them to their owners whom they are working with. And it is in the interests of all parties concerned, the government, land owners and slaves, that the slaves should remain to work on the farms. If the policy of encouraging the slaves to leave the work on the farms continues and to beg in the towns, it will produce nothing but evil. We hope the government should consider this matter seriously and that it will issue orders to its officials in authority, not to give any freedom documents, unless the slaves prove their ill-treatment by their masters.[14]

Colonel Jackson believed this line. His encouragement of the Arabs to continue with local slavery may be recalled. "Sudanese slaves will remain with their masters, so long as they are well treated." The postindependence governments of Sudan, which became involved in the modern forms of slavery, have used the same arguments as above not only to deny the existence of the practices, but also to justify whatever form of slavery they admit to when cornered. For example, the present militant Islamic government has been confronted on many occasions about the ill-treatment meted out against the southern "street children" in Khartoum. The children have routinely been rounded up, beaten, forced to convert to Islam and drop their African names, and often sent to the war front in the South. In response to these claims, the government has argued that these children are better off in the Islamic schools than on the streets. This echoes the colonial and early twentieth century Arab contention that "slaves have no sense of social responsibility." What is common between the past and the present regarding slavery has been that the Arabs have always given themselves the right to decide what is in the best interest of the Southerners.

The second basis for my assertion is that, as the letters have shown above, the Arabs have always had the advantage of being listened to, so that their views of the issue of slavery were better known to the colonial officials than the views of the victims. The opinions of the slaves were never sought, so no one cared to document how they felt about the institution. Even so, evidence gleaned between the lines in official and personal letters indicates that the slaves did not want to stay with their masters. Their constant attempts to escape despite the risks of being killed or recaptured and resold can attest to their desire to be free. Consider the following letter, which Richard Owen of the Slavery Suppression Department wrote to his father during his early days in Sudan about the difficulty he faced in his efforts to suppress slavery among the Rashaida of eastern Sudan and in obtaining freedom for Muwalladin.[15]

Muwalladin had come in and asked for freedom papers; Hannim had given them papers, but unwisely insisted on their going back to their master's tribes. One of them was chained up by her master to prevent her going away again, when she eventually managed to escape, was re-caught by him, threshed, and doubly shackled with iron camel shackles! The other one has disappeared, her master says "she said she would not come with me, and walked off to Gadaref"; the general rumour and matter of common knowledge is that he tied her by a rope behind a camel and proceeded to drag her behind, under the midday sun, for home. By the time they had gone 6 miles she collapsed, her eyes bulged and her tongue came out, and she died! So they buried her where she was. It's common knowledge, but you can't get any Rashaida to witness to it, and I am trying to find the corpse and prove it, but it's like looking for a needle in a haystack.[16]

Therefore, the allegations by the Arab leaders that slavery worked in the interest of both slaves and masters, are easily countered by the reference in the same letters to the slaves' constant attempts to get away. They opted to be "prostitutes and alcoholics," instead of choosing the alleged "joys" of being slaves. Why would they run away even when they were born in the master's family and did not have or know any alternative families? Despite being born into slavery and having never experienced life to be otherwise, these so-called lawful slaves were aware that something was not right about their status and were constantly trying to change it. It was obviously better to be free and hungry or poor than to live in bondage, even when one was treated fairly.

History has repeated itself once again. While thousands of people from South Sudan suffer through a grave tragedy, the government of Sudan has consistently denied it and the world has decided to listen to the oppressor once more instead of taking a stance against one of the most cruel acts against humanity. Newspapers from around the western world have written about it. The United Nations Special Rapporteur on human rights has documented it. Individual researchers have witnessed it. The U.S. Congress has discussed it and has asked experts on Sudan to testify on the issue. The U.S. Committee for Refugees has given heart-breaking testimony to the U.S. Congress. Many members of nongovernmental organizations have pleaded with their own governments to pay attention to the suffering of South Sudanese, but their requests have gone unheeded, just as the pleas of the British Anti-Slavery Society went unanswered by the Colonial Service. In the same fashion that the British colonial administration refused to put the antislavery policy into action and ignored the British public opinion on abolition, the government of Sudan has gotten away with tragic violations while the world looks on.

This chapter has taken us from British colonial efforts against slavery, to their change of heart about it in order to appease the Arabs of northern Sudan, to a comparison of their ideas and practices, to the current Sudan government's promotion of slavery in the South. And what have we learned which we did not already know or suspect? Have we really discovered a new way of reading colonial records and interpreting the Sudan government's behavior over slavery?

The example of the British colonial policies and their deliberate evasion of the real issues fueling slavery in Sudan serves to remind us that new forms of slavery practiced today in Sudan are carried out with full aid from the government, but they are not divorced from past practices.

These practices have been systematic methods followed by many imperial governments that have ruled Sudan since 1821. They have all used racial ideology as a springboard for slavery. Scholars once believed that the British colonial government had embarked upon a full-scale policy of eradicating slavery from Sudan, and that slavery had been reduced or ended then.

Today, with the resurgence of chattel slavery, it seems that British colonial ambivalence towards slavery and its production of different definitions continued to influence the attitude of the Sudanese government regarding slavery for decades following colonialism. By analogy, then, I would like to draw attention to enduring racist attitudes in modern Sudan. Slavery in Sudan should not be studied through the traditional divides between precolonial, colonial, and postcolonial periods as if these periods are divorced from one another, as modern scholarship has tended to do so far. Nor should it be studied as a purely economic practice. Current slavery should not be treated as if it is entirely a recent isolated development, as many researchers do when they blame it all on the war. The history of Sudanese slavery has often suffered from a divorce between the study of nineteenth-century slavery and British policy regarding it, on the one hand, and the new form that is in place today, on the other. The latter can be evaluated only by examining how much it is a remnant of the archaic system left behind by the regimes that have ruled the country and whose views on race relations were closer to the Arab North than to the African South.

Sudanese slavery, especially the enslavement of South Sudanese and the Nuba, is as old as the first alien encroachment in the region. It has almost always been a product of the state system. The imperial powers have all used slaves, and the only twist to this history was the British claim to an antislavery stand. The Slavery Suppression Department lacked the full government assistance it needed, and the policy was neither practically seen through nor did it have the full backing of the colonial government. And this state denial of the existence of slavery continued even after the states which first invented it had disappeared. The Turco-Egyptian government, British colonial government, and postcolonial Sudanese governments all put the slaves to different uses and maintained a facade of the illegality of slavery on paper, but it cannot be said that any of them actually was fully interested in abolishing it, and especially not if the abolition policy risked turning the Northerners against the government of the day.

It is certainly possible to examine, using various historical sources, what these successive governments have learned from one another in terms of juggling the hostile Western and local public opinion against slavery and their reliance on slavery to pacify the Africans. It is a fair conclusion that these governments not only failed to suppress slavery, but also never had the intention to end it, as nothing in their policies quite demonstrates that as far as the documents can tell us. It would be wrong, however, to conclude from the forgoing that slavery was a product of racist attitudes alone. Slavery is only one symptom of the destructive nature of polarized race relations in the Sudan, which have produced many other social, economic, and political ills in the country. Moreover, to conclude that the present pathological state of South-North relations is entirely attributable to race would also be myopic. The history of racial interaction and Sudanese slavery is a component of the way in which the relations between African and Arab Sudanese must be addressed. At this point what matters is not how much damage racism has done in the lives of Sudanese people, but rather the influence it continues to exert on their relations and its potential for more serious damage now and in the future.

Chapter Five

The South-North Population Displacement

One of the most puzzling issues in Sudan's conflict is the displacement of South Sudanese to the North. The number of displaced South Sudanese in the North begs the question as to what prompts them to migrate to what is supposedly an enemy territory. There are no easy answers to this question. But despite the prevalent sense among the southern population that the North is a hostile environment, many factors have forced the people of the South, particularly the Dinka and the Nuer of Bahr el-Ghazal and the Upper Nile, respectively, to brave the North over the past four decades. This chapter addresses these factors and argues that the experiences of Southerners and the subservient position they have occupied in the North have served as recipes for slavery ever since the 1960s, when the numbers of Southerners in the North began to increase.

During 1960–61, massive flooding displaced many people from the Dinka section of Bor of the Jonglei region and Nuer from various parts of the central southern Upper Nile region. Other people living in the Sudd region from Mongalla to the confluence of Bahr el-Jebel and the Sobat downstream of the swamp system and to Malakal were also displaced. Practically all the people who live in this region are traditionally cattle-herding people who seek grazing in the more elevated portions on the west bank of the Nile or far east during the flooding season. But certain floods are still remembered in the history of these groups as inescapable. In 1961, the Bor Dinka lost a large percentage of their herds, they lost their crops, and whole villages were under the water for months. Their response was to vacate their inundated homeland, and many of them migrated to the North. This was the first single large migration to the North by a southern group because of a calamity that was not manmade. The government of General Ibrahim Aboud welcomed them on condition that they adopt Islam. Their children were not enrolled in schools until they adopted Arab/Muslim names. It was a culturally violent experience only comparable to and reminiscent of the Turkiyya and the Mahdiyya. It

was also the first time these groups of Dinka and Nuer came face to face
with racial and cultural segregation, for they had successfully escaped
or resisted slave raids with vigor during the Turkiyya and the Mahdiyya
because of their terrain. Slave-raiding parties of the nineteenth century
were not capable of penetrating the swamps of the Upper Nile, so the
people there were comparatively less exposed to the slave trade of the old
days.[1] These people had also confronted the colonial administration with
dignity and pride in the 1920s and the 1930s and were incorporated into
the state polity only after a comparative recognition of their traditions by
British colonial officials. In other words, no government had ever managed to successfully challenge their identity and pride. But in the 1960s
when the floods uprooted their livelihoods and displaced them to the
North, the Khartoum government exploited the fact of their impoverished condition and used it as justification for their subordination. It was
an opportunity to implement the policy of Islamizing and Arabicizing the
South without sending any missionaries there. The hope and the plan of
Sudan Islamists was that any Southerner who became Muslim during this
period could soon help extend the faith to their original home areas.

In the 1970s, following the Addis Ababa agreement that ended the first
civil war in Sudan, many Dinka and Nuer migrated in large numbers to
Kordofan and Darfur as well as the central region to work in agricultural
projects as farm wage laborers. Many more traveled as far as Khartoum to
work in the construction industry that was booming because of Nimeiri's
postwar reconstruction plans.[2] Although most of them were seasonal migrant laborers who spent the dry season in the North and returned to
their agricultural fields or cattle grazing in the South during the rainy season, their presence in large numbers in northern cities was not received
well by Northerners. It was the first time that some Northerners began to
see so many Southerners around their neighborhoods and some uneasi-
ness concerning the religious identity of the South was often expressed.
Moreover, many Northerners believed that Southerners did not have a
religion. There was a concern among Northerners that the presence of a
large number of "unbelievers" in Muslim communities was a menace and
threat to public Islamic morals.

Northern Views of Southerners

The presence of many Southerners in the North and the central region
also raised concerns among Northerners over the question of Sudan's
national identity. A series of governments in Khartoum had attempted
for a long period of time to establish a Sudanese national identity on
the foundation of Arabic language, Arab culture, and Islam. All the suc-

cessive Khartoum governments have worked diligently to persuade the world that Sudan is an Arab country, a reality that South Sudanese are, of course, extremely bitter about. But now to have the face of the capital city and other big northern towns, places that were historically claimed to be Arab, "littered" with people whose appearance and culture differed significantly from that of the North, was seen by Pan-Arabists as a challenge to the Arab and Muslim cultural project. If displaced Southerners could at least become coreligionists, that would spare the North the embarrassment of having to explain the religious identity of the country to the rest of the Islamic world. It is a matter of common knowledge that North Sudanese are uneasy when asked by Middle Eastern Muslims and Arabs about the religious and cultural identity of Sudan. Their response is that Sudan is a Muslim and an Arab country, but the presence of a large number of people whose culture and religion differs from the rest of the Middle East complicates the explanation. The whole northern society embarked on a mission to explain away the African and non-Muslim character of Sudan by portraying southern migrants as a burden intruding on the Arab communities of the North. The fact that they were citizens of the same country made poor partly by politics and policies of the northern government was disregarded.

Increasing crime rates at the time in such places as Khartoum, Madani, and el-Obeid were often blamed on "the large number of the undocumented labor migrants from the South," according to a local daily. In May 1976, one of the oldest Arabic newspapers in Khartoum, *Al-Ayam* carried a news article on an incident of a fight in Khartoum that involved Dinka men against Nuba men. Some Nuer men jumped into the fight on the side of the Dinka and a Nuba man was killed. The slayer, a Nuer man, was never found by the police since most Nuer migrant workers never use their real names while in the North. The article said that the public in Khartoum was terrified by such incidents, "which were new but becoming more frequent because of labor migrants."[3] In those days, stereotypes abounded in northern public discourse and in warnings that if the government did not pay attention to the increasing number of rural and "backward" people in the cities, the North was going to be taken over by crime. It was particularly at this time that Northerners began to create negative jokes descriptive of Southerners. To this day, northern humor involves depiction of Southerners as crime-prone, uncivilized, unfit for city life, and undeserving of equality with Northerners. It was not uncommon to hear government officials in the North talking of Southerners' natural incompetence in carrying out simple tasks. This has made it difficult for Southerners to be employed in the North.

Violence Against Southerners in the North

The negative characterization of Southerners displayed itself openly in the manner in which northern government officials and public service staff treated any Southerner seeking service. Southerners were often openly denied service in hospitals. Excuses were created to turn them away from any public assistance that other Sudanese received. Abusive words, especially the term *abd* or slave, were always hurled at people in public transportation and in lines at the post office or bank. It is my contention that such characterizations of a whole race of people is at the root of even more horrendous practices of discrimination. Physical violence always begins with verbal violence. The abusive characterization of Southerners gave license to the police to conduct racial profiling in response to crime in the cities. Periodically the police were instructed to round up groups of migrant laborers or any other Southerners found in a large gathering and send them to jail without specific charges or trial. Secret police usually broke into houses to arrest Southerners simply because there were "too many of them living in one house." Given that most of the migrants could not afford housing individually, it was not uncommon to find up to ten young men living in a two-bedroom house. For some reason, this did not sit well with either the police or neighboring Muslim families. The police often alleged that such places were hideouts for criminals, and the Muslim families imagined something immoral about young unmarried men living in their neighborhoods.[4] All of this was possible through the backing or complicity of the courts and the entire legal system. When they were tried, they often had no legal representation. Bogus charges could be brought against individuals who did not understand the language, and without legal defense they were sent to jail without even understanding what crimes they had supposedly committed.

While in detention, Southerners were severely beaten, electrocuted, starved, and occasionally raped.[5] Their detention sites were usually not disclosed to any asking family members or friends for many days. The early 1980s practice of the most hated policy of *kasha* was born out of this hatred and fear caused by the presence of Southerners in the North. *Kasha* was a practice that the Nimeiri government introduced to cleanse the capital city of all the undocumented rural migrants, mainly from the South and the Nuba Mountains. Such people were to be captured and repatriated to their home regions. They were usually rounded up and packed into lorries and trains headed South. But the practice was so arbitrary that the police did not distinguish among the student, the laborer who had a job, and the "redundant." The only criteria for arrests were physical appearance, especially complexion, attire, and Arabic language skills or accent. If one was black and did not speak proper Arabic, he was perfect candidate for forced repatriation. Those who looked unquestionably northern in terms of their physical appearance were not asked to provide identification even when found loitering in the same area with those who were obviously southern. The practice was also very violent and almost gave the ordinary North Sudanese a notion that a Southerner was truly undeserving of respect or dignity. Since the legal system was so biased and violent against Southerners, there was no reason for a Southerner to expect the civilian population of the North to be fair either. It was the characterization of Southerners as naturally *abd* that allowed Northerners to promote physical aggression toward the South. The current complicity of the northern populace over the issue of slavery is also a direct consequence of the subordinate position assigned to Southerners over the years. It is probably the negative perceptions of the South and the fact that slaves are largely from the South that makes it difficult for North Sudanese to rally against slavery.

The Case of the Ngok Dinka

In the 1970s, the people of a Dinka section called Ngok of Abyei district became part of Kordofan by the virtue of the Addis Ababa accord and found themselves thrust onto the battlefield of identity politics in Sudan.[6] The Ngok Dinka are the only Dinka group whose territory falls outside the established boundaries of South Sudan (i.e., the former Southern Region, 1972–82). They occupy the southeastern part of the government-controlled state of West Kordofan (formerly part of South Kordofan). Their immediate neighbors in Kordofan are the Misseria, a Baggara branch. The Ngok Dinka, under their leader, the late Deng Kuol Arop (Deng Majok), opted to remain part of Kordofan at independence in 1956 rather than join the Dinka groups in Bahr el-Ghazal. Deng Majok, as paramount chief, was incorporated into the native administration of Kordofan as Nazir, as northerners call their tribal chiefs. The Addis Ababa agreement of 1972, which ended the first civil war in Sudan, included a provision for a referendum on Abyei to decide whether it should remain part of the North or be incorporated into Bahr el-Ghazal. This provision was never fulfilled due to both the ambivalence of the Ngok people and the Nimeiri government's evasion of the issue.

Over time, the Ngok of Abyei fell through the cracks of the volatile arguments between the government of Sudan and the government of the Southern Region on the issues of allocating development projects and the cultural position of the Ngok in terms of education. The Ngok therefore found themselves almost without a choice but to seek jobs in the North as a way to find acceptance into the northern identity. Because of their proximity to northern administrative centers and their incorporation within the political and cultural boundaries of the North, the Ngok Dinka of Abyei have had greater access to education and employment in the cash economy of Sudan than other Dinka groups. They therefore have greater familiarity with northern Sudanese culture and operate more easily within it than other Dinka. Yet, their access to education and employment in the North came at a high premium and continues to work against their aspirations for autonomy. For example, during the period following independence, especially when General Ibrahim Aboud was in power, the school system had an Islamic orientation and the Ngok were required to drop their Dinka names and religious beliefs and adopt Islamic practices in order to be admitted into government schools. Ngok laborers in agricultural schemes and domestic workers in Arab households were given Arab names. Many of the prominent Ngok individuals today were once forced to adopt Muslim names and were made to memorize the Koran as conditions upon which to access education. But despite their relative incorporation into the northern culture, the Ngok, like all the Southerners, continue to be disdained in the North, and consequently harbor hostility toward Northerners. They have abandoned their foreign names and use them now in jest only. Although most of them have dropped these practices after completion of school, their bitterness over the previous government's attempts to recreate their identity is evident in the large number of Ngok Dinka who have joined the SPLA, where many of them have achieved high rank.

In addition, a large number of Ngok women during the period of migration worked as domestic servants in Muslim households in many northern cities, particularly in Khartoum. Their relationships with their employers were not governed by economic and class relations alone as they were between the northern dominant groups and northern lower class. Dinka domestic workers had a double utility: first, as cheap, malleable labor; and second as a subordinate client group that can be managed, manipulated, and even abused. Local leaders, merchants, and households have all used these workers in different ways. At the same time, the desperate conditions of most workers forced them to accept deplorable and demeaning roles that they did not know would become part of their jobs in northern households.

Suppression of the Dinka language was also a common practice. Since the employer communities were predominantly Arabic speaking, the workers were subject to the symbolic violence of having to communicate in the language of the "master." For example, the female domestic workers were denied the freedom to use the language that they knew best and which they would enjoy using, meaning their native language. While inside the compound of the employer, the woman was prevented from uttering even a word in Dinka for fear that she might influence Arab children. The employers usually even opposed the congregation of these women after work to converse in their own language. Given the strong restrictions on their movement, these women's desires to speak their own language were so strong that these women would sneak out of their employers' houses at night so as to meet one another for an opportunity to talk about home in their own language. It was common in the 1970s to find numerous Dinka Ngok women gathered to talk in open areas at night throughout Khartoum.

Equally oppressive was the fact that domestic workers were often given Muslim/Arab names. The act of forcing on the housemaids new names other than their ethnic names given at birth is a part of the verbal violence that gave these workers a feeling of cultural inferiority, since the new names were the cultural and religious names of their superiors. These new names did not accord the worker a recognizable social status in the North; nor did they make them part of the family in which they worked. But such names were used as a sign of each family's ability to convert a southern woman, something that is regarded highly among Northerners. Muslim families would boast to neighbors and friends about having converted a Southerner. The new names were also intended to spare the Arabs the supposedly torturous effort of pronouncing "difficult" Dinka names. The Ngok domestic workers were also victims of denigrating and abusive language used by the "master" or his children in the daily terms of address. The term *abd* was often used to call the woman.

Their living conditions, in the case of those who lived within the household where they worked, were usually appalling, and most of them could not afford to rent separate living quarters, for their pay was often pathetic. But of particular importance in terms of violence was the sexual abuse that many domestic workers experienced. For example, domestic workers of various ages were made to provide sexual gratification for the employers as well as to their male relatives and guests, a clear contradiction to the religious morals that they espoused. There were several variations to this type of abuse. A young woman (Ngok domestic workers were almost all young unmarried women) was sometimes raped by the man who employed her; she was sometimes forced to perform as a sex educator to minor boys; and she was often forced to undergo the Muslim ritual of female genital mutilation.[7]

All of these abuses constitute a system of dominance. They have become integral to the institution of slavery. These practices were often reported by these women when they returned to their home villages, but the number of cases informally reported was usually minimal due to the fear among these women of ruining their reputation. Despite this under-reporting, it became commonly known among the Dinka that many of their women were abused in the 1970s; after that time many families started restricting the migration of their female workers. Nonetheless, many years of subjugation of Southerners had given Northerners an appetite for southern female workers, and had promoted the notion that Southerners could be used as slaves. This notion is still held and is responsible for the perpetuation of the practice of slavery and for northern complicity in slave raiding and the slave trade in Baggaraland.

The Ngok relationship with the Misseria since independence has been marked not only by subtle and sometimes more blatant discrimination, but also by several incidents of large-scale physical violence. Some of the most notable of these incidents were the killing of several hundred Ngok Dinka in Babanusa town in 1965, following clashes in the Ngok area the previous year, and a series of attacks on trucks carrying Dinka passengers to Abyei in 1977. Upon the defeat of the government army by the SPLA in most of the South in the mid-1980s, there was an upsurge of Baggara violence against the Dinka, and the Ngok response to the raids was to abandon almost all the rural areas of their territory. Some of the inhabitants of these areas migrated to northern towns; others were displaced by repeated raids and went southward with their cattle to SPLA-controlled Tuic Dinka territory; the remainder stayed in Abyei town under constant harassment by the government of Sudan soldiers controlling the town. To this day, the rural areas of Abyei north of the Kiir River are almost completely deserted.

Although migration and displacement, especially to the North, turned out to be destructive in every sense, Southerners initially had viewed them as survival strategies when all other strategies failed in the face of the government's scorched earth policy. Because of this migration, part preemptive and part actually forced, the Ngok Dinka have suffered the loss of assets more than other Dinka groups in the area and have benefited less from international aid services rendered by the United Nations–led Operation Life-line Sudan than all the Southerners. Yet, they have probably fared better than Dinka in northern Bahr el-Ghazal in terms of physical survival. The majority of the Ngok people today live outside their traditional homeland. Their culture is totally reconfigured and their traditional administration is mutilated. For example, the SPLA commissioner of Abyei is resident in Tuic, and consequently their native administrative courts have been transferred to either Tuic or to Khartoum. The Ngok living in the North suffer the most. Their severely impoverished conditions have exposed them to all forms of exploitation and have caused Northerners to view the Ngok with utter contempt, indeed as people who can be nothing other than slaves.

"Kill a Slave by Using Another Slave"

By early 1985, the second round of civil war was extended not only into all areas of the South, but also into the Nuba Mountains of central Sudan. When the army of the government of Sudan was continuously losing ground to the SPLA, the field commanders of the government forces in the southern region resorted to revamping the practice of tribal militia. The use of the militia was aimed at pitting Southerners against one another in accordance with the popular northern phrase *ektul el-abid bil-abid* (kill a slave by using another slave). This was tantamount to a scorched earth tactic. The result was that many people among the Dinka, especially in the Upper Nile region, escaped the onslaught by moving northward. They reasoned that once in the government-controlled areas, the government might afford them protection and they might find jobs and international aid. The movement was also a preemptive act based on the calculation that physical mobility is better than staying put. In addition to the use of the militia force to fight the SPLA by proxy, the government army, finding it difficult to confront the SPLA, arbitrarily struck civilian villages, burning them, destroying property, killing the invalid and capturing scores of the able-bodied to be enslaved in the North. The result was massive displacement into the North from the Dinka areas that were within reach of the militia and the military. Three sections of Dinka nearest to the Baggara were hit worst—the Malwal Dinka of Aweil, the Tuic, and the Ngok Dinka.

In Upper Nile, the government used the Murle, who had historically engaged in raiding and counterraiding with the Dinka of Bor, to fight the SPLA. The government also found an opportunity to weaken the SPLA through its usual designs to pit Southerners against one another. A small force composed of Nuer tribesmen emanating from what was Anyanya Two became a government instrument in the civil war. Anyanya Two, an offshoot of the southern rebel movement that fought for independence of the South in the first civil war, was in disagreement with the SPLA during the current war on the issue of independence versus the overthrow of the Arab-dominated system and establishment of a united democratic Sudan. The SPLA's stated goal has been to liberate all of Sudan from tyranny and domination by the minority Arab clique. Although many in the movement saw the calls for unity as merely a tactic and separation as the desired goal, the SPLA was so persuasive about issues of underdevelopment in the whole Sudan that people living in areas historically underserved joined the "revolution." But the Anyanya Two leaders believed that Northerners could not be trusted and that the South would be better off as an independent state. This group had been unambiguous about its goals. Being a direct descendant of the secessionist movement during the first war, Anyanya Two had learned the lesson that the North Sudanese were not yet ready to commit themselves unconditionally to a secular and democratic state. Most South Sudanese found it ironic, however, for Anyanya Two, as a group that was so resolute about secession and which had actually started the rebellion, to have allowed itself to be manipulated into the government's arms. But Anyanya Two was a group with meager military successes. Its initial leadership, which was more sophisticated in articulating their political goals, was eliminated soon after the formation of the SPLA. What remained was an amalgamation of many guerrilla bands operating locally without a definite purpose. Their confrontation with the SPLA soon took on aspects of a Nuer civil war against the Dinka.

To illustrate, when the SPLA was formed with the backing of the Ethiopian Dergue regime, Mengistu had insisted on a unified political and military command under John Garang. Some of the older former Anyanya commanders such as Akwot Atem and Samuel Gai Tut resisted this policy and war ensued between the SPLA and the residual Anyanya Two. The latter lost access to international borders and was left without a source of adequate military supplies. Al-Mahdi's government took advantage of Anyanya Two's weakness and secretly extended its support to some members of Anyanya Two. In desperation, these groups joined the government's forces to fight the SPLA in Upper Nile, and al-Mahdi's government called them the "friendly forces." The SPLA found itself with no choice but to fight them with the same vigor as it fought the government army. The rural masses were caught off-guard by this turn of events and were soon swept up in a spiral of military raids and counterraids with little hope of mediation. To enact the policy of "kill a slave through another slave," the Khartoum government actively fanned the flames of these conflicts—especially that between rival southern military leaders—as part of its long-standing efforts to wage a proxy war against the SPLA. The confrontation between Anyanya Two and the SPLA caused serious destabilization of the region and massive displacement of Dinka and Nuer. The numbers of displaced Nuer increased in the North and their conditions in camps around Khartoum are appalling.[8] Pitting Southerners against Southerners as a mechanism of pacification continued and became more vigorous after the SPLA split in 1991, when various Nuer against Nuer militia confrontations became the norm through the 1990s.

The Militia Policy and Displacement

During the reign of Sadiq al-Mahdi, the elected prime minister of Sudan (1986–89), the government was particularly unable to defeat the SPLA forces in the South. It was then that the decision was reached to revamp Nimeiri's militia policy in pursuance of the possibility of weakening the SPLA through the use of southern tribal militias. The program was initiated everywhere in the South, especially in eastern Equatoria where the Mandari and Toposa tribesmen were trained and armed to fight the SPLA, which the government described as a Dinka occupation force of non-Dinka areas. To sell the concept of tribal militias, the government portrayed the SPLA as a Dinka clique intent on occupying non-Dinka areas without regard for the interests of all the ethnic groups in the South.

Although these forces did not really lead to the defeat of the SPLA as the government had hoped, they surely caused some weakness in the southern opposition as a whole. For one, the tribal militia's anti-SPLA stance made it impossible for the SPLA to gain badly needed new recruits from these tribal groups. Secondly, when the SPLA responded to these militia forces by treating them as enemy forces, which meant that the SPLA attacked and killed large numbers of them, such confrontations led to a more hostile relationship between the tribes where the militias came from and the SPLA. Such hostility and the SPLA campaign to win over these groups was the cause of worldwide criticism and condemnation of the SPLA for human rights violations, a criticism that continues to haunt it to date.

In addition to eroding the sympathy that the SPLA enjoyed internationally, the government of Sudan fueled the confrontation with the tribal militias in order to achieve three more objectives: First, to expose the SPLA in a bad light as a violent organization, one without a political cause. Second, to show its critics that the South is not a homogenous political unit and that SPLA claims of representing the whole South were baseless. This was particularly the line maintained by the government in response to criticism over its dismal human rights record. The government's usual propaganda argument relating to the militia policy, which dates back to the days of Nimeiri, asserts that the war in the South is really a product of internal southern tribal hatred and therefore is unrelated to national policies. Third, the government intended to create havoc in rural areas of the South to cause the people to move to government-held towns. When people left SPLA-controlled areas en masse, the government claimed it to be a military, political, and economic victory over the rebels. The government propaganda machinery, particularly the media (print, television, and radio) depicted these population movements as evidence of its ability to attract the people away from the more "impoverished, hostile, and disorganized conditions under the SPLA rule."[9]

The SPLA eventually overcame these hurdles and was able to gain support among most of the ethnic groups previously hostile to it. One of the reasons for this turnabout was the realization among the Southerners, especially after the massive displacement to the North in 1987, that the Northerners treated all Southerners as second- or third-class citizens without distinction. In 1987 the SPLA began to adopt an approach to the southern ethnic militias that won over some militia groups and helped lay the foundation for later military successes in the South and expansion into parts of the North. The SPLA regularized its quest for supplies by imposing a food tax which, once settled, generally freed the civilian population from arbitrary collection. Throughout 1987 and 1988, the SPLA gained in popularity and its relations with civilians began to improve. But the government army retaliated against the civilian population in areas recently vacated by the SPLA. This further pushed them into areas held by the SPLA and further led to the demise of the militia program. In 1988 and 1989 the SPLA won over a series of local militias to its side, including the most formidable of all, the Anyanya Two. Despite continuous criticism of the SPLA among many of these ethnic groups, especially the Nuer, who expressed their hostility to the SPLA in no unequivocal terms, there was no doubt that they all regarded the SPLA as the only hope for the southern cause. But by this time all the fighting between the SPLA and various militias had already caused a massive influx of extremely impoverished rural people, especially from Upper Nile, into the North. Like the earlier movements due to floods in the 1960s, or in search of employment in the 1970s, all of which exposed the southern migrants to northern disdain, the war-provoked migrations of the 1980s were equally demeaning.[10] The movement of desperately poor people into a hostile environment such as Baggaraland played into the hands of Northerners who had slaving intentions.

The government militia policy particularly faltered after the rapprochement between the Anyanya Two and the SPLA. The understanding between the two movements meant that SPLA supply lines were now secure. By 1988, the SPLA was able to move through much of the countryside in South Sudan without major obstacles. It was able at this point to concentrate its forces around the main government garrisons, and secured the international borders to the east and south. Civilians in these border areas, faced with frequent government aggression such as the aerial bombardment that had become the norm, were able to flee into the neighboring countries rather than government-held towns.

However, in Bahr el-Ghazal, where no Dinka militia could be formed against the SPLA, General Burma Nasr, military commander of the government forces in Bahr el-Ghazal, launched a different kind of militia. These militias were to be created in the North among the Baggara of Kordofan and Darfur. As Ushari Mahmoud and Suleiman Baldo wrote, "the core strategy to undermine SPLA support in the Dinka area was to resurrect and fuel the historical Dinka-Rizayqat (Baqqara) strife."[11] The

Baggara were recruited, armed well, and instructed to function as a proxy counterinsurgency force in Bahr el-Ghazal, giving them, in effect, license to raid Dinka villages and cattle camps and abduct their inhabitants. The Baggara at this time did not need persuasion from the government since they, on their own, had historically been engaged in conflict with the Dinka over the grazing valleys of the Kiir River and had raided northern Bahr el-Ghazal since the time of the Mahdiyya. A government offer of arms, although a politically motivated action far beyond the Baggara interests, was a welcome initiative for the Baggara, at least for the moment. The Baggara seemed to have not grasped the far-reaching consequences of their government-sponsored hostility to the Dinka and the proliferation of arms. Although some Baggara leaders may have recognized other government motives for supplying arms, they could also see the rewards to their own people. Having government backing meant to the Baggara that they would have an upper hand in their competition for resources with the Dinka.

When Sadiq al-Mahdi became prime minister in 1986, his government was under the impression that it held a stronger military position than the SPLA. It appeared that al-Mahdi was of the idea that the "rebellion movement," as the SPLA was called in the official discourse, would collapse in the face of a prolonged conflict. Libya was now on the side of the Sudanese government, U.S. military assistance was still coming in, and the Transitional Military Council (TMC) had rallied the Arab Middle East to the defense of Islam and Arabism. This may have increased al-Mahdi's unwillingness to deal seriously with the SPLA. Yet al-Mahdi's political support in the army was weak, especially among the high-ranking officers. His traditional political rivals, the Khatmiyya Sect and the Muslim Brothers, were dominant in the army. There were also indications that the army was exhausted by war. For this reason, al-Mahdi tried to circumvent the army in his own war strategy, by channeling supplies to pro-Ansar militias. This strategy did not achieve the desired goal of weakening the SPLA. In fact, it backfired. The distribution of arms to civilians caused serious security problems in Kordofan and Darfur. Armed robbery and other abuses became rampant in western Sudan.

Although the use of tribal militias to fight the SPLA began in 1985 during Nimeiri's era, it became a more significant factor in the war after the fall of Nimeiri. The Misseria and Rezeigat Murahileen of Kordofan and Darfur received support from the transitional government that replaced Nimeiri, and large well-armed raiding parties began attacking the Dinka sections of Ngok, Tuic, Abiem, and Malwal. Just as in the nineteenth century, the main incentive to join the raiding band in the 1980s was economic. The Baggara had been marginalized by Nimeiri's government, partly because of their support for the Ansar Sect and the Umma

Party. Therefore, the coming to power of some western Sudanese who were members of the TMC was received by the Baggara as their chance to rectify the situation. The western members of the TMC government pushed for provision of arms to the Baggara. The Baggaras' ambition was to control the water, pasture, and land resources of the Dinka and the Nuba. With arms supplied by the government increasing their firepower, they intended to chase the Dinka away from the grazing valleys of the Kiir River. They wanted to seize Dinka cattle to be sold in the North, an activity that became so lucrative that the pro-Umma merchants, politicians, and officers supported it. For example, David Keen asserts that the pro-Umma merchants contributed heavily towards financing the militia raids and seizing of Dinka cattle. This lowered the price of cattle in western Sudan, so the merchants bought them at wholesale prices and then shipped them to Khartoum.[12] Government support to the Baggara increased in 1986 when Sadiq al-Mahdi became prime minister, as the Misseria and Rezeigat were generally members of the Ansar Sect and supporters of the Umma Party.

Unlike the old times when the level of weaponry between the Baggara and the Dinka was relatively similar, the Baggara, better equipped this time, launched devastating raids into northern Bahr el-Ghazal. The Baggara raids peaked in 1986 and 1987. The firepower of their modern automatic assault rifles (AK-47s) against the Dinka spears and hippopotamus skin shields enabled the Baggara to annihilate whole villages indiscriminately, killing all those who resisted, capturing women and children and looting the cattle. Their impact in creating famine and spreading human rights abuses has been well documented in reports by Human Rights Watch and other human rights groups. The United Nations Commission for Human Rights has sent two Special Rapporteurs, Gaspar Biro and Leonardo Franco, to Sudan over the past four years. Both men have written reports describing the atrocities of the Murahileen and the practice of slavery.[13] Sometimes, the army undertakes a joint operation together with the Baggara tribal militia to attack SPLA positions or civilian villages deemed sympathetic to the SPLA. In two such operations in 1987 and 1988 the Rezeigat joined hands with the army unit from el-Da'ein and went on a raid that went as far south as Gok Machar in Aweil West. Upon their return, a celebration was organized in Abu Matariq[14] for the victorious militia. Witnesses reported that the militiamen had Dinka children and young women that they brought with them from the operation.

It was these joint operations between the militias and the Sudanese army that became the principal cause of displacement from northern Bahr el-Ghazal into Darfur. The displaced Dinka, especially from Aweil, usually move to ed-Da'ein town when the raids destroy their villages, where they find foreign aid and look for a way into other northern cities. International aid agencies have initiated relief programs to house some of these displaced Dinka in Baggara territory. But the displaced Dinka who are resident in relief camps are constantly vulnerable to Baggara attacks in revenge for any SPLA victories back in the South. The presence of a large number of Dinka in Baggara areas increased the Baggara enmity towards Southerners as it has done over the course of the current war in the North as a whole. As Ushari Mahmud and Suleiman Baldo wrote in 1987: "Thousands of Dinka moving north to escape war and famine exacerbated animosity. Ethnic chauvinism among the Rizayqat is being fuelled by social changes related to the migration of thousands of drought and war-affected people, the increasingly complex nature of the economy and inter-ethnic competition over resources and services, local political animosities, class disparities and general strife. The government, to reach its ends of self-preservation, has begun a war within a war." [15]

During the 1987–88 period, the combination of war, drought, breakdown of local economies, and declining prospects for decent living caused many Southerners, including Equatorians who in the past sought refuge in the East African states of Uganda and Kenya, to move to the North. The cumulative effects of raiding and war-provoked destruction of regional economies within the South have driven Dinka villagers into the North for both relief and security. This increases the availability of cheap, exploitable labor in the North in general. It also diminishes the presence of Dinka herds in the grazing land along the Kiir River, increasing its availability to Baggara herdsmen. This was regarded in the North, both in government circles and among the Baggara, as an indication of the success of the militia operations. For the government it was used as proof that the SPLA is hated in the South, and that continuation of the militia system would soon result in the collapse of the SPLA. For the Baggara, the success of the program was measured by the amount of grazing area vacated by the Dinka and by the displacement and influx into Darfur of a large number of desperately poor people ready to be exploited. The more destruction the Baggara meted out, the more agitated against the Dinka they became. It became a circular process beginning with the Baggara need for grazing and government need for a force to destabilize the Dinka, which grew into atrocious raiding, substantial destruction and displacement, the Baggara contempt for the displaced, and finally the enslavement of the despised Dinka. This process continues today. Throughout the period 1987–99, the Baggara militia pounded at the Dinka so long as there was no local defense force to resist the raids successfully. Raiding is still taking place today.

False Hopes of Security and Dinka Migration to the North

In 1988 the Dinka land in northern Bahr el-Ghazal was subjected to a massive famine. Sorghum grain ran out, agricultural activity was fatally disrupted because of the security situation, the cattle were mostly looted, and the people from Gogrial, Aweil West, and Aweil East Counties moved away from their areas into Darfur and Kordofan. As thousands of Dinka families were fleeing the famine in their areas and passing the Kiir River northward, the Baggara devised ways to exploit the famine-stricken migrating Dinka. The most horrifying was the formation of committees to meet every Dinka family that was passing through with children. These committees would encounter the migrating families, whose assets had been stripped, and offer them certain deals. One of the offers relating to slavery was that the Dinka families leave their children with the Arabs to herd their cattle for a year in return for a large amount of money—a wage for the child and money for the family as well. The family could then use that amount to buy food and cover transport costs. The family would be given money and a paper containing the name of the person who took the child, and after a year they could come to retrieve the child and the money in Safaha. Some Dinka were desperately in need and did not understand the meaning of this document, and therefore, accepted the offer. Others rejected the offer, saying that they would prefer that they or their children die than put them up in a transaction that was clearly a sale of children by their own parents. But many Dinka who refused to offer their children in that way were coerced to do so and their children were snatched from them. They were told openly that either they accepted the deal or their children would be taken by force in any event. In fact, some had their children forcibly taken from them in this manner. This deceit combined with force led to the enslavement of over 2,000 Dinka children by the Rezeigat during the dry season of 1988 alone. When the families returned to Safaha a year later as was promised during the transaction, they found no one to talk to and they did not find the children. This was when they realized that the whole operation was a hoax.

The assumption among South Sudanese, however, that the North would provide security and relief had been noted throughout the recent history as a miscalculation. In 1987, as mentioned in Chapter 3, Rezeigat massacred approximately two thousand unarmed Aweil Dinka migrants in the railway station in ed-Da'ein. Prior to this event, as mentioned above, throughout the 1970s there were large-scale killings of Ngok Dinka by Misseria in various places in southern Kordofan. Many Southerners traveling on the train passing through the Baggara territory to the North have been victims of organized Baggara hostility towards the Southerners. In most of these cases local authorities were implicated in

the events, and in none were any legal measures taken against the perpetrators.

In the minds of desperate Dinka, however, the displaced persons'
camps in southern Darfur represent, in one sense, a place of relative
security. The presence of international NGOs in these camps gives the
displaced persons the illusion that the Baggara would be deterred from
attacking them. But this does not mean that they are safe either from
exploitation or attack. As a visiting team of consultants on behalf of the
European Commission Humanitarian Office (ECHO) noted in a report,
"camps have, on frequent occasions, been abandoned after northern militias have suffered a defeat at the hands of the SPLA, for fear of revenge
attacks. In such circumstances the camps are generally looted. There is
no recorded instance of the return of goods or livestock either to the displaced or to the NGOs that provided them."[16]

Sadiq al-Mahdi's Policy Toward the South

Although the South remained critical of the Khartoum government long
after the fall of Nimeiri and transfer of power from the TMC to the coalition of Umma, Democratic Unionist Party (DUP), and NIF, it is safe to
say that Southerners also remained hopeful that a "democratic" period
might bring a change in the government attitude toward the South. These
hopes were dashed by the glaring contradictions in Sadiq al-Mahdi's political stance. It became very clear that he was fully committed to the
establishment of an Islamic state in Sudan. His articulation of this position was in direct opposition to the secular state Nimeiri presided over up
to 1983. When al-Mahdi became prime minister he aligned himself with
an international expansionary Islamic ideology. His reluctance to give
serious consideration to southern proposals was apparent, and his utter
contempt for southern leaders was underlined by his inclusion in his government of only those southern leaders who lacked a political constitu-
ency of their own. His views became closer to the views of Iranian leaders,
and he offered no real compromise either on the issue of an Islamic state
or on southern autonomy.

His earlier criticism of Nimeiri's September laws imposing Islamic legal
code was not directed against the very idea of applying Islamic laws in
Sudan, but rather to point out that the way Nimeiri applied them was
not based on sound Islamic principles. His coalition partners, the DUP
and the NIF, adopted an even harder line, which saw any concession to
regional autonomy or federalism in the South as undermining a future
Islamic state. Although the DUP and NIF accepted that in a regional
or federal system individual regions could choose whether or not to be
governed by *shari'a*, such a concession came with preconditions. Fore-

most was that non-Muslims living in the North would also be governed by Islamic jurisdiction. The NIF was particularly unwilling to see the old Southern Region reinstated. Rather, it preferred the maintenance of the three separate regions of Bahr el-Ghazal, Upper Nile, and Equatoria. In this way, the idea of homogeneous identity of the South would be challenged easier, especially since the Muslim radicals of the NIF calculated that Islam could be pushed faster into Bahr el-Ghazal and Upper Nile. The two regions are both historically and geographically in closer contact with the North. They already have pockets where Islam has taken root, and therefore, the NIF hopes that Islam can be extended here with ease.[17] The coalition government worked very hard to fan the conflicts among the three regions, either through recruitment of tribal militias within the South to fight the SPLA, as stated above, or by causing rifts among the southern opposition groups and in the government.

The policies of al-Madhi's coalition government did nothing but fuel the war with no prospects for an end to the country's mounting economic and social problems. By 1988 dissatisfaction had increased within the North. Obviously, the war was not affecting the South alone. The country's economy was stripped by the war, poverty abounded in the North just as in the South, and families were increasingly agitated by the continuous deaths of their children in war. Northerners had also become uneasy with al-Mahdi's failure to address the major issues facing the country. The war was ever more expensive in terms of both material and human resources and was more unlikely to be won, production was steadily declining, foreign debt had reached historical highs, and the disunity of North and South was set on a path of no return. The army issued al-Mahdi with an ultimatum: either ensure that the army takes an upper hand in the war, or find mechanisms for a peaceful settlement.[18] The choice between fighting the war properly or making peace with the South became the question for political parties as the next elections were approaching. Seeing that an effort to bring peace would sit better with the voters, the DUP pulled out of the coalition and made contacts with the SPLA. The head of the DUP, Mohammed Uthman al-Mirghani, went to meet John Garang in Addis Ababa, where the two signed a declaration to suspend the *shari'a* and convene a constitutional conference to decide on the crucial issues facing the country. The public in Khartoum and elsewhere in the North received the news of this agreement with jubilation. When al-Mirghani returned to Khartoum from Addis Ababa, the public went out on the streets to support his effort, an event that was an illustration of how desperate for peace the Sudanese had become.

When Sadiq al-Mahdi realized that the popular support that Northerners were giving to the DUP-initiated peace plan would weaken the position of any party that stood in the way, he reluctantly agreed to work closely with al-Mirghani to negotiate a peace settlement with the SPLA. Attempts were made to restore the Umma-DUP-NIF coalition, but the NIF left the coalition because of what it saw as peace negotiations that compromised their goal of an Islamic state. The Umma and the DUP would have pushed ahead with negotiating a peace settlement, but a group of radical Muslim officers in the army, supported by the NIF, staged a military coup on June 30, 1989, and overthrew Sadiq al-Mahdi's elected government.

NIF Militarism and Slavery

The overthrow of al-Madhi's government could be regarded as a great set-back for the hopes that were raised by the DUP peace initiative. Al-Mahdi, having been forced by the political situation in the North to show commitment to a peaceful solution for Sudan's problems, had made breakthroughs toward reconciliation with the SPLA. But all the prospects for peace were shattered once more by the coup, and a new era of militarism was ushered in again. But just as Sadiq al-Mahdi had done in the early days of his premiership, the new military government in Khartoum calculated on gaining military ground in the South and saw no immediate need for making concessions to the SPLA. The junta vigorously pursued the military option. However, in 1990 their military initiative failed to reap any recognizable benefits. Many factors played against them, including the Gulf crisis caused by the Iraqi invasion of Kuwait. The military government, which by this time had demonstrated itself as an NIF government despite its incessant denial, supported Iraq; and in the process alienated Egypt, the oil-rich Gulf countries, and a greater number of the world's nations. Foreign aid and military assistance dried up even from Iraq's Saddam Hussein who had been a staunch supporter of the North in the war against the South. Hussein could no longer provide military hardware or financial assistance due to his own confrontation with most of the world.

The events in the Gulf region and the consequences for the Sudan government also coincided with the SPLA's improved military situation when the movement found a new source of supplies in southern Africa and more secure supply routes of its own through East Africa. By the end of 1990, the hopes of the Khartoum government for gaining military ground in the South had not been realized, and the government decided to return to the policy of tribal militias. The difference this time was the slogans and the incentives for recruitment. Whereas Nimeiri's government capitalized on southern ethnic differences and anti-Dinka politics in Equatoria to recruit for militias, al-Madhi's government used its strong relations with the Baggara to introduce the Popular Defense Forces in early 1989 to destabilize Bahr el-Ghazal. The NIF-backed military government, however, resorted to jihad.

Although recruitment for the Popular Defense Forces continued and was expanded under al-Bashir, the promised incentives were different. It is important to note that when al-Mahdi's proposal for Popular Defense Forces was first made, it was opposed by most of the senior officers in the army. The army argued that it would destroy the image of the army as a national institution. But there were some officers who supported the militia policy. One of the few officers who had been involved in supporting the militias in the field was Brigadier Omar Hassan al-Bashir. Al-Bashir continued the policy even after he overthrew al-Mahdi.[19] The new recruits were told that the war in the South was to defend Muslim land from aggression of the infidels. The militia acquired the name Mujahideen or holy warriors. In the same style as the Iranian slogans during its war against Iraq, NIF militias were promised points toward heaven because they were an Islamic army fighting to spread the word of God and to stand up against the "Zionist and American influence in the South." As John Ryle wrote: "Attacks by northern militias on the Dinka to the South have been given an air of legitimacy in northern Sudan, in the first instance by a history of racial discrimination and slavery—by the categorization of Southerners as inferior to Arab Northerners—and latterly by the notion of *Jihad*, of holy war. The Murahileen could be characterized, in this sense, as a predatory religious formation. This notion is expressed in a saying current in the north: *Dead you are a martyr; alive you benefit* (i.e., from looting)."[20]

Under the NIF, the Baggara militia attacks on the Dinka were ever more atrocious, and ever larger numbers of people from northern Bahr el-Ghazal were displaced to the North. During this phase of displacement, NIF contempt for Southerners reached new and unprecedented heights. Hassan al-Turabi, the ideologue of the Muslim Brotherhood and mentor of Omar al-Bashir, appeared particularly anti-South and saw no need for decent treatment toward the displaced. Southern politicians who voiced the concerns of the displaced were simply shunned, or arrested. Al-Turabi openly showed disrespect for southern politicians whom he regarded as power-thirsty and job-hungry. He simply either ignored them or pitted them against one another over the government ministerial posts. Al-Turabi is said to have made two statements that Southerners hold as indications of his negative attitude towards the South. On the issue of rivalry between southern politicians and factional fighting in the South he once advised Northerners to "let Southerners fight one another and we will make peace with whoever wins."[21] On the issue of the displaced Southerners, he also reportedly said that all southern politicians could be bought so that they do not keep complaining about the plight of their people displaced into the North. These statements were made in an effort to evade responsibility for the displaced in the North and blame their suffering on the "corrupt" southern politicians.

Factional Fighting Within the South and More Displacement

Al-Turabi's perceptions of the South became even more evident after 1991, when the SPLA experienced a nearly catastrophic split. The split occurred in August when an ethnic Nuer commander, Dr. Riek Machar, announced a coup against an ethnic Dinka, Dr. John Garang. Initially, "the two doctors" were divided over the question of whether or not the SPLA should abandon its declared aim of creating a united, democratic, secular Sudan in favor of political independence for the South. Resentment over Garang's notoriously heavy-handed rule had also been building within the movement for years. These were the factors that triggered the 1991 coup attempt by Machar and others. It is worth mentioning that another precipitating factor was the May 1991 loss of the SPLA's main supply lines and military bases in southwestern Ethiopia, following the collapse of Mengistu's Dergue government. This event also provoked the mass exodus of some 350,000 South Sudanese refugees from their Ethiopian hiding places. The Khartoum government promptly bombed the returning refugees, scattering them to diverse regions where they later became vulnerable to the predations of rival southern factions.

Faced with this chaotic situation, it was not long before issues of nationalism gave way to the more basic need for self-preservation. Both Garang and Machar reached for the ethnic card, and from there the conflict spiraled downwards into the hands of numerous independent warlords, each preying upon one another's civilian populations. Several months into the split, nearly 70 percent of the Bor Dinka in the southern Upper Nile region had been displaced, with hundreds of civilians having been killed or wounded, in what became know as the Bor massacre.[22] Nuer communities in the central and western Upper Nile also experienced devastating military raids by Garang's forces, particularly in the areas of Ayod, Ganyliel, and Mayom.[23] By 1992, the economic fabric of the extended regions—based on a mixed agro-pastoralism supplemented by seasonal fishing—stood in tatters. This precipitated another mass exodus of Dinka and Nuer to the North. The government found this factional fighting in the South beneficial for its policies of "divide and conquer." It was much easier for the government of Sudan to argue against southern political rights as a united front. Such South-on-South violence also furthered the government's propaganda efforts to portray the destruction of the South as the result of internal tendencies toward "tribalism," rather than as the consequence of its own discriminatory and militaristic policies.

Another factor that increased the movement of Southerners to the North was the havoc wrought by Kerebino Kuanyin Bol in Bahr el-Ghazal from 1994 to 1998. This confrontation displaced thousands of people from Gogrial and Tuic Counties to Abyei and further north up to Khartoum. Kerebino was a founding member of the SPLA. In 1987, he and a number of other SPLA officers were detained by the SPLA commander in chief John Garang for reportedly having plotted a coup against Garang. When they broke out of prison in 1992, they fled to Uganda and then to Kenya where they were granted political asylum. While in Kenya, they joined the SPLA breakaway faction led by Riek Machar and they all formed SPLA-United, a movement that was later renamed the South Sudan Independence Movement/Army (SSIM/A). As mentioned earlier, a combination of their anger with Garang and lack of their own supplies eventually drove them to form an alliance with the NIF government against the SPLA.[24]

Kerebino formed a separate fighting force and attracted a number of Nuer soldiers who broke away from the SPLA as well as proceeding to recruit followers from among his own Dinka of Bahr el-Ghazal. In 1994, he declared war on the SPLA and with his predominantly Nuer force he managed to fight his way into the government-held town of Gogrial. Most of the fighting took place in his own native district of Tuic, and with his new base and an NIF supply station in Gogrial his war against the SPLA went on until the end of 1997. During this period, Kerebino inflicted substantial damage on his own people in Tuic, Abyei, and Gogrial Counties, and parts of Aweil East and Wau Counties, all in Dinka territory. In January 1998, Kerebino switched sides again and rejoined the SPLA, but his activities had already caused an unspeakable misery among the Dinka and were responsible for the subsequent famines that struck northern Bahr el-Ghazal during this period. The displacement of the Dinka population, which continued well into 1999, was primarily due to the demolition of the meager civilian infrastructure. Huts, clinics, and other facilities were burned to the ground. The fighting made it difficult for the population to stay in one place, to find food, to protect their animals from capture, or to cultivate.[25] Large segments of the population migrated to the North where they experienced even more indignities. Their racial status, their political stance, and poverty exposed them to various forms of enslavement and reinforced the negative images Northerners always held about the South.

Northern Popular Perceptions of the
Displaced and the Revival of Slavery

The movement of South Sudanese to the North, without the necessary skills for city life, and without the political leverage that rural Northerners usually have in the cities, forced the Southerners to take marginal and petty jobs. Holding certain kinds of jobs in Sudanese societies dictates the jobholder's social standing. Because Southerners took up the occupations that are regarded as very lowly, it was almost automatic that they should also hold subservient positions in any other aspect of life, including being equated with slaves, thus the word abeed[26] that is used by Northerners to address Southerners.

Dinka laborers in the North, working for little more than the food they eat, contribute to the profitability of agricultural production in Sudan, while losing their social standing in the eyes of the Northerners. Destitute laborers are treated as the property of the prosperous merchants and large agricultural landowners. Those advocating against slavery in Sudan, including human rights-based NGOs and UN agencies, appear to have forgotten this simple truth. Displaced Southerners are at the bottom of the racial hierarchy in northern Sudan. Having few or no resources, they are highly dependent on a complex set of patron-client and exploitative relations linking them to local groups and power brokers, including merchants, farm owners, and aid agencies. Within this system of dominance, relations range from servitude through various forms of bonded work, to providing cheap agricultural and urban labor, and being used by local power brokers to attract foreign aid.[27] Within such a complex and integrated system structured by relations of dominance, the lines dividing slavery and cheap labor, especially for an outsider, are blurred. As a result, slavery in its various forms is simultaneously enforced and changed by the humanitarian assistance provided through the government.

Aid agencies appear to inadvertently sustain the exploitation of Southerners in the camps. Even the displaced persons' camps structured and maintained by international aid agencies, especially in Darfur, despite their important work in saving lives, facilitate northern domination. Humanitarian aid for the displaced Southerners represents opportunities and benefits to the northern groups, including the government. The government of Sudan has sometimes chosen to emphasize that the displaced are full Sudanese citizens. This has tended to facilitate their strategic incorporation into the labor force and to legitimize cultural suppression. At the same time, local authorities, especially in Darfur and Kordofan, have sometimes emphasized a separate identity for the displaced in order to attract NGOs and outside assistance into a resource-poor area. These displaced Southerners work for the Baggara as agricultural day labor in the cultivation season and do various forms of menial work in the off-season. The role of relief agencies, it seems, is to keep the agricultural workforce in good condition in conveniently situated holding camps. It is as if they were being fed so as to go to work during the rainy season. Currently, slave raiding is driven by this environment of contradiction between the Baggara hate for Dinka on the one hand, and the usefulness of the displaced in attracting foreign aid and providing cheap labor on the other.

Chapter Six
The Political-Economic Conflict

> We are under the northern attack because our land is rich. Rizeigat Arabs to the north first took our wildlife, then our cattle, and now they are taking our people to be used as *alony*, slaves.

The Baggara-Dinka conflict is a microcosm of the overall North-South confrontation. The national-level issues underlying Sudan's civil war are clearly displayed in the way Baggara-Dinka strife has evolved over the past two decades. Admittedly, the war between North and South was broadly responsible for both the more voluminous resurgence and concealment of slavery in the 1980s and 1990s. But in the same manner that the northern effort to exploit southern resources has caused the war, it was the economic and political desperation in Kordofan and Darfur that can help account for the sharpening of the Baggara assault on the Dinka.

The successive governments in Khartoum have helped magnify the Dinka-Baggara hostilities by political design in efforts to harvest the southern wealth. Attempts by Nimeiri's government to redraw the North-South borders, the issue of the Jonglei Canal, and the issue of Sudan's oil, most of which is to be found in the South, all became central to the conflict and the second round of war. Within the North, the political and economic dominance of the central region at the expense of other regions has prompted the Baggara to take their anger out on the Dinka of Bahr el-Ghazal. The Khartoum government, moreover, discovered that the historical strife between the Dinka and the Baggara could be a potential political and military tool. It was something that could be used to combat the insurgency in the South as well as to persuade the Baggara against possible violent dissension. Therefore, when the government experienced many difficulties fighting the guerrilla army of the SPLA in the 1980s, it resorted to the use of Baggara militias, known as the Murahileen, as low-cost counterinsurgency forces. This chapter chronicles the recent historical evolution of this conflict and how slavery became reinstitutionalized in the course of this recent history.

Border Conflicts

The border issue at first revolved around those areas adjacent to the Southern Region, which by the provisions of the Addis Ababa agreement were under consideration for transfer to that region. These included the mineral-bearing areas of Kafia Kingi and Hofrat al-Nahas, ceded to Darfur in the 1960s, the Dinka district of Abyei in southern Kordofan, and the Kurmuk and Chali districts of Blue Nile Province. The border issue was sensitive for a number of reasons. The Muslim rulers in Khartoum actually viewed the border demarcation as a colonial legacy biased against Arabs and Muslims of the North. Therefore, being prejudiced against the borders set in colonial times, the Arab officials disregarded the status quo on the Dinka-Baggara border and asserted that the separate grazing and fishing areas of the two ethnic groups must be merged. The officials contended that the merger would accelerate national integration and maintenance of peace and stability on the borders. Consequently, the border demarcations were practically abolished, giving the Baggara Arab pastoralists the freedom to cross the Kiir River to graze and water their livestock, and fish and hunt with impunity in the Dinka areas of the borderlands. These borderlands became known in North-South political discourse as "contact areas."

During the first civil war, which took place between the South and the North from 1955 to 1972, the Baggara Arab pastoralists did not take part in the conflict. They considered it to be a war between northern and central riveraine Arabs and South Sudanese over political, economic, social, religious, and cultural matters that did not immediately concern the Baggara. Having decided to be neutral in the conflict, the Baggara continued to use the Dinka grazing plains, fishing in the Dinka pools and lagoons without problems. They also carried on their traditional barter trade with the Dinka as well as the South Sudanese rebel forces of the Anyanya. But when the second civil conflict broke out in 1983, Dinka and Baggara Arab relations of relative understanding turned into mutual hostilities. The hostilities stemmed from the entry of the many Arab and Fellata[1] pastoralists into the Dinka and Jo-Luo territories to graze livestock during the 1970s drought. As the lack of rain resulted in the loss of a lot of livestock to Baggara Arab and Fellata pastoralists, they entered northern Bahr el-Ghazal in large numbers with cattle, sheep, goats, horses, donkeys, and camels, causing serious problems of overgrazing and degradation of the Dinka pastures. The Arab and Fellata influx into the territory resulted not only in overuse of the grazing plains, but also in overfishing, burning of grass, and cutting down of valuable trees as fodder for the livestock. In addition, these pastoralists became hunters, killing small and big game in the nearby forests. This is what provoked the Dinka to attempt to limit the Arab entry into their territory.

In Kordofan and Darfur the prolonged drought of the 1970s meant increased hardship for Arab cattle herders who shared the dry season pastures of the Kiir River with the Dinka of Abyei and Aweil.[2] So there was some concern in the North that should the above-mentioned territory be transferred to the southern region, pastoralist Arabs would be denied access to the river. This concern suggested that the government of Sudan was always aware and fearful that sooner or later the South would secede or gain greater autonomy.[3] During the time of Nimeiri, the expressed concern for the welfare of the Baggara was a political ploy that did not necessarily mean serious support for the Baggara. It was rather a political move to deflect the Baggara hostility by pointing them towards the South. Through various media, the government portrayed the Dinka as the enemy of the Baggara rather than the government. Government officials preached to the Baggara that there was more in common between the Baggara and the government than between the Baggara and the Dinka; and that indeed, their livelihoods were more endangered by the Dinka than by anything the government could do. Nimeiri had never had much support among the Baggara and always feared their wrath. A gesture of the kind expressed in the border question was intended to generate support for Nimeiri among the Baggara.

Throughout the late 1970s, and with increasing ferocity during the early 1980s, gangs of armed Arabs (both Misseria and Rezeigat) attacked Dinka villages with the intent of driving the Ngok Dinka out of Kordofan into Tuic, or pushing the Dinka of Aweil south of the Kiir River. The Umma Party almost openly waged this policy. Its leaders were involved in arming and encouraging the nomads. This is because the area had been the stronghold of the Umma Party and because of the Baggara belief that the Baggara were the Ansar, or supporters of the Mahdi during his revolution against Turco-Egyptian rule in 1881. Their support for the Umma Party, which has also been led by the descendents of the Mahdi, has been very staunch throughout until Nimeiri came to power in 1969. When the Addis Ababa agreement was signed, the Umma Party was opposed to some of its provisions because they may have seemed disadvantageous to the Umma support base among the Baggara. When the second civil war broke out in 1983, the Baggara, particularly the Rezeigat, found an opportunity to address their economically and politically marginalized position throughout the Nimeiri years. The government of Sadiq al-Mahdi, following its ascendance to power after Nimeiri, diverged from the Nimeiri policy of acting as a constraint on intertribal raiding, and adopted a policy of arming militias, most particularly the Rezeigat. Since the beginning of the war, these militias have enjoyed almost complete immunity from legal redress.

Border Policies, the Discovery of Oil, and Southern Reactions

The issue of the Southern Region's borders became entwined with the issue of oil and economic development. In November 1980 the new National Assembly, in considering a bill to set the boundaries of the new regions in the North, attempted to redraw the Southern Region's boundaries, placing the oil fields of Bentiu and agriculturally productive areas of Upper Nile Province inside neighboring northern provinces. Opposition of the Southern Region to this ludicrous proposal was unanimous, and transcended the political divisions which were already at work within the region. The unified front forced President Nimeiri to slow down the process of border carving, but he did not decide in favor of the Southern Region's rejection of his border policy. Nimeiri was at the time still cognizant of the importance of southern supporters in maintaining his power, and keeping the South pleased nearly guaranteed him a support base in the military.

The southern opposition to the redrawing of the North-South borders echoed far and wide throughout the Southern Region as well as in the North. Many southern politicians in the government, in both the national and the regional parliaments, who openly opposed Nimeiri on this issue were imprisoned. Student demonstrations all over South Sudan in 1982 shook the political scene and threatened local governments in what some feared was the beginning of the end for the Nimeiri's reign. Given that Sudan was a police state at this time, local officials were held accountable and swiftly purged from the central government when they failed to put down the demonstrations. Orders were issued to local police to use force to break up the demonstrations. Massive student protests occurred throughout Bahr el-Ghazal in February 1982. In one particular incident in Wau, the commissioner of the province, Alfred Deng Aluk, instructed the army to join forces with various law enforcement agencies to end the protests. The army and police opened fire on the demonstrating students. Twelve students were killed on the spot. Hundreds were severely injured, leaving many of them permanently disabled. This incident and many other similar incidents throughout the South practically spurred a second period of North-South strife. The country was headed for war from that time on. One year after the incident, most of the students who participated in these demonstrations were quick to join the southern revolt when the war started in 1983.

The Southern Region's main asset is oil. This was discovered after the

Addis Ababa agreement had been signed and the regional government for the South established. Almost all of Sudan's oil reserves are located in Upper Nile and Jonglei Provinces, but the regional government was not consulted on the granting of concessions to the Chevron and Total oil companies.[4] Because the oil deposits are found in the South and the Addis Ababa accord barred the central government, at least on paper, from treating it as a national resource without the agreement of the South, many signatories of the agreement, including Nimeiri, turned against the agreement. Nimeiri was a Northerner, after all, and could only support the South to a certain degree until he had a complete grip on power. For example, the agreement made provisions for the regional government to levy a corporation tax on any non-government-owned factory in the region, as well as to tax the profits from the export of products from the region. This would have given the South considerable revenues from any oil refinery sites in the region, and on the export of any refined or unrefined petroleum products. But Nimeiri saw this as too many concessions in favor of the South. The regional government insisted that a proposed oil refinery to be built by Chevron should be placed inside Upper Nile Province, close to the oil fields, so that consequential development in the region would benefit the immediate local population. President Nimeiri, however, ordered the construction of the refinery outside the Southern Region, in the North.

Southerners' objection to the building of the refinery in Port Sudan was unanimous. Students, politicians and political activists put together massive demonstrations all over Sudan just as they did on the issue of the boundaries, and the government's response was as harsh as ever. Many Southerners went to jail, were tortured, killed in captivity, or simply declared missing. The national intelligence agency headed by the notorious torturer Omer Muhammad Taib was instrumental in crushing the southern opposition to Nimeiri's policies. What was an exercise of democratic rights by South Sudanese, as the Addis Ababa agreement had provided, was treated by the North as an act of defiance, despite the fact that all protests and demonstrations were peaceful actions. The government abused the support that the South had given Nimeiri and that he was now beginning to lose quickly.

Commercialization of Nilotic Traditional Livelihoods

One economic asset that also holds important cultural symbols for the South is livestock, particularly the cattle of the vast Dinka-Nuer belt of Upper Nile and Bahr el-Ghazal. Cattle are also deemed the mainstay of the Nilotic economy. But a concerted effort by Northerners to commercialize Dinka and Nuer cattle has been an issue of serious ideological as well as physical clashes between the state and the ethnic nationalities concerned. As far back as the British colonial period, the government of Sudan has always regarded Dinka and Nuer cattle as a stumbling block to any kind of modernization project. Sharon Hutchinson writes that in 1946, in a bid to persuade the Nuer about the easy convertibility of money as opposed to cattle, an assistant district commissioner proposed to require the Nuer to pay their tribute in cattle.[5] The government of independent Sudan continued this system with the view that if the Dinka and Nuer were to be incorporated into the state and develop respect for the authority of the government, one must first undermine their source of pride and wealth. The successive Khartoum governments have all pursued this policy of uprooting cattle-based economies.

The present NIF government seems convinced that it is the Nilotic perceived wealth that generates enough fodder for the war. Without it, the government believes, the Nilotic people would not be able to feed the war. The successive governments since the fall of Nimeiri, including the government of Sadiq al-Mahdi and the NIF government, have repeatedly gone on record stating that it is this wealth which enables the Nilotics to provide material support to the SPLA and all other insurgents, and that destabilizing their economic base reduces their ability to sustain the SPLA forces and undermines the source of their cultural pride. This assumption was soon supported by the events relating to the current war. When the government armed Baggara militias with new weapons, they surged into Dinka and Nuer areas of Bahr el-Ghazal and Upper Nile during the winter of 1986 and 1987, burned villages, seized livestock, and enslaved men, women, and children. Massive displacement to the North was the result. As more and more Dinka and Nuer became impoverished by the war and were displaced into the North, Islamic organizations in northern cities exploited their vulnerability and escalated the conversion effort to make Muslims out of Southerners. The more Southerners moved into the North, the more northern Arabs/Muslims found it legitimate and easier to undermine the African cultures. Once persuaded through the Islamicization and Arabicization project that Southerners and their cultures are inferior to Northerners, a Northerner is also persuaded to take up the task of emasculating the South's identity by all means available.

The Jonglei Canal: Development or Exploitation?

The South's other main asset is water. The South enjoys higher rainfall than the North, and it is at the confluence of rivers arising in East Africa, Ethiopia, and central Africa. Northern Sudan has had its eyes on the vast and better-watered southern region for its irrigation schemes, but such projects have always been hindered by the complex political and historical relationships between North and South. One move by the North, which became another strong factor in the conflict, was the Jonglei Canal. As a great deal of water which flows into Sudan from East Africa is dispersed through the great central swamps of the South and never reaches the North, both northern Sudan and Egypt resumed an old plan and in 1974 proposed the digging of a canal.[6] It was to begin at Jonglei on the Bahr el-Jabal and end at the White Nile near the Sobat River mouth. The project was presented as one which would simultaneously control flooding and increase water availability, both within the South and farther North. When the central ministries of irrigation and agriculture presented the proposed project to the president of the High Executive Council (HEC),[7] the argument for the project was that the canal was crucial for expansion and to meet the agro-industrial needs of the country. Benefits to accrue for the South, such as improved transportation, agricultural schemes to produce cash crops, and clean drinking water and hygiene, were emphasized. The HEC, unsure about such benefits, was hesitant about the value of the project. But the southern government agreed to pilot projects as a way to test the central government's intentions regarding its socioeconomic development plans in the project area.

Over the next few years the commitments of the central government to development in the Jonglei area proved unworthy of southern trust. The government argued that the pilot project in mechanized farming was far too expensive to keep up. In other words, the northern government demonstrated to the Southerners that the expansion of "national" irrigation schemes in the North was far more important than the localized development of the South. Even the pleas of environmentalists about the danger that the canal presents for wildlife and the traditional cattle herding in the region, questions that the South would have ignored in return for development projects, were not heeded.

Throughout the early 1980s the southern regional government became engaged in confrontation with the central government because the president of the Republic was considerably involved in the process by which the president of the High Executive Council was chosen. This meant that political rivalries between southern politicians to win Nimeiri's support gave President Nimeiri powers that were not part of the Addis Ababa covenant. Provisions beneficial to the Southern Region were not observed. There was considerable dissatisfaction with the failure of the central government to fulfill its financial obligations to the Southern Region. No development projects ever really got under way in the South, not even those proposed in exchange for southern agreement to the Jonglei project. And to make matters worse, the central government often evades responsibility for the underdevelopment of the South by blaming it on alleged "corruption" of southern politicians, or on inefficiency of the southern workforce. This has infuriated Southerners and has caused them to feel that they do not belong in a united Sudan.

The Overall Impact of Nimeiri's Policies on North-South Relations

With these policies regarding southern oil, cattle, wildlife, water, and grazing, the government proved itself to be more concerned with the extraction of the South's resources than with southern development. So economic confrontation between Khartoum and the regional government, which escalated into the current war, has to be seen within the context of the failure of the Sudan government to realize its desire of becoming the "bread basket," as it had been called, in the Middle East. Successive Khartoum governments have all attempted to accomplish the goal of making Sudan the bread basket of the Arab world at the expense of the South. The attitude in the North has always been that benefits of development in the North will trickle down to reach the South eventually. The emphasis has been on how to make southern resources available for development in the North. South Sudanese were quick to note these policies as typical of the way the Khartoum governments, from Turco-Egyptian rule to the Mahdiyya through the Anglo-Egyptian Condominium to the independent state, had dealt with them since the initial contact. Southerners sought to challenge the policies of the Nimeiri government as they had done on numerous other policy issues over the last forty-four years of the country's independence.

The first round of civil war from 1955 to 1972 was an unforgettable exercise in resistance. And although the situation between North and South by the 1980s had been more confounded by new social and political developments, as we have already noted, the present ongoing war is a direct descendant of the previous war. For instance, the first round of the conflict was ended by means of an agreement reached in Addis Ababa, Ethiopia, between then-president Jaafar Nimeiri and the Anyanya forces. The agreement, which granted the South autonomous status, had serious loopholes, and Nimeiri was quick to take advantage of these weaknesses. He contravened the pillar clauses of the agreement including the integrity of the autonomous government itself without consulting with the southern leaders. In the early 1980s, Nimeiri touched old wounds in the heart of the South. He redesigned the North-South boundaries and planned to build a refinery in the North for exploitation of the southern oil resources in ports far away from the origin. He also divided the South into smaller and weaker states of Bahr el-Ghazal, Upper Nile, and Equatoria, and finally declared the imposition of shari'a, Islamic law, throughout the country. Nimeiri's policies angered Southerners, and although they had initially been strong supporters of Nimeiri for ending the first civil war, many people in the South organized into opposition.

Although many Southerners, especially the veterans of the Anyanya guerrilla movement, had noticed the double face of Nimeiri and had mobilized to oppose him since 1980, it was particularly in 1983 that the people of the South saw their special constitutional status—the regional parliament and government—undermined by Khartoum. Nimeiri had been heard boasting that the Addis Ababa agreement was "neither a Koran nor Bible."[8] He no longer felt bound by the provisions of the agreement, especially that he had by now found some weakness among southern politicians. For instance, when one southern leader began to show signs of taking a more active role in questioning Nimeiri's decisions and authority, Nimeiri aligned himself with another southern leader.

This was particularly the case between Abel Alier and Joseph Lagu.[9] When Alier appeared actively involved in safeguarding southern interests on certain economic matters, Nimeiri turned to Lagu over the issue of further "decentralization." Through a succession of constitutional amendments and utter disregard for the Addis Ababa agreement, Nimeiri divided the South into three smaller regions in order to weaken it. So although many Southerners hailed the formation of smaller regional states as reflecting more freedoms, the South was no longer capable of putting up a strong block against the North. Nimeiri was easily able to run southern affairs as he wished. The governors of these regions, whom Nimeiri appointed, and the weaker regional assemblies had no power to oppose him as he had given himself "constitutional" rights to dismiss them at will. Now, even the people of Equatoria who demanded the redivision of the South as a response to "Dinka domination" in Juba were already beginning to regret their move. The powers that they had thought would transfer to them when the Dinka exited Equatoria were not available, as Nimeiri had stripped the authority of regional governments to a minimum. Regional demands for constitutional rights from the central government, when pressed hard, resulted in the leaders losing their posts. Those wanting whatever government post the central government could offer to a southern politician remained in the government and endured the humiliation that came with it, and those believing that the South deserved more began to mobilize against Nimeiri. Despite some strong southern voices against Nimeiri, whether among civilians in the cities or the SPLA war activity, the southern political voice has never experienced the strong unity that it needs in order to present the North with a real challenge.

The Genesis of the Current Round of the War

The period of relative calm brought by the Addis Ababa agreement and the serious attempts to pacify the South and unite the country by allowing the South to have an autonomous status within a united Sudan were interrupted in 1983. A group of former Anyanya officers who had been absorbed into the National Army mutinied in the southern towns of Bor, Pibor, and Pochalla. What triggered their mutiny was their refusal of orders to move to the North in January 1983. They viewed the transfer to the North as a breach of the Addis Ababa agreement, which stated that the absorbed Anyanya were to serve only in the South. John Garang (a former Anyanya soldier himself), then a lecturer at the Sudan Military College and head of the Sudan Military Research Bureau in Khartoum, went to Bor, supposedly to mediate. But in fact, Garang was already party to a conspiracy among some officers in the Southern Command planning the defection of the Battalion 105 at Bor. The Sudanese army, in an effort to curb the rebellion, attacked Bor, and the mutineers pulled out of Bor. During this chaos, Garang left by another route, and ended up in the bush with the mutineers. They started a guerrilla movement and went to Ethiopia to solicit arms and training bases. Further action by Khartoum regarding other southern garrison towns pushed more southern groups into active alliance. A combination of the attack on Bor and the subsequent dissolution of the Southern Region prompted more mutinies. By the middle of 1983 about 2,500 soldiers had defected to the new guerrilla base being established in Ethiopia, and another 500 remained in the field in Bahr el-Ghazal. Nimeiri's government sent close to 15,000 northern troops to the South armed with American weapons, including jet fighters and transport planes. Shortly afterward, by the end of July 1983, the Sudan Peoples' Liberation Army and Movement (SPLA/M) were formed, with Ethiopian backing, under the leadership of Colonel John Garang de Mabior. The formation of a large army composed almost entirely of South Sudanese who had been forced into rebellion by the abrogation of the Addis Ababa agreement immediately resurrected the prospect of a second war for South Sudan's independence. The years of peace changed swiftly into years of war, reviving all the North-South animosities, raiding, slavery, and northern scorn for Southerners. Many of the old Anyanya veterans had never been comfortable with the Addis Ababa agreement, and now was their second opportunity to dedicate themselves to the separation of the South from the North. A full-fledged second round of war between the North and the South ensued immediately, and with Ethiopian and Libyan support, the SPLA made significant military gains against Nimeiri's government in 1984.

The SPLA's immediate problem was Nimeiri. The overthrow of Nimeiri was thus the first practical goal to be achieved, a difficult one given the huge U.S. military support to Sudan at the time, both in terms of hardware and expertise. This goal prompted the SPLA to seek alliance with other opposition groups. Gathering the needed force against Nimeiri required a different way of thinking about the southern grievances. For tactical reasons—in order to enlist the support of other regions in Sudan and the military aid of Ethiopia and Libya, which were both against Nimeiri— the idea of secession for the South had to be put aside until the fall of Nimeiri. It is for all these reasons that the SPLA called upon all the people of Sudan to fight for change in the entire structure of the Sudanese system rather than to simply depose Nimeiri. The SPLA issued a manifesto, which highlighted the specific grievances of the South, but treated them as issues of underdevelopment in the entire country. This stance appealed to other regions and sectors of Sudanese society that had their own grievances against Nimeiri and the central government, but who would have been hostile to a southern independence movement.

John Garang regularly addressed the nation through Radio SPLA, and he redefined the so-called Southern Problem as a problem of the underdeveloped areas in the whole country. He gave an historical overview of the pattern of marginalization of certain areas in Sudan, particularly the west, the east, the south, and the far north, in favor of the central region. He also pointed out the failure of the first Anyanya movement, and how the Addis Ababa agreement was a sham accord, which allowed Nimeiri to maneuver against it, and which caused corrupt southern leaders to care only about their own personal gains. Just as the manifesto had done, Garang focused on the issues of racism, tribalism, and ethnicity as the tools the central region had used to manipulate and cheat the rest of Sudan. Throughout history, Garang claimed, the central region had sapped the resources of other regions, leading to a pattern of unequal development because the government had been in the hands of people from the most developed areas. Garang suggested that the southern grievance was in fact, a common grievance shared with other regions, and that this fact was obscured by the question of religion because all the Khartoum governments had aspired to establish a Sudanese national identity on the foundation of Islamic and Arabic culture. "What about the tongues of Dinka, Nuer, Moro Nuba or Hadandawa," Garang asked the Sudanese on SPLA radio, which was airing from Ethiopia and was received clearly all over Sudan. Various groups in the underdeveloped areas of Sudan saw Garang's point and reacted in a myriad of ways.

When the SPLA forces penetrated the Nuba Mountains and southern Blue Nile for recruitment and to spread the rebellion against the Arab and Muslim domination in the Sudan, many young Nuba and Ingessana men and women from urban and rural areas immediately joined the ranks

of the South Sudanese rebels. Consequently, their participation in the rebellion changed the trend of the civil war from 1985 to the present time
from being a conflict between the South and the North to being one between African or non-Arab ethnic groups and Arabized ethnic groups in
the country. Such African unity, which had never existed before, and the
widespread rebellion in South Sudan, western Sudan, and southern Blue
Nile instilled fear in the Arab and Islamist rulers of the Sudan.

Traditionally, the African and non-Arab groups such as the Beja of eastern Sudan, the Fur and the Nuba of western Sudan, and the Ingessana
in southern Blue Nile, provided the Sudan army under the command of
the Arab officer corps with most of its fighting men. This was the case,
for instance, during the first civil war. However, the present civil war has
changed all that. Many of these ethnic groups carried out numerous acts
of defiance against the Nimeiri government. As the Nuba and the Ingessana ethnic groups regarded this war as a total liberation of the African
and non-Arab ethnic groups from the Arab minority rule and the res-
toration of their geopolitical, economic, cultural, social, and religious
rights in Sudan, they became seriously involved in the rebellion against
the Arab-dominated government in Khartoum. This is the political situation that became responsible for the Baggara-Dinka strife and resurgence
of slavery.

Having found it difficult to recruit troops from the Nuba and the other
non-Arab groups in the North, as they had done in the past, the various
Arab governments in Khartoum turned to recruit most of their troops
from Arab ethnic groups in both urban and rural areas. While the urban
Arabs formed the core of the army, the rural Arabs, especially the pastoralists and peasants, became the militia forces or the so-called Popular Defense Forces. In order to inspire, unite, and rally these forces behind them, the Khartoum governments (both Nimeiri and later, Sadiq
al-Mahdi) presented the conflict to these northern Arab groups as a direct threat to their immediate livelihoods.

The process that finally brought Nimeiri down after sixteen years in
power was credited by many observers to the SPLA, as the force that weakened Nimeiri economically—the war was reportedly consuming $1 mil-
lion a day. The SPLA was also credited for the fall of Nimeiri due to
Garang's influence and encouragement of the northern populace to act
at the right moment.[10] After sixteen years in power, Nimeiri was deposed
through a popular uprising supported by the Sudanese army in Khartoum on April 6, 1985. Nimeiri was visiting the United States at the time,
trying to persuade Washington to continue aid and military support,
which was tending toward reduction because of the growing Western unease about the human rights situation in Sudan. Nimeiri was replaced
by a junta, the Transitional Military Council (TMC). This council began

to make preparations for elections so as to change to civilian govern-ment. The transitional government called upon the SPLA to join the elections, suggesting that the only obstacle to democracy and human rights had been removed. The dictator had been overthrown. But the SPLA rejected the call, arguing that the change in Khartoum was a mere change of personalities, not a change in the system. There were ideologi-cal differences between the SPLA and the rest of the Sudanese opposition groups, especially the major sectarian parties, which were very eager to grab the power, and there was very little cooperation between them dur-ing the struggle against Nimeiri. The only agreement between the SPLA and the northern opposition groups was the vitality of working together to overthrow Nimeiri. It was understood that a constitutional conference would then be held for the Sudanese people to decide on the identity and the future of Sudan.

When Nimeiri fell, all the major northern opposition groups rushed back to Khartoum to take part in the government, but the SPLA kept away, despite vigorous criticism by most northern Sudanese. The SPLA leader, John Garang, was heavily criticized and even accused of aimless warmongering. "What is he still fighting for when Nimeiri the dictator has been removed?" was the question all over North Sudan and even among some South Sudanese politicians. The elections were concluded without most of the South. Only the three main cities of Wau, Malakal, and Juba participated in the elections since most of the South at this time was under SPLA control. Sadiq al-Mahdi came to power as an elected prime minister, leading a coalition of his Umma and Democratic Union-ist Parties that had alternated in power in the previous parliamentary periods since independence. The coalition also included the fast growing National Islamic Front (NIF) of Hassan al-Turabi.

It is safe to say that many Sudanese hoped that Sadiq al-Mahdi, once in power, would use the contacts established with the SPLA during the opposition period to seek a peaceful resolution to the conflict. But al-Mahdi repudiated his party's earlier understanding with the SPLA and refused to commit himself to a reconciliatory policy. The SPLA had been watching him closely over the question of Nimeiri's hated September laws, the Islamic laws which al-Mahdi had publicly denounced when he was in opposition. Al-Mahdi could not commit himself to a plan to repeal these laws. Instead he denounced the SPLA for continuing the war and expressed wonderment over SPLA's rationale. Al-Mahdi was particularly unhappy with what he termed as Garang's "incitement" of hatred for the central region among many people in Sudan. It is worth noting here that Garang was repeatedly accused in the government's official discourse of reverse racism and anti-Islam propaganda. "Garang claims to be fighting against injustice but he is obviously influenced by foreign forces to preach

hate against the Arabs and Muslims . . . he is causing rifts in the Sudanese society, and his dangerous views must be exposed," al-Mahdi once
remarked on national television.[11] The result was his decision to continue
the military approach as the only way to deal with the "southern problem," as Northerners call Sudan's conflict. Al-Mahdi's government, like
Nimeiri's, met with a lot of difficulties in the battlefields.

In 1986, military gains by the SPLA against the government forces, particularly in Bahr el-Ghazal, led the government of Prime Minister Sadiq
al-Mahdi to transform Nimeiri's militia policy into a more creative system. He revamped the recruitment of Baggara militias, arming them with
even more powerful automatic weapons. Again, the government's purpose in arming these tribal militias, the Murahileen, was to conduct an
inexpensive counterinsurgency war against the SPLA, which the government claimed was a Dinka movement. The same recruitment tactic used
during the Nimeiri years was applied again, that the people most immediately vulnerable to the SPLA attacks were the Baggara, who stood to lose
the grazing areas of the Kiir River. So a war against the Dinka was warranted, and General Burma Nasr, the commander of all the government
forces in Bahr el-Ghazal, drew up the plan of how the militias were to
operate in conjunction with the government troops. As was observed in
an article in an English-language newspaper published in Khartoum: "It
would seem that because most of the SPLA is composed of Dinkas the
government feels free to wage a war on Dinkas and other southern civilians and to conduct a scorched-earth policy. It is against this politico-
religious and racial tapestry that the militias, manned by traditional ad-
versaries of the Dinkas, were formed."[12]

The strategy was to undermine SPLA support in the Dinka areas by re-
igniting and fueling the historical Dinka-Baggara conflict.[13] The practice
of militia forces was aimed at incapacitating the SPLA support base in the
Nilotic areas of Dinka and Nuer populations. This was evident in the fact
that the militias became so diligent in avoiding any attacks on SPLA military targets. The Murahileen did not attack any villages where the SPLA
might be present.[14] Their purpose was to abduct, loot, destroy, and kill.
They were not ready to risk themselves in combat. Their "military" effort
was directed exclusively toward civilians, and gross violations of international laws of war were meted out on a scale unseen anywhere else since
World War II.

When Sadiq al-Mahdi left office after the NIF-backed military government came to power in 1989, the militia recruitment tactic changed again.
In addition to presenting the North-South conflict to the potential Baggara recruits as a mission to augment their resources and gain wealth,
the Khartoum government also declared jihad against Christian, African,
and non-Arab ethnic groups. The Baggara were also given freedom to kill

these groups, loot their wealth, capture slaves, expel the rest from the territories, and forcefully settle in their lands. In short, they had to carry out what clearly amounted to ethnic cleansing in order to resettle Arab ethnic groups in the Christian, African, and non-Arab lands.

Resettling Arab farmers and herders in areas belonging to other groups has been most successful in the Nuba Mountains. Whole Nuba villages were forcibly relocated to barren areas of Kordofan, which the government euphemistically called "peace camps," while the Arabs took their land. Traditionally, the Nuba had lived in relative peace with their neighbors, the Misseria Arab pastoralists, for over a century. But as it had done in Dinka-Rezeigat relations, the government upset the Nuba-Misseria balance by two actions—by enabling merchant farmers to take more and more Misseria land, and by arming Misseria clans to take the fertile lowlands on which the Nuba used to farm.[15]

Northern Economic Policies and the Revival of Slavery

The southern opposition to the central government's water policy was one of the most directly influential objections to northern policies that related to the issue of current slavery. The halting of the Jonglei Canal project in 1983 due to war had dashed the hopes of the Sudan government for the growth of irrigated mechanized farming, and the government had to concentrate on rain-fed mechanized agriculture for production of cash crops. The government's own plan was to see the growth of agro-industry in Sudan through increased investment in mechanized farming and high-profile projects such as the Kenana Sugar factory. This was all to be accomplished through a successful Jonglei Canal, but the faltering of the project meant that rain-fed agricultural schemes expanded far more than irrigated schemes. This coincided with the growth of demand for Sudanese sorghum and millet in the Middle East, especially in Saudi Arabia where this grain is used as fodder in the growing livestock industry. The opening up of an international market for Sudanese crops, which were largely subsistence crops, turned them into cash crops and created land disputes on the border areas between South and North.

Investment in mechanized agricultural schemes by civil servants and merchants in North Sudan has had a long history and has been part of the struggle for control of the levers of government by the various nationalist parties. Islamic banks and their heavy investment in rain-fed mechanized projects, especially in western Sudan, were at the center of development programs in the late 1970s. Although instrumental in the growing economic power of certain political groups, the financial contribution of the Islamic banks in the success of many schemes has accelerated a process of social and economic disruption. By using legal backing of the courts, the well-placed merchants and government elite started to circumvent customary land rights for both small landholding farmers and pastoralists in Kordofan and elsewhere. The traditional practices governing land use were eroded by the legal system that rural people were not a part of. Those who can no longer work the land on their own have been brought into a large wage-earning agricultural work force. In Kordofan and Darfur, herders were doubly hit by the drought of the late 1970s and the interference of large schemes in their access to pastures and water. It was this dispossession that contributed with more weight to the outbreak of hostilities between northern militias and southern Sudanese in northern Bahr el-Ghazal right before and during the early years of the current war. When the Baggara pastoralists lost large portions of their land to mechanized agriculture and the remainder to drought, they have been prompted to compensate for it by attacking the Dinka. They received support from the government to conduct the raiding without fear of legal action against them.

To reiterate, the main incentive to join the Murahileen in the early 1980s was economic. Many pastoralists had lost large herds of livestock in the drought of the late 1970s. But the advent of mechanized agricultural schemes had also been very damaging to Baggara livelihoods in that it dispossessed the Baggara of land use rights. Like a chain reaction, these desperate Northerners were impelled toward the exploitation of South Sudan to make up for their own loss of entitlements to those politically well situated within the North. As already argued, since the Dinka were already rendered vulnerable by their political stance in the North-South conflict, their property became fair game for the surrounding groups, notably the Baggara pastoralists and semipastoralists of western Sudan. The Baggara were themselves politically recalcitrant in part because of the threat of mechanized farming to their grazing land. Khartoum deflected the frustrations of such groups into raiding of the South. This policy of pitting two dissenting groups against one another was marked by the government's act of abolishing the native administrations on tribal borders between North and South. The policy was aimed at subordination of ethnic representation so that no tribal group claimed ownership of land; in other words the government of Sudan was attempting to de-ethnicize South Sudanese. For this policy to work, it had to be accompanied by a process of acculturation and Islamization. Tribal fighting forces of the Rezeigat and the Misseria (particularly the Misseria Humr) organized and carried out violent raids on Dinka villages and cattle camps with the intent of seizing Dinka cattle and clearing pastures for themselves. They criminally kidnapped children and women to be sold into slavery in Darfur and Kordofan. The slaves were then incorporated into the labor system of the agro-pastoralist production complex of Darfur and Kordofan. There have also been groups of armed Baggara militias that accompany the army in military operations supposedly targeting the SPLA and SPLA-sympathizing villages. But they all avoided attacking the SPLA bases directly and instead targeted the civilian villages for the purpose of slave taking. Some of these groups rode the train between el-Meiram and Aweil, getting off and on along the way to target the cattle camps of the Dinka in northern Bahr el-Ghazal. They would then take the captives and the booty back to the train, which took them to Aweil, where they prepared to take them further North when the train returned. Despite all this coordinated activity between the government and the militias, the former continued to deny its involvement in slavery.

The Sudan government, as mentioned earlier, has claimed that the so-called slave raids are nothing other than a feud over grazing land or water resources between competing tribes. But contrary to these claims, the nature of the organized raiding and the work that the captors are subsequently made to do indicate that this is slavery with all the relations that this practice has evoked throughout history. Many human rights groups and the United Nations Human Rights Commission have investigated and issued reports since 1995 that described slave raids, slave trade, and slavery. These reports characterize the structure of the current slave raids and the subsequent exploitation of the slaves as very similar to those of the historical slave raids (*Ghazwa*) of the nineteenth century in the same area. The contemporary raiders' intentions are the capture of slave children and women and the unlawful acquisition of cattle and other property. The structure of the organized slave raid also gives evidence that slavery in that part of Sudan is not an isolated or erratic phenomenon, but rather an institution in which many partners are involved in direct and indirect ways. These partners include the enslaving community, the native administration leaders such as the *nazir*, the *umdas*, and the sheikhs, the army, the government officials who work in the enslaving communities such as judges, policemen, the local administrator, and security men. Another partner was the Umma Party of Sadiq al-Mahdi, whose main electoral support base was to be found among these enslaving communities. All these partners are accountable for acts of commission and or of omission that protected, maintained, and helped to reproduce the phenomenon of slavery.[16]

Other factors about the Baggara need to be highlighted and may explain their reasoning about raiding and slavery. Certainly drought and desertification in their region has put a constraint on grazing, driving the Baggara, particularly the Rezeigat cattle owners south of the Kiir River, in search of grass and water for their livestock in the dry season. Many Rezeigat lost livestock in the famine of 1983–85,[17] and cattle raiding to the South, in the Dinka area, has been a means of replenishing depleted herds. In addition, like other peoples of the western parts of the country, the Rezeigat have been marginalized in terms of development inputs from the central government. They may have perceived themselves in some sense as victims and their raiding of the Dinka as a survival strategy. The Rezeigat may have calculated raiding the Dinka to serve two main purposes: to clear grazing regions south of Kiir River, and to displace and render the Dinka so desperate that they would become a source of cheap, exploitable agro-pastoral labor. The Baggara may have also reasoned that displaced Dinka would become a magnet for foreign aid, which can be used to the benefit of the local Baggara community in general, to which the Baggara may, indeed, feel entitled as the hosts.

An indication that the Baggara regarded themselves as entitled to relief items provided by international NGOs in the name of displaced Southerners may be found in their various efforts to loot these items. Since displaced Southerners first began arriving in Baggara areas in the late 1980s, more powerful surrounding groups have frequently seized the relief inputs provided by the aid agencies as a part of an effort to promote economic self-sufficiency among the displaced. Such assistance, from the perspective of the Baggara, defeats the whole purpose of raiding the Dinka. If allowed to keep their assets, these Dinka would not be available for exploitation as cheap labor. So asset seizure by the Baggara became a frequent occurrence and the possession of such assets proved dangerous for the Dinka, as people often get killed in the process. It was therefore quite common in the 1990s that dry season grazing tensions would arise as the Rezeigat herdsmen began their annual move into northern Bahr el-Ghazal. From time to time, the Baggara met with resistance by the SPLA and a number of Rezeigat would be killed. This usually prompted violence against the displaced settled in such important Rezeigat towns as Abu Matariq. The camps were often looted, and the Dinka would flee the camps to other areas such as Nyala. To avoid the violence that the Baggara meted out against the displaced Dinka over relief assets, the displaced devised mechanisms to "pay off" the host community. A review on behalf of Operation Lifeline Sudan estimated that 20 percent of relief items were being discretely "allocated" to the host community under an agreement with the local relief committee. In addition to all other host community machinations, the displaced were, in effect, only receiving about half of what they were originally intended to receive.[18] Cheated of aid, many displaced persons were forced to work for their hosts in some of the most demeaning occupations in order to supplement their food needs. Further evidence for relief diversion from the displaced is indicated by the high malnutrition rates in one of the displaced persons' camp called Khor Omer in 1998, despite the distribution of huge amounts of food aid in the camp shortly before the assessment was undertaken.[19]

Apart from the exercise of unaccountable force used to coerce South Sudanese into the labor force, a variety of political and commercial measures have been used to reproduce the cheap and desocialized labor on which the commercial agrarian economy of North Sudan (irrigated production, mechanized rain-fed farming schemes, and so on) depends. The Rezeigat, like other Baggara groups in the North, have come to rely on southern labor to perform low-status agricultural work. Land ownership among the Baggara is through repetitive use and ability to maintain labor. Clearing brush from the fields is one of the difficult tasks that the Dinka labor force is usually required for. Once a field has been cleared and used, year in and year out, it becomes the property of the person who uses it, although the Dinka have no such entitlement. But even when one has cleared a field, it has to be used continuously for ownership to be established. When it is left uncultivated it becomes fair game. So in an environment of competition for land caused by mechanization, as described above, for Baggara without access to large-scale mechanization, obtaining labor—whether through raiding or forced migration—is the key means of overcoming production constraints and the loss of land entitlements. The result is that the Dinka victims of raiding, who have been displaced and are living among the Baggara, are caught up in the resulting conflict. As well as serving as a cheap labor force, they are, in effect, hostages to the tides of war. For example, a defeat of a Baggara raiding force by the SPLA in the South may be avenged by killing, looting of Dinka possessions in the Baggara area, and taking them to work land they can never own.

Of particular importance in regards to the violence against the displaced Dinka is their role as sharecroppers in the commercial production of groundnuts and other crops in the Baggara area. The sharecropping arrangement involves a verbal agreement entitling the cultivators to half of the harvest in exchange for their labor and means of sustenance. Historically, there were traditional tribal structures that regulated labor in certain areas of Darfur and Kordofan. For example, the commercial production of groundnuts has developed in these areas since the 1960s, relying heavily on migrant labor from the Dinka areas of northern Bahr el-Ghazal, especially from Malwal of Aweil. Migrants from Nuer areas also went to Kordofan to work as sharecroppers. This system of seasonal labor migration has increased significantly among the Dinka since the 1970s. They became engaged in sharecropping with the Baggara, often replacing other sources of labor. The war in 1983 temporarily stemmed the tide of migrants, but then growing insecurity and famine due to Baggara raids greatly increased the flow of Dinka migrants to the North. The Dinka have now been integrated into the Baggara areas as the backbone of the agricultural labor force. But the system is now significantly different from the prewar migration and sharecropping. What used to be a voluntary migratory system has been transformed into structures of slavery. The Rezeigat and the Misseria Humr used to employ agricultural laborers and herders from the Dinka and Nuer on a seasonal basis. The Baggara farmers and herders have now been supported by a government policy of pacification of the South to create an opportunity for them to accumulate wealth through slave raids and forced migrations resulting from the raids.

The way this circular process works could be summarized as follows: by supporting Baggara raids on the Dinka, the Khartoum government hopes to find one solution to two problems. First, it throttles the SPLA support base in the Nilotic areas with as little expense as possible. Second, fearing dissent among the Baggara for having been marginalized for so long, it gives the latter a free rein to loot and displace without fear of being punished. The Baggara then benefit from the raids by displacing the Dinka and exploiting them as well as through the capturing of slaves. The displaced in Baggara areas are kept as magnets for foreign food aid and as hostages in the tides of war. Aid provided by foreign NGOs is then looted by the host community and used to pay for labor or loaned out to displaced sharecroppers, which means the displaced end up paying for the relief items with their labor instead of getting it free as was intended.

Apart from the necessary agricultural inputs, the farm owner provides food and water to the laborers during the period of cultivation. Water is important since distant farms usually lack any source of drinking water. A farm owner is therefore expected to deliver water to the workers. This pattern of employment has particular significance for displaced Dinka. So the Baggara view food aid to the Dinka with contradictory feelings. If the Dinka receive it, they would have no reason to work for the Baggara. If it is stopped, the Dinka might have no reason to migrate to Baggaraland, even when pounded by raids. They may decide to run southward, and a great incentive for raiding, that is, labor exploitation, would be removed. This is partly why the Baggara often seize the relief assets given to the displaced Dinka so as to use it as food payment to the laborers, who were supposedly the beneficiaries of the relief items to begin with.

The crucial problem for the displaced is that the food provided by the farm owner during cultivation, whether from relief or from his own sources, is usually insufficient to support the entire family of the sharecropper. This is especially so because the women and children are not allowed to work as sharecroppers, for the farm owner does not want to spend valuable food and water on individuals whom he deems physically incapable of producing much. So to cover the food needs of their families, the sharecroppers take loans, which are either paid for by relief goods seized from them or deducted with interest from the sharecropper's half of the harvest. In such cases, it is not uncommon for sharecroppers to finish the season with little or nothing to show for their endeavors. In the end, the combined food from relief and income returns of all the activities open to the displaced fall significantly short of basic requirements for survival. The displaced, therefore, are caught in a collective effort by the Baggara to create a hostile and exploitative web around the displaced. "The result for many is malnutrition, ill-health and premature death." [20] This is most particularly true of what one might call pure slaves, that is, those who were abducted and sold or offered as gifts to families of slave raiders. They do not receive even the minimal pay that the displaced receive.

As stated earlier, the exploitation of the displaced Dinka by the Rezeigat in Darfur and by the Misseria in Kordofan also rests on the ability of the latter groups to exert violence, without fear of legal measures. Another major economic activity which thousands of the displaced or abducted Dinka slaves are forced to do is herding of livestock in western Kordofan, southern Kordofan, and southern Darfur. Interviews with former slaves who escaped from bondage indicated that this activity extends as far as western and northern Darfur. Herding in this region is a difficult endeavor and the Dinka would not have done it if they were not physically coerced. Many former slaves said that they would not have done it even with pay. Herding involves continuous movement with the herds of cattle, sheep, and goats through rough terrain that spans great distances, in pursuit of water and grass. Herds require close supervision; herders must keep them from straying into farmed land. Herders have to fetch water from the wells, cut tree branches for the animals to feed on, and build enclosures for the animals.

Displaced and abducted Dinka slaves also engage in agricultural labor different from the sharecropping mentioned above. In many cases, the slaves combine agricultural labor with herding according to variable cultivation and herding cycles and to the respective intensity of work and level of hardship incurred. At times when there is no relief food or when it has been looted, displaced Dinka work as day laborers on the farms of smaller farmers. Some younger men also migrate to large agricultural schemes in central and eastern Sudan. When possible, women also perform domestic work. If the camps are too distant from town for women to have the opportunity to do domestic work, they resort to a range of strategies, including collecting firewood, weaving grass mats, brewing beer, and engaging in prostitution. For a large number of Dinka, the main reason for engaging in these terribly under-rewarded occupations is the need for cash to enable them to search for their family members who have been abducted and enslaved. As will be explained in the last chapter, there have been myriad efforts to buy the freedom of slaves by paying an Arab middleman who traces the slaves, buys them, and returns them to their

families. For an impoverished Dinka family to generate enough money
for this endeavor, it takes the labor of many individuals to obtain the freedom of one.

To summarize, for the Dinka who are purely slaves, unlike the displaced
who have a comparative opportunity to work, the slave is always given the
harder work when the Baggara must themselves participate. Some slaves
participate in the agricultural labor and at the same time must help with
herding, for example drawing well water for the herds. In addition, when
there are no agricultural activities, the slaves are sent back to herding.
Thus, it could be argued that the enslavement of the victims of political
and economic conflict, whether of those abducted during the raids or
those displaced by war and raid-induced famine, has become part of an
institutionalized system of slavery. This is true in light of the following.
First, the displaced and slaves became essential components for production in Arab communities in Kordofan and Darfur. Second, the enslaving
communities have developed an elaborate system for the perpetuation of
the conditions that make slavery and other forms of exploitation thrive
in the shadow of the civil war. Third, enslaving communities have capitalized on religious and racial ideology, which accord inferior status to the
enslaved communities.

The subhuman status ascribed to the enslaved communities because
of their race and religious beliefs has functioned to justify slavery, both
in the minds of those who recruit for it and those who actually carry it
out. Sudan's slavery is a product of historical, economical, racial, cultural, religious, ideological, and military factors, and it is within this context that it can be accounted for. The interaction of all these factors has
produced asymmetrical power relations between the enslaving communities and the targeted communities. These asymmetrical power relations
are embedded in a context of evolving race relations in which violence is
communal, where violence has reached high levels of brutality, and where
it involves exploitation at very high levels and is supported by dominant
ideologies.[21]

Has No One Heard Us Call for Help?
Sudanese Slavery and International Opinion

In describing his experiences during his explorations in southern and central Africa, David Livingstone once wrote: "The strangest disease I have seen in this country seems really to be broken-heartedness, and it attacks free men who have been captured and made slaves."[1] With these words Livingstone may well have been talking about South Sudanese slaves in northern captivity today. One might find some similarities between the experiences of African slaves in the hands of the Swahili traders of the nineteenth century that Livingstone was writing about and the lives of Dinka slaves in the hands of North Sudanese at present. The difference, however, is that Dinka slaves are undergoing their tragedy during a period in human history when slavery is almost the dividing line between civilization and barbarism.

In a world where international intervention in crises has become a common practice, South Sudan has witnessed the worst human tragedy since World War II. The catastrophe in Sudan has been described as one of the greatest humanitarian crises in the modern world.[2] Two million people have died during the course of the current war, slavery has been revived, four million people are living in displacement, and famines continue to threaten more lives.[3] Since the National Islamic Front took power in Khartoum by force in 1989, South Sudan has been turned into a killing field. Determined to impose its version of Islam on the whole country, the regime has conducted a "holy war." Slave raiding has been the chosen weapon of terror, whereby Arab militias storm African villages in the South, killing men and taking slaves. The holy war is also conducted through bombing of villages, including schools and hospitals, and starving people by denying aid agencies access to the famished population. The denial of access to food aid as a weapon of war caused the death of 60,000 people in Bahr el-Ghazal alone in 1998.[4]

Yet, the international family has shown very little effort to alleviate the tragedy. The humanitarian effort undertaken by Operation Life-line

Sudan (OLS) has been greatly appreciated by the people of the South,[5] but the operation is perceived as merely treating the symptoms of the crisis and not addressing the most crucial aspect of it, that is, the root causes of the crisis.[6] In fact, the operation has been criticized as inadvertently promoting the war—particularly when food is appropriated by soldiers—and as providing a kind of alibi for international donors, encouraging and legitimating a failure to address the political roots of an emergency. The operation has been widely blamed for allowing the powerful countries to evade their responsibility in seeking a diplomatic solution, and for causing a dependency syndrome among the war-affected populations. Part of this "dependency" is seen as arising from the way relief discourages productive activity by pulling people away from their home areas. It is also seen as creating dependency by offering people an easy alternative to hard work and local coping techniques. Another important element of the widespread fears of dependency is the possible role of relief in undermining both local institutional capacity and the willingness of local authorities to take responsibility for welfare.[7] Humanitarian assistance has also been criticized for functioning as a magnet for displaced Southerners in Darfur and Kordofan, where the Arabs are exploiting them under the noses of the aid agencies.[8] Having been at war for the past seventeen years, South Sudan has been described as a wasteland.[9] There is no working economy, poverty is total, and then a procession of foreign aid workers, most of whom do not speak local languages, arrive in their "birds of steel," as planes are sometimes called. These affluent representatives of a different world make the gap between the haves and have-nots only too glaring. They bring meager relief handouts and their arrogant attitudes toward the people only make the material poverty of South Sudanese even more real. It is the inattention to this gap that has increased the brokenheartedness.

The feeling among South Sudanese that foreign aid workers do not accord them the respect and dignity they deserve as human beings was particularly heightened in 1999 when the U.S. Congress passed a law that would allow the president of the United States to send food to the SPLA directly. This proposition was opposed out of hand by all the major private aid agencies operating in South Sudan such as Care International and World Vision International. Their objection was based on the assumption that if the U.S. government circumvented the established channels for humanitarian aid delivery, that might place their neutrality in jeopardy. They also argued that such action would move the United States away from the principle that humanitarian aid should not be used as a weapon of war. The other argument against the proposal came from human rights groups such as Human Rights Watch and Amnesty International. They said that the SPLA is implicated in human rights violations just as the government of Sudan is, and direct humanitarian assistance to the SPLA sends a signal that the U.S. government condones its abusive treatment of civilians. The attitude of the aid agencies and human rights groups was typical of the arrogance with which they have always delivered their services. Their understanding of South Sudan has been one that views southern cultures as cultures of war. That war may change culture but that people continue to cling to their ideas of pride and dignity seems lost from the view of foreign aid workers. Just as they never ask how the people would want to be helped, or what kind of services the people prefer, the opinion of the people they "serve" was not solicited on the issue of direct assistance to the SPLA.

Naturally, all the intellectuals from South Sudan, whether in diaspora or within Sudan, welcomed the proposition, even though they were aware that it might not happen. For a people who have been neglected by the world for so long, a gesture like this from a major power like the United States was more than the people of the South could have hoped for. However, they were greatly disappointed when all the aid agencies serving in the South and portraying themselves as concerned for the people of the South opposed the one thing that might have made a step toward ending the misery of African Sudanese.

In regard to the slavery problem, direct food assistance to the SPLA would have enabled its forces on the borders between the North and South—the slavery zone—to keep guard against the Murahileen raids. One of the biggest problems for the SPLA troops guarding the North-South border areas is that the civil population has deserted the area for security reasons. And given that the SPLA forces rely almost exclusively on the civilians for sustenance, the soldiers are forced to travel back and forth between their positions and the civilian villages farther south to look for food and other supplies. This is an expansive and rough terrain and the soldiers do not have means of transportation. So when they have collected their necessary supplies from the villages, they have to carry them on their shoulders back to their posts. South Sudanese who supported the proposition for direct U.S. assistance to the SPLA believed that such assistance would have mitigated this situation and would have enabled the SPLA to protect the people from slave raids more effectively and efficiently.

The conclusion reached by southern communities in Sudan and abroad was that the private nongovernmental organizations within OLS are in the business of humanitarian assistance merely because of their own private greed. In fact, the accusation of complicity in the suffering of South Sudanese went so far as to suggest that these NGOs do not want peace to come to Sudan, for that would mean losing the huge funding that has turned humanitarian assistance into a fast-growing enterprise. The local suspicion was that NGOs were opposed to the idea of U.S. direct aid to South Sudanese because these NGOs thought that it would take the jobs away from the expatriate aid workers.[10] Although this may be an unfair characterization, given that these organizations have spent large amounts of money to deliver relief to South Sudan since 1989, the sentiments were not completely unfounded. The position of South Sudanese in East Africa over U.S. aid was summarized by a letter to Kenya's *Daily Nation* as follows: "The opposition of some NGOs working in South Sudan to the U.S. government's humanitarian gesture towards South Sudan as reported recently was a very unfortunate action. While South Sudan appreciates any genuine humanitarian aid to its oppressed and hungry people, it, however, deplores any aid done mainly on self-interest and profit."[11] Clearly, the people of South Sudan believed that the NGOs objected to American food aid to the SPLA essentially out of fear that they might lose their business in Sudan.

When the people of South Sudan made pleas to the world to deliver them from the new forms of slavery revived by the North, the international reaction has been to blame the abductions and slavery on the war. And the international attitude is one which seems to suggest to the southern slaves to wait in bondage until the war is brought to an end. In other words, the question of slavery has fallen by the wayside in the face of the spectacular and devastating poverty and famines. In fact, slavery is at times blamed on the war-provoked poverty of South Sudanese. Notice the stand taken by United Nations Children's Fund (UNICEF): "To roll back and eventually bring a halt to slavery in Sudan, UNICEF believes the main effort should be directed at enlisting the support of the warring parties in ending the armed conflict and all its practices."[12]

As the earlier chapters have shown, the history of the current slavery in Sudan is a history of the North's political domination, economic ambitions, racism, and cultural and religious intolerance. It is also a history of southern determination to retain its identity, of resistance against assimilation and "ethnocide," and of a stand against a policy of extermination perpetrated by the successive regimes in Khartoum. The relationships between the South and the North remained influenced by this history because of two opposing views that have become the reality of Sudan over the past seventeen years. First, given this background, the North continues to hold the notion that Sudan will see unity and harmony only after its Arab and Islamic culture has completely dominated every aspect of life in both the North and the South. Second, in response to the northern views of forced unity, the South has developed a strong feeling of animosity toward the North in a way that will prove difficult to reconcile.

Reports on Slavery

The first reports of slavery that appeared in the media were championed by South Sudanese journalist and politician Bona Malwal, who was the editor of the *Sudan Times*, the only English-language newspaper in Khartoum during Sadiq al-Mahdi's reign as prime minister of Sudan. When the allegations of slavery became widespread in 1987, Bona Malwal and Macram Max Gassis, the bishop of the diocese of el-Obeid, at the request of some members of the U.S. Congress, went to testify in Washington. Northerners regarded these developments as damaging to the image of the country and some northern writers began to grapple with the issue, sometimes accusing Malwal of defaming the country simply because of his disagreement with the prime minister. The question of slavery heightened the North-South divide. Instead of investigating it, many educated Northerners concluded that the allegations of slavery were meant to tarnish the image of the North, especially its Islamic character, which is supposedly a humane character,[13] a suggestion that outraged the South even more. "Why would anybody make up a story about human suffering?" was the question one heard very often in Khartoum in the late 1980s.

On the issue of slavery, the current southern animosity toward the North as a whole may have been slightly ameliorated by the commitment shown by the two university professors Ushari Mahmud and Suleiman Baldo, who reported the massacre of Dinka refugees in the town of ed-Da'ein in 1987 with heartbreaking detail.[14] Their report raised the alarm, especially among the Northerners who were skeptical about the stories of slavery carried by the *Sudan Times*. In addition, the few North Sudanese—like the political advisor to John Garang, Mansour Khalid, and the SPLA spokesperson in Eritrea, Yasir Arman—who had joined hands with the South to fight the Khartoum government may have also mitigated the North-South polarization. Because of these few Northerners, many Southerners argued strongly against the often-generalized notion of the wicked North. But as for the rest of the North, the South, no doubt, believes that most Northerners sanction the practice of slavery. It is the omnipresent opinion among Southerners that Northerners are denying the practice of slavery only because it is shameful for a modern country to tolerate and even encourage what is deemed to be one of the worst crimes against humanity. Although I have no specific written documentation or a systematic polling of southern opinion about this notion, this is the opinion that has been expressed to me during my interviews with Southerners from all walks of life within South Sudan. I have also followed discussions among diaspora South Sudanese on the Internet over the last two years, and the dominant sentiment has been that Northerners really hate the people of the South. Whether or not this is true is irrelevant. What matters is that such a notion exists among South Sudanese, and this feeling has and will have negative impact on North-South relations. It makes the possibility of future reconciliation remote. Indeed, many southern intellectuals have already spoken out on many platforms that it is too late for unity.[15]

This image regarding slavery was particularly and irreversibly painted by the reaction of Sadiq al-Mahdi's government to the reports of the reemergence of slavery. Although Mahmud and Baldo did not initially set out to report on slavery but rather to prove wrong the "southern allegations," as the northern intelligentsia called them, their document made the South regard them as heroes nevertheless. But instead of investigating the allegations of monstrous slavery put forward in their report, the government opted to demonize them, describing them as "fifth column" collaborators with the SPLA. Since 1987, any Sudanese citizen living inside Sudan who mentioned the existence of slavery has been jailed on charges of defaming the country or even treason.[16]

Due to the government's hostile reactions against those reporting about slavery, the question of slavery was almost eliminated from the list of concerns of the international bodies such as the UN and NGOs operating in Sudan from that day on. Apart from the continued efforts of local journalists like Bona Malwal,[17] Sudan's slavery was to remain unreported to the outside world for the next several years until the Children's Rights Project of Human Rights Watch/Africa issued its famous booklet in 1995.[18] This document described the practice of slavery and provided testimonies of its victims where the abducted children and women often lead lives of extreme deprivation and cruelty at the hands of their masters. The booklet also documented that many of the captives are physically and sexually abused, and forced to live at a standard well below that of their captors (sleeping on the floor, minimum food, and no chance for education). In addition, the document revealed the horrendous activities of the Sudanese government in forcing the displaced children from the South into Islam, army, and labor. These children were denied their ethnic heritage, language, religion, and identity as they were cut off from their families and were held by Arabic-speaking captors, most of whom forced the children to take Arabic names in place of their African names.

In the usual human rights writing, using a neutral tone in a search for balance, the Human Rights Watch's document also accused the SPLA of recruiting minors into the rebel army. In response to this document, the SPLA has openly argued in various forums that in a state where certain identities are targeted for elimination by an organization that calls itself a government, young people, including those that some cultures may consider to be children, have to go to war. SPLA commanders were quick to make the point that recruitment of boys into opposition forces, where they may be better able to defend themselves and their families, is a lesser evil than the possibility of being taken into slavery. The Khartoum regime, however, responded to accusations of human rights violation, including slavery, as mere allegations in an effort to smear the good name of the Islamic government.

Perhaps one of the reports most damaging to the government of Sudan's case for denying the existence of slavery was the report by the Special Rapporteur of the United Nations Commission on Human Rights, Gaspar Biro. In a 1994 report, Biro cited the raids carried out by government-sponsored Murahileen militias used as proxy fighting forces. Biro said this had led to "an alarming increase in cases of slavery, servitude, slave trade and forced labor." He also noted that the total passivity of the government can only be regarded as tacit political approval and support of the institution of slavery."[19] The Sudanese government's response to Biro's report was expectedly one of outrage. The government accused the Special Rapporteur of hate for Islam, and requested the United Nations to ask him to rethink his report. The Sudan government also requested that Biro be removed as the Special Rapporteur on Sudan, a request that was not heeded but one which caused a serious row during the following reporting period, when Biro was dispatched to Sudan again. His second report was equally critical of the government of Sudan on the question of the joint raids by the Murahileen, Popular Defense Forces, and government army, and the labor exploitation that the captives were subjected to.

Although the reports listed above did not immediately arouse discernable progress in steering concern worth noting among international agencies, the government of Sudan felt the pinch. It became engaged in a discourse of denial. Government officials started a campaign to label accusations against all those concerned about and reporting the horrors of slavery. They were accused of carrying a grudge against the government because of its Islamic orientation. But these officials were aware that the time was close when they would be required to respond to the allegations with more evidence to show that the government was acting against the practice of slavery.

The antislavery reporting and the campaign being waged by church groups against the slave trade eventually forced the government to investigate the reports, or at least to put up a facade in which it appear as if it was doing something about it. The government has masqueraded as concerned over the years, but has not come clean on a world stage. Following the publication of the report on ed-Da'ein massacre, Hassan al-Turabi, then Sudan's attorney general in al-Mahdi's government, sent a journalist who was a lawyer and a member of the National Islamic Front, Majid Yousef, to "investigate the allegations of slavery." Majid Yousef was said to have told al-Turabi that the report by Mahmud and Baldo was accurate, but his report was never published. The first admission by someone close to government circles that slavery exists was to come from al-Turabi himself, when he was no longer a member of al-Mahdi's government. When he was in opposition to al-Mahdi's government, in an interview on Voice of America radio he commented, "the so-called slaves were in reality prisoners of war treated like slaves."

When the elected government of Sadiq al-Mahdi was overthrown in a military coup that brought the NIF to power in 1989, al-Turabi, who was widely known to be the force behind the military government, and the ideologue of the Islamic regime, started to categorically deny the existence of slavery in Sudan. Al-Turabi began to give lengthy interviews in newspapers in Khartoum and in the Middle East, where he presented his strongest denial of slavery, and his views on the nature of the word "slavery" in the Sudanese context. In an interview published in *Anbaa* newspaper on January 21, 1998, he focused on the illegality of slavery in Sudan. He said, "Sudanese law not only bans slavery, it also forbids any forced labor or exploitation of the individual. Our system forbids that you could coerce anyone to work, even if you were paying that person for the work." He also characterized the slavery reports as "malicious propaganda behind which stands the United States of America." Because of al-Turabi's skills at playing with words and the government's emphasis on the unconstitutionality of slavery in Sudan, the government managed to misrepresent the facts surrounding slavery. In fact, the international community was drawn into the government of Sudan's whitewashing exercise. The NIF delights in remarks such as that the government is "investigating" and working with the legal system to "eradicate" the abductions. The world almost believed the line that Sudan's slavery was the result of war, and that it could only be addressed through bringing peace to Sudan. The attitude of the government was that slavery-like practices happen only because the SPLA evades peace negotiations, and that if the international community wishes to end slavery then Western countries need to pressure the SPLA to accept a peaceful solution to the conflict. History attests to the ability of tyrants to deceive the world. One only has to remember the disbelief of the international community concerning reports coming out of Rwanda in 1994 to know how easy this can be.

The combination of the Human Rights Watch document, the press reports coming out of Sudan, and eyewitness accounts between 1986 and 1995 prompted a degree of curiosity among non-Sudanese writers. Journalists from the United States started traveling to South Sudan and writing about slavery in the mid-1990s. In 1995 Clarence Page of the *Washington Times* traveled to northern Bahr el-Ghazal and came back to write moving editorials about the plight of Sudan's slaves.[20] Also deserving of mention is the 1995 *Washington Times* article, "Southern Sudan's Kids Vanish into Slavery," by Shyam Bhatia. The *Washington Post* and the *Boston Globe* also spearheaded a campaign to expose Sudan's slavery. Many powerful people in the United States, like the Nation of Islam's Louis Farrakhan, were quick to denounce journalistic reports as a "white man's" concoction to show Africans in a bad light. It is worth noting here that the reaction of many people of African descent to reports of modern African slavery has often been one of skepticism, especially in North America. They perceive news of African slavery as an attempt of racist whites to deflect attention from the horrors of the transatlantic slave trade and to make light of the role of racism in the slave trade. There has been a great deal of literature attempting to distinguish between *benign* slavery (usually Muslim slavery) and *harsh* slavery (normally plantation slavery in the New World). This has indeed turned African-Americans into apologists on behalf of Muslim slavers. It is as if they wish to deflect the embarrassing historical reality that the Muslims of North Africa as well as from Arabia had engaged in slavery to an equal or even at times worse degree than the American plantation owners, and they continue to hold slaves at present.[21] Farrakhan challenged journalists to provide evidence, and journalists did just what he had asked for. The NBC television program *Dateline* sent a crew to Bahr el-Ghazal only to return with horrifying scenes. These journalistic reports raised a storm of indignation from around the world. It later became evident that Farrakhan actually denounces in public the allegations of Sudan's slavery but admits privately to South Sudanese that he has seen horrible things happening to Southerners who live in the North as displaced people. For example, at a Pan-African conference in Ghana, Farrakhan suggested that the claims of slavery in Sudan were made out of Southerners' inferiority complex, for "they are very very black."[22] But in an encounter at a Nairobi hotel in 1998, after having just arrived from Khartoum, he intimated to Bona Malwal that Southerners were indeed denied full citizenship in Khartoum.[23] So it appears that Farrakhan is simply unwilling to publicly admit the suffering he witnessed in Sudan, lest he loses his favored status among Muslims in Africa. It is common knowledge that the Nation of Islam receives considerable financial assistance from Sudan and Libya.

Antislavery Activities by Christian and Other Organizations

Frustrated by the indifference of Western governments and the world community at large, Christian organizations from the Western world started the campaign to raise money for the purpose of freeing abducted and enslaved children. Foremost of these organizations was the Swiss-based Christian Solidarity International (CSI). This is a small "organization which grew out of smuggling Bibles behind the then Iron Curtain. It discovered slavery in Southern Sudan by accident, when it was the guest of the Khartoum government in 1994."[24] When CSI could not find answers to the questions they put to the government, they went to the South, without the Khartoum government's permission, to investigate the matter further from the areas controlled by the SPLA. While in the South, CSI stumbled upon the small-scale "redemption" of slaves that the Dinka communities had been carrying out whenever they could raise enough cattle to sell. Since then, the group, led by an American, John Eibner, began journeys into border areas between South Sudan and the Baggara territory in Darfur and Kordofan. The object of their trips was to obtain the freedom of any children they could locate. While on the borders, the group "redeemed" the slaves by paying an Arab middleman to locate them and purchase them from their masters, and then took them back to their villages in the South. CSI's president, Hans Stuckelberger, related the history of their involvement in the slave redemption program in Sudan: "We first heard of slavery in Sudan through rumours. But in 1994, we realized during a trip to Sudan that there is slavery and that people, in rare cases, are able to buy the slaves back. They were collecting money for this; it was a practice that was in existence. In 1995 we had our first slave redemption trip, which was filmed by ZDF German TV. Through an Arab retriever, we were able to free 15 slaves. That was the beginning. We decided this was something we must do something about as our Christian duty. It slowly built up."[25]

In 1995, the Boston-based American Anti-Slavery Group (AASG) kicked off the antislavery campaign in coordination with smaller South Sudanese community groups on the east coast of the United States. The American Anti-Slavery Group's president, Charles Jacobs, started the campaign by writing lucid newspaper articles and letters to the editors of such prominent papers as the *Boston Globe*, the *New York Times*, the *Los Angeles Times*, the *Washington Times*, and the *Washington Post*. Like CSI, AASG was outraged by the inaction of Western governments, especially the U.S. The group declared that "we cannot remain silent in the face of such fundamental human rights violations."[26] By this statement Charles Jacobs gained much popularity and appreciation among South Sudanese in exile. Letters poured to his Internet Web site from all over the world where exiled South Sudanese have resettled and have access to computers.

Two main areas of antislavery activity were the focus of AASG. First was raising funds to support CSI slave redemption programs, and second was to build awareness in the United States. The awareness campaign also involved pleading to the American people and government to put pressure on the government of Sudan on the issue of slavery. The campaign also entails asking Americans to divest from companies that do business in Sudan such as the Canadian oil company, the Calgary-based Talisman Energy. Against the Canadian government's recommendation and the threats from opposition armies in South Sudan, Talisman initiated oil ventures in South Sudan. Its operations have so far been criticized as promoting the war and the slave taking by providing the government of Sudan with the cash that enables it to purchase arms.

In 1998, fifth-grade schoolchildren in Aurora, Colorado, upon learning that children their ages were being held in bondage and that their freedom could be obtained for a mere $50, established an abolitionist movement called Slavery That Oppresses People (STOP). Their campaign attracted spectacular media coverage. Their teacher, Barbara Vogel, along with a few of these students went to Washington to testify before the U.S. Congress. The students of Highline Community School of Aurora became a sensation in the fall of 1998 and the spring of 1999, especially over the eloquence with which they spoke about the suffering of South Sudanese children. The media was equally stunned by the degree of financial commitment shown by these children, who collected their lunch allowances every day for a cause that even more knowledgeable adults were unable to commit to. One writer said that for a ten-year-old child, "donating 10 dollars is like you and I donating 10,000 dollars." The children collected more than $50,000 and sent it to CSI, which sent more emissaries to Sudan with the money to purchase and free more slaves.

The children's campaign aroused the sympathy of many people from all corners imaginable, be it a Hebrew school in British Columbia, a Texas retiree, a priest in Canada, a pastor in Mississippi, or a Jewish novelist.[27] Barbara Vogel received hundreds of letters and electronic mail messages from exiled South Sudanese as well as from many Americans who had been touched by the children's commitment to justice. In August 1999, Vogel traveled to northern Bahr el-Ghazal with CSI's John Eibner with the mission to secure the redemption of another group of children. On this trip, the group bought the freedom of 1,050 women and children, bringing the total of slaves redeemed since 1995 to 7,725 slaves, each redeemed for about $50 each. The children in Colorado received the news of this redemption with cheers and tears of joy.[28]

Debate over the Evidence of Slavery

By 1998, whether or not slavery existed in Sudan was no longer the subject of thorny debate that it had been since 1987. The evidence had become conclusive as to the fact of its existence, and the remaining debate was now about why it is happening and what should be done to end it. But as far as the government of Sudan was concerned, allegations of the existence of slavery were the creations of its foes bent on tarnishing the name of the Islamic state. Due to increasing pressure from the international community, the Khartoum regime seemed to have relaxed the yoke of slavery. More and more slaves regained their liberty. They obtained their freedom through some discreet legal measures or through escape. Many of the former slaves interviewed for this study stated that they were set free after they secretly managed to report their cases to the police. As one of them said, "If you are lucky to find a non-Baggara police agent, he could assist you to get on a bus heading north, and then after you have passed the Baggara territory, you can get on the train to take you to el-Meiram. From there you can walk home."[29] Others escaped right out of bondage, a risky venture that can result in death should one be caught in the act. Yet a good number were set free after their former masters were paid in cash or cattle, amounts and numbers of which were dependent on a number of factors, including the age and sex of the slave. Young adult males and "beautiful" girls were priced higher than all the others were. Prices can also be subject to the discretion of the master. A more compassionate slaveholder may pity the relatives and lower the price.

The narratives of the increasing number of freed slaves exposed the practice more widely. They told of their use as laborers on farms, as herdsmen or domestic servants. Women and girls related stories of having been taken in by Arab men as concubines. Evidence mounted and Khartoum could no longer dismiss the allegations offhand. To deny the existence of slavery, the government needed to show genuine commitment to ameliorating the situation. But to the frustration of all, the Khartoum regime continued its stonewalling tactics. However, in an effort to conceal this tactic, the government formed a committee in 1996 to investigate the allegations, but still refused to call it "slavery." This committee was established by the minister of justice to investigate what was called "involuntary disappearance." Made up of representatives from government agencies—the Humanitarian Affairs Commission and the Ministries of External Affairs, the Interior, State Security, and Military Intelligence—the committee was headed by a lawyer, Ali Ahmed al-Nasri. It has to be noted, however, that this committee was put together by another government body called the Human Rights Consultative Council under the minister of justice. The committee traveled to Darfur and Kordofan, but did not publish a full report. It only issued several statements, often verbal, to the press in which it insinuated that it had not found any case of slavery in Sudan. Little could be expected from a committee composed of representatives of the government branches most closely involved in the war and slavery. The Ministry of Military Intelligence, the police, the judges, and the National Security Ministry were all the parts of government the escaped slaves and their relatives had pointed out as the culprits. They could not have reported their own misdeeds, and the government knew that the committee would not genuinely investigate anything. It was a mockery of the international legal system and antislavery conventions.

The antislavery activities of Baroness Caroline Cox from the British House of Lords were ever more embarrassing to the government of Sudan. The government, therefore, decided to invite a colleague of Lady Cox in the British House of Lords, Lord McNair to examine the situation in Sudan. He was taken to various places within Sudan, including the transition zone, but he had no opportunity to visit areas of his own choice. Lord McNair, having been guided through superficial tours of prearranged areas of the capital city and displaced persons' camps in Kordofan by the government's security agents, returned to England satisfied that there was no slavery in Sudan. He presented his report to the House of Lords in October 1997. In a vicious attack on his colleague Lady Cox, his report suggested that the allegations of slavery in Sudan were unfounded. With this, the government of Sudan had beaten human rights and antislavery groups at their game. These groups knew perfectly well that a government's guest taken to specific areas does not account for much, but by such activities, the government had enough room to use the situation to its advantage. Aware that real international verifiers of slavery will have no access to the actual areas of slavery and the slave trade, the government of Sudan could easily downplay the international concern. Khartoum knew that the international legal system does not have the ability or the political will to force them to open up the "slavery zone." Much like in the old days when the European explorers of central Africa were subjected to scrutiny by the Arab and Swahili slave traders, the northern Sudanese slavers are very skilled at getting away with the crime. The Baggara slavers in Darfur and Kordofan and the government know too well that if allowed access to the slavery zone, any foreigners or educated Southerners would provide a full account of the atrocities the Arabs were committing in the area.

As is the case with all pariah states, the triumph of the government of Sudan over finding a new ally in Lord McNair was ephemeral. Lord McNair had quickly learned the government's vocabulary. He pressed the fact that during the past fifteen years or so, the population of Khartoum has increased by several million, and the fact that most of the new inhabitants were refugees from the war in the South. The visiting lord took this as evidence for lack of slavery, and suggested that if the Northerners wanted slaves, indeed, why would they go raiding in the South when they could easily take them from among the refugees. In addition, against all the reports from NGOs about the depressing conditions of the displaced Southerners in the North, Lord McNair "observed" that the government was "sharing" its meager resources with their brothers and sisters from the South. Perhaps the situation of the displaced in Khartoum really did seem like this to a passing tourist whose expenses were paid by the local government, but to anyone who knew the real facts about the current Islamic government and the racial tension, Lord McNair's account is completely absurd. The displaced in the North are not at peace and their life there is on the point of total misery, except that the displaced cannot be made slaves because the government fears the inquisitive foreign journalists, human rights activists, and foreign diplomats. But it still manages to maintain religious schools where southern "street children" live in conditions well below those of their northern counterparts.

Expecting more international outcry, the government established another investigative body in 1999. The Committee for the Eradication of Abduction of Women and Children allegedly started working on its mission at the beginning of 1999, but nothing materialized beyond remarks that the "abductions" were rooted in the civil war and tribal conflict. By the middle of the year, the government sent reports to the United Nations in which it tried to disprove the allegations against Sudan of the practice of slavery, but none of these reports seemed to have persuaded the UN to make them public. This only left room for more reporting and efforts to collect more evidence.[30]

The UN Commission on Human Rights sent a second Special Rapporteur, the Argentinean lawyer Leonardo Franco, to investigate slavery and other human rights violations. His report made plain that men, women, and children were taken as chattel slaves, although boys, girls, and women were the principal targets. The report indicated that the government of Sudan was using this practice of slavery as a tactic of war to recruit one set of tribal allies and displace another set of tribal enemies from their homelands. The practice of religious persecution, which is a component of the practice of slavery and a root cause of the war, was also addressed in the report. Franco reported the activities of Murahileen, the PDF, and the government's army that ride on the "slave train," as the military supply train has become known in South Sudan. While in Wau town, Franco received reports about the continuing capture of women and children in South Sudan for the purpose of reducing them to slavery. The UN official examined slavery in light of the human rights abuses being perpetrated in the context of the conflict; his report characterized the situation as follows:

Raids by militia are a major source of violations of human rights. In Bahr-el-Ghazal, the Murahileen militia (or Mujahideen) often accompany the state-owned military supply train escorted by the popular defense forces (PDF), which travels down to Wau, and from Wau back to Babanusa. According to consistent and reliable sources, the Murahileen ride on horseback along both sides of the railroad tracks, fanning out within a radius of up to 50 km, and systematically raid villages, torch houses, steal cattle, kill men and capture women and children as booty. Often abducted women and children are taken up north and remain in possession of the captors or other persons. The PDF are also said to take part in the raids.[31]

Despite this strong evidence, the government of Sudan continued to make a mockery of the clear international legal opinion on any form of exploitation. Many third world countries ruled through brutal force found it easy to vote in favor of the government of Sudan on issues of human rights violations at the UN. So, evidence such as is provided by the Special Rapporteur does not go a long way toward forcing the country in question to change its ways. The only way to do this is by action of the Security Council, but this needs the commitment of a strong and politically willing Western country to steer through a Security Council resolution of condemnation, and to follow that with concrete action, should the country fail to comply with the resolution. The government of Sudan counted on the knowledge that there is no such country with the willingness to stand up against the tragic situation in South Sudan. However, a combination of events finally sent a strong message to Khartoum on the issue of slavery. The Special Rapporteur's report was part of this. In addition, a month earlier, CSI had made a statement that it had "bought back" a total of 5,066 slaves in Sudan over the last four years for $52,000. Although people, governments, and organizations were unable to condone the slave buyback initiative, the program had highlighted the tragic reality of Sudan's slavery. These events demonstrated that there was no room for denial, and there was increased moral pressure on the international community. Moral obligations and UN condemnations, however, do not necessarily lead to action, and the case of Sudan provides strong evidence of double standards in the international system.

The hardest blow to Sudan's case came when it was most unexpected. In March 1999 UNICEF executive director Carol Bellamy stated for the first time that UNICEF was concerned about abduction of children and women in Sudan's war. She declared, "Now that there is irrefutable evidence of an established and on-going slave trade in Sudan, UNICEF hopes to cooperate effectively with the government of Sudan, and other interested members of the international community to end the slave trade in Sudan."[32] UNICEF referred in particular to the need of cooperation with the Office of the High Commissioner for Human Rights, which had been actively concerned about and engaged in the issue. UNICEF demanded firm commitment from all those directly and indirectly responsible to end the slave trade in Sudan. The agency also highlighted the necessity of granting freedom of movement for international investigators, and of starting a program to trace and retrieve slaves and to reunify them with their families.

This announcement infuriated the government of Sudan, and the country's foreign under-secretary Hassan Abdin summoned UNICEF's country representative in Khartoum, Thomas Ekvall, and conveyed the government's official rejection of the statement that slavery existed in Sudan. The following is an excerpt from the statement that was given to Ekvall as well as to news agencies: "The Sudanese government is dismayed and astonished that such a statement is made by a UN agency well acquainted with the situation in Sudan. . . . The Sudanese law is opposed to all forms of enslavement . . . negative practices arising from conditions of the civil war and tribal conflict cannot be classified as a sort of slavery." [33] The government of Sudan demanded that UNICEF retract what it called an "unfair and unfounded accusation against Sudan." Abdin warned, "the future relationship between Sudan and UNICEF will depend on the organization's response to this request." Bellamy later retracted her statement and has refrained from calling it "slavery" since then. The slave trade was to become "abduction" and slaves were called "captives of tribal raiding" in UNICEF's vocabulary, just as the government of Sudan had described it since the beginning.

On April 23, 1999, the United Nations Commission on Human Rights issued a resolution on the situation of human rights in Sudan following the publication of the Special Rapporteur's document. The resolution completely disregarded the strong evidence furnished by the UN's own official, and it failed to confront fully the practice of slavery in Sudan. The resolution decided against the use of the word "slavery." The use of euphemisms in the resolution—"forced or involuntary disappearance" and "abduction of women and children to be subjected to forced labor or similar conditions"—fell short of describing the exact situation of slave raiding in the areas of northern Bahr el-Ghazal, Abyei, and the Nuba mountains. The resolution failed to address the enslavement of captured Dinka in Darfur and Kordofan. The United States Mission to the United Nations issued a statement in protest of the language used in the resolution. In its protest, the mission stated, "the failure to use the word 'slavery' in the resolution will be seen as ignoring an abominable practice, for which there should be zero tolerance. That failure also undermines the report of the Special Rapporteur, which uses the term and discusses the issue at length." [34]

The government of Sudan was under such serious attack from all directions that it had to respond differently to the slavery claims. It continued to deny the existence of slavery, but in different language. For example, on April 30, 1999, President Omar al-Bashir told journalists that the accusations were merely part of a campaign to distort Sudan's image through all sorts of propaganda, because of its Islamic orientation. The United States and Israel were particularly attacked as the masterminds behind the slavery allegations. He suggested that "the claim will make anyone familiar with the situation in Sudan laugh." A week later, however, the government accepted that there were cases of "forced labor and similar conditions" in Sudan. Having said this, the government of Sudan then agreed to collaborate with the UN agencies. The government requested the assistance of UNICEF to work with Sudan's Human Rights Advisory Council in addressing the slavery problem.

Denials by government officials that slavery existed were, however, not based on serious investigation, nor did they have any credibility. It was clear that the government instinctively rebutted as propaganda any claims about slavery when made by organizations suspected of supporting the SPLA. But many people from different parts of the world were determined to show that slavery is not a propaganda issue that can be dodged simply by calling it "forced labor," as the government had been doing. It was obviously not enough, either, for antislavery activists to argue about the role of the government in slavery without showing concrete evidence.

The International Failure to Respond to Sudan's Crisis

Despite the increasing media coverage, Sudan's case of slavery did not receive the attention it deserved from the quarters of the world's governments. The indifference of the world community to Sudan's slavery could be explained in a myriad of ways. African countries are too embroiled in their own economic and political problems to even have an understanding about Sudan's problems. The Organization of African Unity (OAU) has no conception of how to deal with such complex conflicts. In fact, given that two-thirds of the world's internal conflicts today are in Africa, many people have concluded that the OAU has proven completely unable to mitigate Africa's crises. One of its charters maintains that national boundaries created by European colonial powers during the scramble for Africa in the nineteenth century must remain unaltered, and therefore, the OAU keeps its distance from countries like Sudan, where the times carry the strong possibility of break up. The OAU has resisted the pleas of many peoples around the continent who want their territories to be exempted from the charter, and the result of this blanket rejection of secessionist sentiments has been lethal wars, as the cases of Sudan, Eritrea, and Western Sahara show.

All of Sudan's neighbors have one kind of problem or another with the government in Khartoum and have shown their inability to mediate in Sudan's conflict. Either out of lack of knowledge or courtesy for the government of Sudan, most African countries' news media have never mentioned the existence of slavery in Sudan, let alone stated an opinion on how to eradicate it. The Europeans were partly responsible for the genesis of the chaos in Sudan to begin with and have decided to have no particular policy on how to resolve the conflict, in the shadow of which slavery thrives. Now under UN economic sanctions, the government of Sudan still enjoys the collaboration of the European Economic Community member states under what these countries have called "constructive engagement." They argue that the best way to deal with Sudan's complex situation is to "diplomatically" engage the government and provide incentives that might persuade it to abandon human rights violations. The evil in this approach is that the European governments have to do this in collaboration with the very government that has violated all the international laws and conventions in regards to the issue of slavery. So, in the final analysis, European governments cannot move beyond the economic promise presented by Sudan to European companies and businesses. It appears that European governments are concerned that to press the government of Sudan on the question of slavery is to jeopardize any future economic deals.

The Americans and the Canadians have not given Sudan's crisis the attention it deserves partly because Sudan is remote and represents no immediate interest, and partly because the United States met with disaster when it sought to intervene in Somalia in the early 1990s. Economic considerations also play an important part in North American silence over Sudan's tragedy.[35] For example, the United States government has put Sudan on the list of countries accused of sponsoring international terrorism. It has also placed a trade embargo on Sudan, and has rebuked Canada over the activities of Talisman Energy and other continuing Canadian commercial operations in Sudan. Yet, in a classic case of shameless double standard, the United States turned a blind eye to a $450 million business in gum arabic conducted by American companies in Sudan. Gum arabic is an essential ingredient in the soft drinks Pepsi and Coca-Cola, and Sudan is the main source of this ingredient.

The Muslim countries in Asia and the Middle East are brethren with North Sudan and blindly support Sudan in international forums. To date, not a single Arab country has expressed sympathy for the South since Libya withdrew its support for the SPLA in the 1980s.[36] This is partly a result of the government of Sudan's portrayal of the conflict as between Muslims and non-Muslims. The grievances of the South have been misrepresented in the Islamic and Arab world as a case of anti-Islam. So, even when the Islamic and Arab countries have not openly supported the government in Khartoum, their silence over its atrocities in the South has been quite evident. They have voted in favor of Sudan on every single issue involving the South in the UN or the Arab League. For example, when Canada took the presidency of the UN Security Council in March 2000, its mission tried to introduce the situation in Sudan for discussion, but all the Arab countries and most Muslim countries opposed the move.

Many countries in the rest of the world are too economically or politically involved with the Sudan government to condemn its dismal human rights record. Countries that are major human rights violators in their own right, such as China and Iran, find it in their interest to side with Sudan on United Nations platforms. South Sudan, in a classic case of history repeating itself, found itself standing alone again just as it did at the time of independence in 1956. There was not a single government that committed itself to aiding the South on pure moral grounds. As usual, it is now the international political and economic interests that will determine the fate of South Sudan. Perhaps the only thing that will save South Sudan from being eliminated as a nation will have to be the resolve of South Sudanese themselves. It is this atmosphere of expressed lack of concern for the oppressed by the major powers of the world that leads small but committed groups and individuals to go it alone and in their own small ways.[37]

South Sudan has had strong allies in the U.S. Congress as well as in the Clinton administration, but their activities have not been able to persuade the president of the United States to act on behalf of the oppressed in South Sudan. During President Bill Clinton's term in office the executive branch of the American government had ample opportunity to act, if the White House had had the will to see justice done or simply to save lives. But Congress has responded to the voices crying for freedom in South Sudan. In June 1999, both houses condemned the Sudanese regime for "deliberately and systematically committing genocide" and for slavery. In November 1999, the Senate unanimously passed the Sudan Peace Act, which enables the president to block American investments in Sudan and to break the food blockade to feed starving populations in South Sudan. These resolutions empowered the president to steer for peace in Sudan, and to protect the population while the search for peace continues. As mentioned earlier, the Congress has made into law a resolution that would allow the president of the United States to provide food aid directly to the SPLA, bypassing United Nations and NGO efforts that depend on Khartoum's approval. In short, the U.S. government has never been in a better position to intervene. The administration has people working full-time on the Sudan crisis, so it would seem that there should be more understanding of Sudan's problems in the executive branch of the U.S. government. Many Americans are already trying to get peace talks going between the government of Sudan and the SPLA, which is more than can be said for the Europeans. Despite the clarity in Congress's position and the commitment of the Africa staff at the State Department, there has been one disappointment after another, and "Clinton himself has been disturbingly silent," as Eric Reeves of Smith College lamented.[38]

Recalling President Clinton's State of the Union address, Reeves suggested that the president has "passed silently over the fact that more than 2 million human beings have perished in Sudan's on-going civil war." According to Reeves, by his inaction on Sudan, Clinton has disregarded a promise he made in April 1999 to Holocaust survivor Elie Wiesel when he said that he would never allow an African nation to suffer the horrific destruction that Wiesel had argued could have been prevented in Rwanda. Clinton had declared in response to Wiesel's assessment of the U.S. failure to respond to news of impending genocide in Rwanda, that "I will do my best to make sure that something like this does not happen again in Africa."[39] Yet, in addition to the dehumanizing enslavement of tens of thousands of Southerners, the deaths in Sudan exceed those of Rwanda, Bosnia, and Kosovo combined, and the president has done nothing to stop it. Sudan's case is the worst man-made tragedy since the Second World War. Was the president's promise to Wiesel a slip of a tongue, or did it exclude the Africans of Sudan?

Worse still, in a meeting in December 1999, the U.S. Secretary of State Madeleine Albright suggested that as much as she deplored the humanitarian situation in Sudan, "The human rights situation in Sudan is not marketable to the American people."[40] This statement was plainly unfounded, for the media coverage of Sudan's slavery and other human rights crises throughout 1998 and 1999 had been unprecedented. Television stations, major U.S. newspapers, and magazines had been carrying stories on slavery, famine, and religious persecution. The coverage was highlighted by "Touched by an Angel," a hit television series, which made carnage in Sudan the subject of its season premier in 1999. In the same year, the U.S. House of Representatives voted 416-1 to condemn the government of Sudan for "committing genocide in Southern Sudan." This does not leave room for a suggestion that the U.S. government's inaction regarding Sudan is about marketing Sudan's crises to the American people. It was about lack of commitment from a strong public figure like Albright.

The Slave Redemption Campaigns

By the close of the twentieth century, the issue of Sudan's slavery was left to the care of individuals and concerned religious groups. The slave buyback programs continued as the only thing within the capacity of these groups. It was initially the redemption campaign that finally put the issue of Sudanese slavery and other human rights violations in the forefront of American media interests anyhow. The slave-buying missions have received wide publicity, helping the organizations to raise money from individuals, corporations, and church groups. Now, in the face of the cold shoulder given by the world community to Sudan's slaves, the campaigns to purchase the freedom of slaves and to divest from Talisman Energy remain the only immediate alternatives. But the slave redemption campaign has been heavily criticized, a criticism that has brought the question of Sudan's slavery into another multidimensional debate.

The heavy media coverage that Sudan's slavery received since 1995, however, has been made extremely controversial by the way Christian and antislavery groups from the Western world have engaged in the effort to obtain the freedom of slaves. Some people find the work being done by Christian Solidarity International and the American Anti-Slavery Group to redeem slaves admirable, even heroic. But it has also drawn criticism from other relief agencies and UN officials who argue that war, not slavery, is the real issue, and that buying and selling people, even to free them, is wrong.

The Arguments Against Slave Redemption

Perhaps there is a need to say at the outset that almost all the points raised against slave redemption programs have been made on the basis of expectations rather than evidence. The problem with this approach is that it is only as good as the assumptions that inform it. None of the statements made by journalists, human rights groups, or the UN in critique of slave redemption programs has cited a specific instance of why and how the initiative is bad. The critics have presumed that there are potentials for fraud because the environment in which these programs take place is highly unregulated.

The first widely publicized wave of criticism of the buyback programs came from UNICEF. Stating that the efforts by nongovernmental organizations to purchase the freedom of slaves from traffickers was not the way to stamp out the scourge, UNICEF proposed to the government of Sudan a plan of action. As stated above, feeling the pressure from the international arena, the government of Sudan in February 1999 invited UNICEF to investigate the phenomenon of slavery on its territory, following widespread reports of the Swiss-based NGO Christian Solidarity International buying back thousands of slaves in order to give them back their freedom. In opposition to the redemption program, UNICEF's Carol Bellamy said that the best way to tackle the phenomenon in Sudan was through a commitment to end the slave trade, freedom for international verifiers, and full support for retrieval, tracing, and reunification programs.

Bellamy became extremely vocal in her opposition to the purchase of slaves by NGOs because, as she said, "the sad truth" was that such actions would not put an end to slavery. UNICEF said that "well-intentioned responses can be flawed. Indeed, we believe the practice has added a clear profit motive to the host of other factors that have allowed slave taking to flourish in that strife-torn country. . . . to pay cash for slaves, even to liberate them, is to enter a vicious circle. At $50 a head in a country where most people subsist on less than $1 a day, the practice has only encouraged more trafficking and criminality."[41] In an ironic adoption of the Khartoum regime's language, UNICEF said the main cause of enslavement was the civil war, which has raged in Sudan for more than eighteen years and has left some two million dead, and displaced another four million people. By this criticism, redemption and antislavery activities were dealt a blow. We have no statistics on how this criticism has affected the fund-raising by the redemption activists, but it seems that the criticism has somewhat affected the media coverage. By the end of 1999, there were fewer television and newspaper reports on Sudan's slavery than there had been a mere six months earlier. Whether this was a result of UNICEF's criticism or a consequence of the usual media fatigue will never be known.

The points raised against the redemption initiative could be summarized as follows: the critics say that pouring hard currency into a nonexistent economy is going to increase the raids. It might also give the slaving communities enough wherewithal for proliferation of arms with which to execute slavery. Another critic said that by paying large sums to free slaves, the Swiss charity undercuts the Dinka living in the North who do the same secretive work for a fraction of the cost.[42] Then there is the moral issue of placing a material value on a human being. For instance, Carol Bellamy once said that "putting a price on a human being is unacceptable," a remark to which Charles Jacobs of the American Anti-Slavery Group retorted, "What is unacceptable is for a human being to be held as property of another human being." Bellamy also suggested that buying slaves and returning them to the war zone and poverty-ridden South Sudan is putting them in harms way. Charles Jacobs was again quick to note that being in bondage is the greatest harm. Jacobs asked, "Could it be that UNICEF does not know what it is like to be a slave?" Which is more evil: to be in bondage or to be poor in South Sudan and face the possibility of being recaptured?

UNICEF's statements were picked up by the American press and the controversy that ensued developed spectacular dimensions. Bruce Finley wrote two instructive, but seriously flawed editorials for the *Denver Post* entitled "Rescue of Slaves Backfiring" and "Good Intentions Gone Awry" on August 22 and 24, 1999, respectively. The claim that the slave redemption program in Sudan had become counterproductive was without evidence as to how the buyback had resulted in the increase of slave raids and in the prices of slaves. Much like UNICEF's claims, there was no empirical evidence for these statements. First, during my trips in almost all the areas where the slaves were taken from, the price for a slave had not increased. It had remained constant at $50. It makes sense from an economic point of view that if slavers have a buyer for their human goods then they will increase the capturing. But there is no indication on the ground that slave raiding has increased simply because CSI is there ready with cash to buy them back. Then, too, there has been no way of telling whether the raids would stop if there were no slave redemptions.

An argument more damaging to the redeemers' cause was written by Richard Miniter in the *Atlantic Monthly* in July 1999. The crux of his argument was that redemption is only worsening matters because it presents lucrative profit opportunities to slave raiders and traders. The magazine article argued that this stems from the fact that the average price of redemption is relatively high compared to the individual income in the country. Miniter argued that the fact that "a typical raiding party has grown from roughly 400 attackers in 1995 [the year that the redemption programs started] to more than 2,500 this year" might indicate that the buyback initiative may provide incentives for more vigorous raids.[43]

Other better-argued criticisms have also been carried by the media, the strongest point being that CSI was not being transparent about how the redemption scheme works. Indeed, they may have allowed themselves to be duped in their dealings with the Arab slave traders, and in the process may have developed an unreliable picture of the exact nature of the problem. If they were trying to right a wrong, it is important not to get involved in other deceptions, the argument went. The reference here was to the SPLA, that some individuals in the rebel army may be taking a cut of the money—probably a large one. For example, the local authorities insist that they are the ones to change the dollars into the Sudanese currency in order to stem the flow of hard currency into the North. The suspicion came from the lack of evidence that even the local currency given to the Arab middleman does indeed go back to Baggaraland. Some critics think that some of the redeemed slaves have possibly not been taken as slaves at all. The argument is that since CSI rarely take with them other foreigners who had been to Sudan before and have extensive knowledge of the internal workings of Sudanese societies, one cannot be sure that they would know if this was what was happening. Some of the critics come from Christian groups who think that if the whole transaction turns out to be a scam, it would be the Dinka people whose image would be tarnished.

Human rights groups are also skeptical about the programs. While not explicitly opposed nor in agreement with slave redemption, but clearly skeptical, Human Rights Watch stated a balanced stance:

Without doubt, the families of the abductees and their chiefs welcome the assistance they receive from outside groups to redeem the slaves. They put the welfare of the individual children and women first, regardless of larger policy consideration raised by concerned agencies and individuals. This is entirely understandable. The danger of continued redemptions is several-fold. Knowledge that there are foreigners (with presumably deep pockets) willing to pay to redeem slaves can only spur on unscrupulous individuals to make a business out of the redemption. The availability of foreign funds poses the risk that those who already conduct slave raids on Dinka may abduct children and women for the explicit purpose of gain from the sale of abductees. Furthermore, such monetary incentive for raiding and abduction may work against local agreements between Baggara and Dinka to halt raiding in exchange for access for Baggara cattle to pastures and rivers during the dry season. Finally, there is the risk of fraud in the redemption process. Redemptions are now conducted without reference to lists of missing children and women; the middlemen seem to secure the release of the abductees from their masters without knowing whether there is a family member ready to assume responsibility for the released abductee. This gives rise to the risk of fraud: for instance, unscrupulous middleman may "borrow" children—with or without the knowledge of their caretakers—who have never been abducted, for the purpose of enlarging a group of slaves. Thus foreigners intending to do good may be deceived by middlemen.[44]

These points are well taken, but the opinions of the Dinka people on the ground differ slightly. As will be demonstrated shortly, communities of the slavery victims initiated the buyback programs and are definitely eager for international assistance to obtain the freedom of their enslaved loved ones, whatever the nature of this assistance.

The Arguments for Slave Redemption

The most valid point raised by defenders of redemption is that it has, at a minimum, raised awareness about slavery in Sudan. Eibner of CSI defended the program by saying he will not pay more than $50 a person. He said he will stop if redemption evolves into a "free market." Defenders of redemption state that "slavery predates CSI's presence here," and that "There is no evidence that there is any more slavery since we started this. The fact is that slavery is not primarily economically motivated. The primary motive is political. The motive is the government using these slave raids as a way to wage war on these people."[45]

UNICEF's statements were criticized by the defenders of redemption as hypocritical and mealymouthed.[46] Charles Jacobs accused UNICEF of selective caring for the world's children. For example, it was during the same volatile period over the question of Sudan's slavery that UNICEF made a statement about providing financial assistance to Indian families whose children had been bonded by wealthy families due to debts accumulated by these poor families. The indebted families, according to

UNICEF's new program, were to be given financial support to pay off the debts so that they are not forced to use their children's labor to pay back the debt. The assistance would enable the families to keep their children from being forced to work to help pay the debt. "Is that not buying freedom for these children? Why is this different from CSI's redemption program that allows families to be united and children to enjoy their liberty?" Jacobs asked. The crux of Jacobs's antislavery campaign and his support for buyback programs were very persuasive. He once declared that "The slaves need to be rescued. Can we leave them there to rot in bondage until 'peace?' Were it your daughter would you say, like UNICEF, 'they must wait until there is genuine peace?' That is an enormous moral error. That is what the world told the Jews under Hitler: 'We win the war first. You wait . . . in gas chambers.' Never again." All the supporters of redemption programs repeated such statements as "while it is not the solution, it makes a difference for the individual child or woman who gets the chance to be free again." Many of them also said, "being released from bondage was the supreme experience of these children's lives." Lady Cox was outraged in October 1999 after being condemned by the United Nations for buying slaves their freedom. She said, "We know it is a dirty business and it is controversial, but you cannot look at a child who is a slave and say to it, 'You have to stay a slave.' "[47]

It may be worthwhile here, however, to recount in Barbara Vogel's own words the circumstances of this endeavor, since it was of such an enormous importance and at the height of the debate. "When we read the article, it just hit us. I was wondering, 'what are we supposed to do? I just got the feeling I have got to stop this,'" she said of the article by Associated Press writer Karin Davies one year earlier. "They sat at my seat, tears just coming down their faces, that this evil had not been taken care of, that we had to hear about it and had to campaign to abolish all over again," Vogel remembered her students' reaction. The children started collecting change in jars to purchase the freedom of one or two slaves. Then publicity started—newspaper stories, radio features, testifying in Congress—and checks began pouring in. By the end of the year, the students had collected $50,000 for the slave redemption programs. Vogel said that it might have been too difficult to grasp the complex problems in Sudan, but "it is never too complicated to help another person."[48] Carol Bellamy of UNICEF also responded specifically to the children's efforts. "While UNICEF understands the humanitarian instincts of schoolchildren . . . the sobering truth is that these efforts will not end the enslavement of human beings."[49] Barbara Vogel retorted, "Using diplomacy to try to end the war that made the slave trade possible is an equally noble cause, but what do we do and what do the slaves and their families do in the meantime?"

Before one explicitly agrees or disagrees with the redemption programs, it is important to note that the buyback programs were not initiated by foreign NGOs. These were efforts the South Sudanese had been engaged in for many years, including networking to identify southern children not living with their families in the North. A variety of other methods were designed to free the identified children and women without attracting the attention of local authorities, which had connived in the enslavement. The families, directly or through "retrievers," had long been paying the slaveholders to secure the freedom of abducted relatives. These local efforts take place as follows: families first try to locate the abducted relatives through a network of sympathetic Arabs, some Southerners who have lived in the slaving communities for a long time, or through other slaves, and then once they have located the slaves, they initiate the transaction.

Alternatively, when there was a truce between some sections of the Baggara and the Dinka, the Dinka chiefs and community elders may form committees that make formal approaches to Baggara chiefs, appealing to them to free the kidnapped or to assist the chiefs in locating them. Note that recurrent local truces have been a feature of the Arab-Dinka relationships. They were signed when the two groups saw that cessation of hostilities might benefit both, and they were broken because of various incidents that have characterized their relationship throughout history. Some of these efforts were reported to have succeeded, but others had failed. During these occasional peaceful periods, the opportunity of social intercourse was utilized to free slaves. These were initiatives that had to be followed very discreetly because they can turn tragic to the retrievers. They may also be cut if the slaving communities among the Baggara or the local Arab authorities find out that large numbers of slaves were being returned to the South in this manner. These measures also required amounts of money beyond the capacity of most Dinka families. In fact, it was financial difficulties that had prohibited most families from embarking on slave redemption. Money was needed for the trip on the train and the bus within Darfur and Kordofan during the search for the whereabouts of the slaves. As a result these measures have been awfully limited. For this reason, John Eibner insisted that "there is no evidence to suggest that our work has undermined local efforts to redeem women and children. In fact, Dinka elders encourage us to press ahead with our activities."[50] Eibner's claim of local support for the redemption program was later backed up by a letter from community leaders of Aweil West, Aweil East, and Tuic counties asking CSI to continue the programs. The letter, dated December 30, 1999, and signed by forty-six chiefs, administrators, and activists, stated: "We, the senior community leaders of the Dinka people of northern Bahr el-Ghazal, denounce the government of Sudan for enslaving our women and children, and express profound thanks to Christian Solidarity International (CSI) for supporting our efforts to redeem them and return them to their families. We ask CSI to continue their program of slave redemption and other forms of community support as long as the government of Sudan's war against our people lasts." In the meantime, as the proponents of redemption suggest, the critics of redemption can pursue alternative measures to end slavery, each according to his/her ability. But what is unacceptable is for people to sit and do nothing about the suffering of other people, said the staunch abolitionist, Charles Jacobs.

To conclude, it is a scandal that aid organizations working in Sudan have downplayed the scale of Sudan's slavery. The people of South Sudan know that the NIF regime is able to perpetrate such horrendous atrocities with impunity, since these acts are perfectly consistent with the nature of all northern governments. What the people of South Sudan find tragic is that the international community does not go beyond feeble condemnations of Khartoum and take more concrete actions to halt the murderous government in its genocidal war. CSI and AASG have made the world take notice of the problem while others failed—or did not try. It is true that CSI and AASG have done this by pandering to the requirements of journalists, but this is the way the modern world works. In the face of the disturbing silence of the outside community, the efforts of these groups seem to be appreciated in South Sudan. They augment local efforts to obtain freedom of slaves. Putting a few hundred dollars into the economy of Bahr el-Ghazal cannot do much harm; probably the opposite. Of course the end of slavery cannot come until there is peace. But peace cannot come until the North realizes that the South has the strength and support of friends to count on. Slavery was there before CSI, and if nobody stops the government of Sudan from waging genocide, slavery and other atrocities will continue whether or not CSI remains. Buying freedom of slaves does not obstruct the progress of diplomatic solutions if indeed there is genuine will to seek these avenues, and these would not require the redemption programs to stop. The problem is the inefficiency of whatever diplomatic efforts have been exerted so far. The only solution is to put pressure on the government of Sudan to end the raids, trace the abducted, and reunify the families.

Notes

Preface

1. See Jok Madut Jok, *Militarization, Gender, and Reproductive Health in South Sudan* (Lewiston, N.Y.: Edwin Mellen Press, 1998).
2. Jok Madut Jok, "Militarization and Gender Violence in South Sudan," *Journal of Asian and African Studies* 34, no. 4 (1999): 427–42.
3. See Robert Collins, *The Southern Sudan in Historical Perspective* (Tel Aviv: Shiloah Center for Middle Eastern and African Studies, 1975). Also see Collins, *Shadows in the Grass: Britain in the Southern Sudan, 1918–1956* (New Haven: Yale University Press, 1983); and *Land Beyond the Rivers: The Southern Sudan, 1898–1918* (New Haven: Yale University Press, 1971).
4. Robert Collins, "Slavery in the Sudan in History," in *Slavery and Abolition* (London: Frank Cass, 1999).
5. Damazo Dut Majak, "The Northern Bahr el-Ghazal: People, Alien Encroachment and Rule, 1856–1956," Ph.D. dissertation, University of California, Santa Barbara, 1990.
6. Martin Daly, *Empire on the Nile: The Anglo-Egyptian Sudan, 1898–1943* (Cambridge: Cambridge University Press, 1986); Douglas Johnson, "The Structure of a Legacy: Military Slavery in Northeast Africa," *Ethnohistory* 36, no. 1 (1989): 72–88.
7. Ahmad Alawad M. Sikainga, "British Policy in the Western Bahr al-Ghazal (Sudan), 1904–1946," Ph.D. dissertation, University of California, Santa Barbara, 1986. Also see Sikainga, *The Western Bahr al-Ghazal Under British Rule, 1898–1956* (Athens: Ohio University Press, 1991).
8. Sharon E. Hutchinson, *Nuer Dilemmas: Coping with Money, War, and the State* (Berkeley: University of California Press, 1996).
9. See Francis Mading Deng, *War of Visions: Conflict of Identities in Sudan* (Washington, D.C.: Brookings Institution, 1995).
10. UN Commission on Human Rights, *Situation of Human Rights in the Sudan: A Report of the Special Rapporteur, Mr. Gaspar Biro, Submitted in Accordance with Commission on Human Rights Resolution 1994/79* (Geneva: UN, 1995).
11. UN Commission on Human Rights, *Situation of Human Rights in the Sudan: Visit of the Special Rapporteur, Mr. Leonardo Franco, to the Republic of Sudan, 13–24 February 1999* (Geneva: UN, addendum to E/CN.4/1999/38, 1999).
12. Although the Guggenheim Foundation's funding proposal did not specify slavery as a topic of research, I came to realize that since slavery is based on

violence and aggression, focusing on it as one form of militarization of ethnic relationships dovetailed with the foundation's interests.

Introduction. Slavery in Sudan

1. The North-South war started in 1955, shortly before independence from Britain, because the South was unjustly made a part of the polity called Sudan while the power was left in the hands of the Arab North. The war ended in 1972 in an agreement that gave the South autonomy. But the agreement faltered in 1983 and the war resumed. The causes of the war have been exhaustively analyzed; see, for example, Donald Patterson, *Inside Sudan: Political Islam, Conflict, and Catastrophe* (Boulder, Colo.: Westview Press, 1999); Millard Burr and Robert Collins, *Africa's Thirty Years' War: Chad, Libya, and the Sudan, 1963–1993* (Boulder, Colo.: Westview Press, 1999); Hutchinson, *Nuer Dilemmas*; Deng A. Ruay, *The Politics of Two Sudans: The North and the South* (Uppsala: Nordiska Afrikainstitutet, 1994); and Deng, *War of Visions.*

2. For estimates of victims of Sudan's tragic years, see reports by the U.S. Committee for Refugees, Washington, D.C. I am also grateful to John Ryle for discussion of this point.

3. *Sudan Times*, 3, No. 624, October 9, 1988.

4. Alan Whitaker, "Slavery in Sudan," reprinted in *Sudan Times*, October 9, 1988.

5. See Collins, "Nilotic Slavery."

6. Kevin Bales lists all the major international conventions on slavery in appendix 2. Of particular interest for this study were the Slavery Convention of the League of Nations (1926), the Universal Declaration of Human Rights (1948), and Supplementary Convention on the Abolition of Slavery, the Slave Trade, and Institutions and Practices Similar to Slavery (1956). See Bales, *Disposable People: New Slavery in the Global Economy* (Berkeley: University of California Press, 1999), 275–78.

7. The *Washington Times* was among the first publications in the Western world to present evidence of the slave trade in Sudan. One of its writers, Clarence Page, who traveled to Bahr el-Ghazal in 1996, made extensive interviews with former slave children. The publication of *Children in Sudan: Slaves, Street Children and Child Soldiers* by Human Rights Watch in 1995 marked the beginning of international documentation of slavery in Sudan.

8. See Bales, *Disposable People*, 6–33.

9. Operation Life-line Sudan (OLS) is a consortium of United Nations agencies and nongovernmental organizations that provide emergency relief for the victims of Sudan's war. See chapter 4 of the report by the European Commission Humanitarian Office (ECHO), *Sudan: Unintended Consequences of Humanitarian Assistance* (Brussels: EC, 1999).

10. Ibid.

11. See Laura Beny, "Legal and Ethical Dimensions of Slavery in the Sudan: The Failure to Address Victims' Testimonies," paper presented at the African Studies Association annual meeting, Philadelphia, November 1999.

12. Cameron Duodo, "Africa's Forgotten War," *Mail and Guardian*, South Africa, January 28, 2000.

13. Khadija Magardie, "A One-Sided View of Civil War," *Mail and Guardian*, South Africa, February 4, 2000.

14. Race in Sudan has become so important that Southerners have been uneasy with the arrangement of colors on the Sudan's flag, which puts the black color on the bottom. When the SPLA designed the flag for New Sudan, the black color was placed on top and the red at the bottom. The Sudanese sensitivity to colors of skin cannot simply be massaged by such remarks as "they all look black."

15. Interview with Lual Ayok, a spiritual leader in Nyamlel village of Aweil West County, June 1998.

16. Akot Akot, a spiritual leader in the Nyamlel area, was interviewed by the author in summer of 1998.

17. See *Human Security in Sudan: The Report of a Canadian Assessment Mission*, prepared by John Harker, a Canadian Ministry of Foreign Affairs special envoy (Ottawa: Ministry of Foreign Affairs, January 2000).

18. See the report to ECHO, *Sudan.*

19. A lecture by Sadiq el-Mahdi at the Islamic University of Omdurman in 1979, quoted by Sirr Anai Kelueljang. See Mom K. N. Arou and B. Yongo-Bure (eds.), *North-South Relations in Sudan Since the Addis Ababa Agreement* (Khartoum: Institute of African and Asian Studies and Khartoum University Printing Press, 1988), 278.

20. This particular wording of the question was made by Simon Wol Mawien, Commissioner of Aweil West, during a conversation with the author in the summer of 1999. The overall wonderment, however, is common among Southerners.

21. See Ahmad Alawad Sikainga, "The Legacy of Slavery and Slave Trade in the Western Bahr al-Ghazal, 1850–1939," *Northeast African Studies* 2, no. 2 (1989): 75–95.

22. It is noteworthy here that the Dinka migratory system of moving between the winter grazing plains and the permanent villages in autumn allows for the pastures to lie fallow, therefore regulating the use of pastures and limiting depletion, despite the large herds of cattle.

23. Muhammad O. Bashir, *The Southern Problem* (Khartoum: Khartoum University Printing Press, 1976).

24. Sudan Archives at Durham University, document identified as SAD 696/8/1-105.

25. See Majak, "The Northern Bahr el-Ghazal."

26. The assertion by many historians that the South had agreed to remain in unity with the North is based on the vaguely reported proceedings of the Juba Conference of 1947. It has now become common knowledge that the few southern representatives at the conference who agreed to unity, some of whom were only semiliterate, were merely manipulated by the highly educated Northerners. See Oliver Albino, *The Sudan: A Southern Viewpoint* (London: Institute of Race Relations and Oxford University Press, 1970).

Chapter 1. The Revival of Slavery During the Civil War

1. Robert Collins, "Nilotic Slavery: Past and Present," in *Human Commodity*, ed. Elizabeth Savage (London: Frank Cass, 1992), 140–61.

2. Antigovernment rebels in Chad with access to the western border of Sudan increased the proliferation of small arms inside Sudan's province of Darfur. Pressed for food supplies, the rebels sometimes sold guns and ammunition to the Baggara for livestock to be slaughtered for rebel armies. See Burr and Collins, *Africa's Thirty Years' War.*

3. Since many Khartoum governments, especially that of Sadiq al-Mahdi

(1986–89), deliberately decided on a policy of genocide against the Dinka, the use of Hitler's phrase "final solution" is indeed fitting in describing North Sudanese views toward the South. The Dinka, whose men were the majority of troops in the SPLA, which the Sudan army could not defeat, were regarded as a menace and a stumbling block to Arab and Islamic expansion into East Africa and central Africa.

4. This is a Sudanese colloquial Arabic term meaning nomadic or mobile, historically used in reference to the Baggara pastoralists. It has become so associated with military raiding that South Sudanese use it to refer to the army of the government of Sudan.

5. See Robert Collins, "Africans, Arabs, and Islamists: From the Conference Tables to the Battlefields in the Sudan," *African Studies Review* 42, no. 2 (1999): 105–23.

6. Interview with Commander Paul Malong of the SPLA. See also the report by Leonardo Franco, the Special Rapporteur on Sudan appointed by the United Nations High Commissioner for Human Rights (Geneva: UN, 1999).

7. In addition to taking children, the regular Sudan army in the South has been notorious for cutting down whole forests both to make charcoal or for timber, and transporting them on military planes and trains returning to the North.

8. See a report written on behalf of the European Commission Humanitarian Office, *Humanitarian Assistance: Consequences Beyond Relief* (Brussels: European Union, November 1999).

9. This information comes from the author's interviews with various people in northern Bahr el-Ghazal, including SPLA officers, civil authorities, Arab traders who have been allowed to trade locally, and former slaves.

10. Interview with Geng Deng, the representative of the Sudan Relief and Rehabilitation Association, the humanitarian wing of the SPLA, Marial Baai, 1998.

11. The Arabic word *tachzin*, which literally means "to store," is the word former slaves said the Arabs normally use to refer to the temporary slave depots.

12. *Zariba* is the Arabic word for fortified stations erected by thorn fences. In the days of the Turkiyya and the Mahdiyya slave trade in Bahr el-Ghazal, the fences were established as depots for ivory, ammunition, barter goods, and for harboring various elements of the slave trade comprising Arabs, North Sudanese, and European traders. In the 1860s, there were a total of eighty *zaribas* in western and northern Bahr el-Ghazal, which had been established in just one decade with a total population of 1,000 individuals. Although the *zaribas* continue to function in similar ways, the Arabs use them temporarily as cattle camps during the dry season. When the slave trade resumed, they were used to keep the slaves before they were taken farther north. They currently serve as military and raiding centers for slavers.

13. On South African apartheid see Edward Roux, *The Black Man's Struggle for Freedom in South Africa* (Madison: University of Wisconsin Press, 1984), and Gail M. Gerhart, *Black Power in South Africa: The Evolution of an Ideology* (Berkeley and Los Angeles: University of California Press, 1978). On the Nazi Holocaust, see Walter Laqueur, *A History of Zionism: From the French Revolution to the Establishment of the State of Israel* (New York: MJF Books, 1972), and Eric Johnson, *The Nazi Terror: Gestapo, Jews and Ordinary Germans* (New York: Basic Books, 1999). On the American West during the early days of occupation by the Europeans, see Gregory Evans Dowd, *A Spirited Resistance: The North American Indian Struggle for Unity, 1745–1815* (Baltimore: Johns Hopkins University Press, 1992), and John E. Kicza, (ed.) *The Indian in Latin American History: Resistance, Resilience, and Acculturation* (Wilmington, Del.:

Scholarly Resource, 1993). It would be interesting to investigate what prompts some Dinka to support the enemies of their own people. As I was unable to meet any collaborators to interview, I only sought explanations to this phenomenon from the communities of victims.

14. Majak, "The Northern Bahr el Ghazal."

15. Collins, "Nilotic Slavery."

16. These terms refer to the structure of the Baggara native administration. They mean "paramount chief," "village head," and "community leader," respectively.

17. The "rest house" is actually the old British District Commissioners compound, which was later turned into a guest house for visiting government officials.

18. Da'wa Islamiyya means "Islamic call." This is an Islamic NGO funded by many Arab and Muslim countries to assist with development in Muslim societies, as well as provide relief to disaster victims. But in Sudan, assistance by this organization to Southerners is contingent upon conversion.

19. Al-Turabi has made many remarks like this since his term as attorney general in Sadiq al-Mahdi's government. For example, in a 1987 radio interview with Voice of America, he flatly denied the existence of slavery. His ideas about slavery and other forms of exploitation being banned in Islam became more prominent when he became the power behind al-Bashir's government.

20. The SPLA local administration in Aweil East and Aweil West Counties have issued many reports during 1997–99 estimating the total number of people from these counties who are in captivity.

21. This story came from an interview tape-recorded by the author, who transcribed it later. The interview took place in Majak Baai, Aweil West County, in July 1998.

22. Interview with a former slave in Marial Baai, Aweil West County, June 1998.

23. Ushari Mahmud and Suleiman Baldo, *Human Rights Abuses in the Sudan, 1987: The ed-Da'ein Massacre. Slavery in the Sudan* (Khartoum), p. 29.

24. Hibiscus is widely liked in northern Sudan. Boiled and strained, with sugar added, it makes a rather pleasant drink, hot or cold.

25. The author interviewed her at this school in June 1999.

26. A slave master's wife is said to be furious at her husband's sexual liaison with slave women because it is extremely demeaning to her if her husband chooses a slave over her.

27. The bulk of the southern women who worked in northern households in the 1960s came from the Dinka of Upper Nile when a mass displacement took place during the floods of the 1960s. Many others came from the Ngok Dinka, who are administratively part of Kordofan. A large number of these women had often reported to their families a myriad of abuses they faced as domestic workers. They included performing as sexual entertainers for minors under the instructions of the boys' fathers.

28. During trips to northern Bahr el-Ghazal during the summers of 1998 and 1999, I visited markets on the border areas, such as Warawar, where the Arabs conduct business when there is some truce between the people.

29. The woman who reported this was interviewed in the summer of 1999 in Malual Kon.

30. Much effort has been put into buying the freedom of many slaves through the use of Arab middlemen. These "buyback programs" were initiated by the Dinka themselves using cows on the North-South borders, or through a tracing network within the North using money. The buyback programs were then picked

up and supported by Christian organizations from the western world, but they have quickly become the subject of a serious controversy; see chapter 8.

31. The interview with Abuk Akot Akot was conducted in June 1999 at Marial Baai village in Aweil West County.

32. Interview with Garang Anei was conducted at Manyiel Market in Aweil West, June 1998.

33. Arop Ajing was interviewed at Turalei village in Tuic County, June 1999.

34. The boy who reported the story was interviewed by the author at Mayen Abun village in Tuic County, June 1999.

Chapter 2. Slavery in the Shadow of the Civil War

1. The United Nations, human rights groups, and nongovernmental organizations that are involved in humanitarian assistance in the Sudan largely use these estimates of the direct and indirect casualties of the war. However, there is no evidence of how this number was reached. In the face of the difficulty of obtaining reliable figures in Sudan, such estimates should be taken with a grain of salt.

2. David Keen, *The Benefits of Famine: A Political Economy of Famine and Relief in Southwestern Sudan, 1983–1989* (Princeton: Princeton University Press, 1994).

3. The two University of Khartoum professors compiled their report in *Human Rights Abuses in the Sudan: The ed-Da'ein Massacre: Slavery in the Sudan* (Khartoum, 1987).

4. See Human Rights Watch, *Children of Sudan.*

5. Patterson, *Inside Sudan.*

6. European Commission Humanitarian Office, *Sudan: Unintended Consequences of Humanitarian Assistance.*

7. Mahmud and Baldo, *Human Rights Abuses in the Sudan.*

8. Bales, *Disposable People.*

9. Attempts by slaveholders to justify slavery on grounds of helping the slaves is as old as the beginning of the transatlantic slavery.

10. During a visit to East Africa in December 1999 and after a meeting with the SPLA leader, John Garang, the U.S. Secretary of State, Madeleine Albright, announced to the press that she had been disappointed by the fact that the activities of Canadian oil company were allowed to go on.

11. *National Post,* November 23, 1999.

12. Harker, *Human Security in Sudan.*

13. Collins, "Nilotic Slavery."

14. The Baggara always call the Dinka *jengai,* which has been translated in different ways, but generally is a demeaning term. The word has been used to describe the Dinka as uncivilized, unintelligent, and closer to animals than humans.

15. Conversation with John Ryle, a consultant for aid agencies, who visited the "slavery zone" in the summer of 1999 and wrote a report on the experiences of displaced Dinka in Darfur and Kordofan.

16. These remarks were made in an unsigned letter claimed by one SPLA officer to have been written by Abdel Bagi Ayii to the SPLA in northern Bahr el-Ghazal. This letter was shown to the author in Malwal Kon in Aweil East in June 1999. Abdel Bagi Ayii's reasoning was corroborated by Dinka and Arab traders at Warawar who have witnessed how he operates in Darfur.

17. Collins, "Nilotic Slavery."

18. Damazo Dut Majak, "Rape of Nature: The Environmental Destruction and

Ethnic Cleansing of the Sudan," paper presented at the American Historical Association Pacific Coast Branch 88th annual meeting, Maui, Hawaii, 1995.

19. *Al-Ayam*, January 3, 1995.

20. See Collins, "Africans, Arabs and Islamists."

21. Majak, "The Northern Bahr al-Ghazal."

22. Ahmad Alawad Sikainga, *Slaves into Workers: Emancipation and Labor in Colonial Sudan* (Austin: University of Texas Press, 1996).

23. Muhammad Ali, the viceroy of the Ottoman sultan in Egypt, ordered the invasion of Sudan from Egypt in 1821 in order to obtain slaves. Zubeir Pasha was the most notorious slaver in Bahr el-Ghazal in the nineteenth century. His real name was Zubeir Rahma Mansour, receiving the Ottoman title "Pasha" only when he was appointed to govern parts of Bahr el-Ghazal and parts of Darfur in 1830s. It is estimated that he has taken more South Sudanese into slavery than anyone else in the history of Sudanese slavery. Muhammad Ahmed, a Muslim clergyman who proclaimed himself as the Mahdi (the expected one or he who will come to deliver the Muslims), started an Islamic revolution, which ended the Ottoman rule in 1881. The reign of the Mahdi did not deliver the South from the shackles of slavery. Instead, slavery continued to be the backbone of his state. Khalifa Abdallahi was the successor of the Mahdi when the latter died in 1885. He continued the same degree of repression and slavery in the South as his predecessor had done. Ansar (the defenders) were the riveraine Arab people of middle Sudan who claim to have been the defenders or followers of the Mahdi and therefore, more deserving of leadership in Sudan because of their historic victory against the foreigners of the Turkiyya.

24. See Douglas Johnson, "Indigenous Religions in the Sudanese Civil War," a paper presented at the conference *Religion and Conflict in Africa*, London, 1998.

25. Of U.S. newspapers, the *Boston Globe* and the *Washington Post* have particularly labored since 1995 to bring the attention of their readers and U.S. policymakers to the issue of slavery in Sudan. The *New York Times* has also carried many articles on the subject.

The Swiss-based Christian Solidarity International, in collaboration with Christian Solidarity World Wide and other smaller church-based groups, has been at the forefront of the battle against slavery in Sudan. Their activities in buying the freedom of thousands of slaves and reuniting them with their families since 1995 have brought a great deal of publicity to this tragedy.

The formidable antislavery organizations that have really touched a chord over the issue of slavery in Sudan have been the Boston-based American Anti-Slavery Group and Slavery that Oppresses People (STOP) of Aurora, Colorado. In 1998, their work was boosted by the campaign waged by elementary-school children in Colorado. The children, through their STOP organization, collected their lunch allowances to enable Christian Solidarity International to purchase Sudanese slave children from bondage and gave them their freedom.

26. These organizations have responded to UNICEF's criticism; I will return to this debate in the last chapter.

27. Mahmud and Baldo, *Human Rights Abuses in the Sudan.*

28. At a conference on slavery in 1998 held at the Museum of Tolerance in Los Angeles, one Khartoum government advocate, David de Chand, a South Sudanese from the Nuer ethnic group, told the conference attendees that slavery in Sudan was a hoax. He said that the SPLA was using it to solicit American military aid.

29. About the nineteenth century slave trade, Richard Gray reports in his *His-*

tory of the Southern Sudan, 1839–1889 (London: Frank Cass, 1961) that colonial officials had estimated that between 1874 and 1879 some 80,000 to 100,000 slaves were exported from Bahr el-Ghazal. But how many have fallen victim since then remains unknown and will probably remain so until the present practices are treated as direct descendents of the past.

30. See Collins, "Nilotic Slavery."
31. Majak, "Rape of Nature."
32. Sikainga, *The Western Bahr al-Ghazal Under British Rule.*
33. William Finnegan, "The Invisible War," *New Yorker,* January 25, 1999, p. 65.
34. Richard Miniter, "The False Promise of Slave Redemption," *Atlantic Monthly,* July 1999.
35. Note that the word *el-Fardus* means "heaven" in Arabic. It is ironic that the Southerners displaced by a horrific government atrocity are housed in a place with a name like this, as if to suggest that the Dinka have moved to a better place.
36. Collins, "Nilotic Slavery."

Chapter 3. The Suffering of the South in the North-South Conflict

1. Interviews with SPLM officials were conducted at Marial Baai village in Aweil West County, June 1998.
2. The raids always take place during the dry season between November and May. This seasonal hostility is caused by three main factors. One is the need by the northern herding Arab tribes for grazing and water in the South. When the southern herding groups meet them with rejection, they resort to violence as the way to clear the grazing land. The second factor is the opposite of the first factor. When there are heavy rains, they not only provide satisfactory grazing and water, but also make it extremely difficult for their horseback raids to take place due to the fact that horses cannot do well in the floodplains of South Sudan. The third reason is the government's constant attempts during the dry season to wage offensives against the SPLA, and the Murahileen, as the raiding force is called, are a cheap and effective way to do so.
3. *Toc* is the Dinka word that refers to the grasslands that emerge soon after the floodplains near the great swamps start drying up. This constitutes the pastures for Dinka cattle during the dry season.
4. The people of Nyamlel have since made many jokes about this incident. They say that the makers of the old maps who have made many mistakes on these maps should be regarded to have done the right thing for once. Placing the town on the wrong side of the river has saved the lives of people in Nyamlel.
5. Wau is the provincial headquarters of the government. It is one of the few towns left under the government's control after the SPLA took control of the bulk of the region.
6. The yearly frequency of raids depends on the climate in the north, the chance of a local truce between the groups, and on the perceived strength of the SPLA to rebuff the attacks that particular season.
7. At times of imminent danger, like the Baggara raids, support for the SPLA and the expectations of the SPLA protection are increased.
8. I came to realize that the authorities did not want to alarm the relief workers by appearing as if there was serious insecurity, lest they be evacuated to Kenya. But they had made arrangements to ensure the security of foreign aid workers if the raid were to take place. Any obvious military activity, population movement,

or postponement of the food drop arrangements would signify existence of security problems and could prompt the UN to cancel the food drops.

9. The Dinka rationalization of the Arab raids will be addressed in the following chapters.

10. As much of the heaviest fighting between the SPLA and government of Sudan–sponsored militias takes place in Dinka territories of northern Bahr el-Ghazal, stripping the area of its resources, and creating famine, large numbers of southern civilians brave the gauntlet of Murahileen forces to move northward into Darfur and Kordofan. There are an estimated two million Southerners in northern cities, and many people, both foreign and South Sudanese find this northward migration into what is supposedly a hostile territory puzzling and disturbing.

11. South Sudanese who are displaced to the north live in crowded dwellings with poor hygiene, no clean drinking water, and inadequate food. See Millard Burr and Robert Collins, *Requiem for the Sudan: Famine and Disaster Relief on the Upper Nile* (Boulder, Colo.: Westview Press, 1995); and Patterson, *Inside Sudan.*

12. OLS is a United Nations–led consortium of relief agencies comprised of UN agencies and nongovernmental organizations (NGOs) established in 1989 to negotiate humanitarian access to the war-affected areas. It has southern and northern sectors to operate in the SPLA-controlled areas and the government-held parts of Sudan, respectively.

13. Alex de Waal, *Famine Crimes: Politics and the Disaster Relief Industry in Africa* (Oxford: James Currey, 1997).

14. U.S. Committee for Refugees, *Quantifying Genocide: War and Disaster in Sudan* (Washington, D.C.: U.S. Committee for Refugees, 1998); U.S. Committee for Refugees, *The Nuba People: Confronting Cultural Liquidation* (Washington, D.C.: U.S. Committee for Refugees, 2000); Dan Connell, "Today's Costliest Civil War: My Trek with the Rebels of Sudan." *Progressive,* June 2000, pp. 24–27; Heather Long, "Pledging His Life to Fight Slavery: Sophomore Works to Free 4,000 Enslaved Africans," *Crimson Online,* September 22, 2000.

15. To understand the scale of devastation in South Sudan, consider that the U.S. Federal Centers for Disease Control hold the view that a mortality rate higher than two per ten thousand per day is an emergency out of control.

16. By 1988, the government was already saying that there were 1.8 million South Sudanese in Khartoum who were living in slums around the city. In August of that year, the worst floods in decades struck the region, demolishing the makeshift housing the displaced had built and causing serious public health problems and food shortages.

17. For more information, consult the various OLS annual reports, which are organized by UNICEF database in Lokichokio, Kenya.

18. See Collins, "Nilotic Slavery."

19. Such statements are a part of popular political discourse. I do not have any documentation as to when this statement was made and by whom, but it is ordinary in Sudanese politics to hear elderly people comparing the systems of government that they remember. Most of the older generation of South Sudanese often referred to the British colonial government as the "real government" in comparison to the Khartoum government.

20. The British colonial government had to choose between the existing two kinds of slavery: modern slavery based on forced cheap labor, composed exclusively of African Sudanese, and the old archaic slave trade, involving raids and selling and buying of Africans—the indigenous population. Fearing that the

northern Arabs, historically accustomed to slavery, might revolt should the government insist on complete abolition, the colonial authorities allowed the slave owners to keep retainers or domestic slaves on condition that no export of slaves be practiced (see Chapter 5 on the racial foundations of slavery).

Due to the difficulties of controlling the vast border areas with what was then Obangui-Shari (modern Central African Republic and Chad), large numbers of southern slaves were still smuggled out into northern Sudan, and were still taken to Arabia under the guise of a pilgrimage voyage. It was not until the colonial authorities concluded an understanding of cooperation with French colonial administrators in the Central African Republic and Chad that the smuggling stopped in the 1930s.

21. See Majak, "Rape of Nature."

22. The movement fighting the current war, the SPLA, is a descendant of the Anyanya movement, the South's guerrilla army of the first civil war. The leader of the SPLA, John Garang, is a veteran of the Anyanya movement.

23. See Keen, *The Benefits of Famine.*

24. The government of Sudan, United Nations agencies, especially UNICEF, some nongovernmental organizations, and foreign diplomats have all chosen to avoid the use of the word "slavery" under the pretext that there are no visible slave markets in Sudan and no concrete evidence of slavery. They have opted to euphemize it as forced labor. The only exception has been the reports by the UN Special Rapporteur on human rights, who has characterized the practices by the government and its militia as amounting to slavery. See the report by the Argentinian lawyer Leonardo Franco in UN Commission on Human Rights, *Situation of Human Rights in the Sudan.*

25. Report of the UN High Commission for Human Rights Special Rapporteur on Sudan (Geneva: UN, 1996).

26. The proposal was written by the UNICEF country office in Khartoum.

27. One of the features of the conflict in Sudan has been the practice by both the government of Sudan and the SPLA of maintaining a civilian population near the army installations. This serves two different functions for the warring parties. The government tries to attract the southern civilians to towns it holds so as to be human shield against possible SPLA attacks. The SPLA, on the other hand, desires to have the civilian population around so that the civilians can pay the cost of war through provision of food, new recruits, and other necessities. For this reason, the government of Sudan attacks the civil population in SPLA-controlled areas simply as a way to push the SPLA behind their line of control, because they cannot do without the civil population.

28. In order to set up two sectors of Operation Lifeline Sudan, one to operate from Kenya into SPLA-held areas and the other from Khartoum into government of Sudan areas, an agreement was signed by the three parties in 1989 to allow humanitarian access to civilian populations.

29. For more information of estimates of war casualty, see reports by U.S. Committee for Refugees: *Quantifying Genocide,* and *The Nuba People.*

30. Historically, the Baggara have always been the supporters of the Umma Party because it is the party led by the descendents of Mohammed Ahmed al-Mahdi, the Muslim revolutionary who fought against the Turko-Egyptian rule in Sudan in the nineteenth century. The Baggara have since called themselves the Ansar al-Mahdi, the followers of the Mahdi.

31. Hutchinson, *Nuer Dilemmas.*

32. This was the language of a statement issued in the summer of 1999 by Bag-

gara chiefs and militia leaders. The document, entitled "Arab Alliance and the Danger of Blacks in Dar Fur: Rezeigat and Dinka Relations — Problems and Solutions," was obtained by the SPLA and was distributed in Nairobi.

33. Collins, "Nilotic Slavery."

34. The massacre of some 2,000 Dinka in one single day in the town of el-Da'ein in 1987, when Sadiq al-Mahdi was prime minister, is one case in point. For details of the massacre, see Mahmud and Baldo, *Human Rights Abuses in the Sudan.*

Chapter 4. The Legacy of Race

1. See Gordon Murray, *Slavery in the Arab World* (New York: New Amsterdam Books, 1989).

2. Zubeir Rahma was the most notorious slave raider and trader in the Bahr el-Ghazal region of South Sudan in the nineteenth century. When Zubeir was absent from the Bahr el-Ghazal, such as when he would travel to Darfur, his son Sulayman would take charge of the affairs of the slave trade. See Majak, "The Northern Bahr al-Ghazal."

3. The British government was very much concerned about what the Americans thought about how any European colonial power dealt with slavery in Africa. Many colonial officials did not know how to deal with the South, which they viewed as uncivilized and unruly, and any measure, slavery-like or not, that might bring law and order to the South was welcome.

4. Collins, "Nilotic Slavery."

5. Daly, *Empire on the Nile,* p. 239.

6. The letter, dated October 2, 1898, and written in Omdurman, was signed by Es Sayed Ahmed el Mirghani, Sheikh Mohammed Sherif Nur ed-Daim, Sayed Meki, Nur Ibrahim el Gereifawi, Hassen Abdel Munim, and Abu el-Kasem Ahmed Hashem. The letter is now in the Sudan Archives at the University of Durham, England, coded as SAD 430/6/5.

7. Bales, *Disposable People.*

8. Johnson, "The Structure of a Legacy," pp. 72–88.

9. Sudan Archives at Durham, SAD 430/6/5.

10. See C. Jackson, *Behind the Modern Sudan* (New York: Macmillan, 1955).

11. Roudolf Slatin (Pasha) was an unwilling Mulazim in the Khalifa's army for years before he was appointed as the inspector general of the Sudan administration following the 1898 conquest.

12. The order to cut off the South from the North grew into a policy that became known as the Southern Policy or the Closed Districts Ordinance. This policy barred Northerners from traveling and living in the South. Its goal was to prevent the extension of Islam to the South, but it was also a recognition of the differences between North and South both in terms of culture and the level of development, which made the South vulnerable to the manipulations of northern merchants.

13. Sudan Archives at Durham, SAD 696/8/85. The letter is dated November 19, 1952.

14. Sudan Archives at Durham, SAD 430/6/5.

15. These were "lawful" domestic slaves — not recently acquired ones, but children of old black slaves, born in the Arab tribe and living on among the slaving tribe as something like retainers.

16. Sudan Archives at Durham, SAD 414/6/9. The letter was written in 1934.

Chapter 5. The South-North Population Displacement

1. Collins, "Nilotic Slavery."
2. See Hutchinson, *Nuer Dilemmas.*
3. *Al-Ayam*, May 3, 1976.
4. It is a common experience of South Sudanese youth in the North that they are often harassed by their neighbors because of the fear that they may become a negative influence on Muslim youth, especially regarding morality. Young southern men living without their families are therefore often interrogated and sometimes arrested every time they are seen in the company of young women.
5. Rape in Sudanese prisons is not only meted out against women. Men also get raped, not by other inmates as is the case in prisons world over, but by prison wardens or by police agents before they are tried and jailed. This is especially the case for those who are considered to have committed grave offenses. Some mention is occasionally made of police agents ramming a wooden or metallic object into a detained man's anus.
6. Francis Mading Deng, *War of Visions: Conflict of Identities in the Sudan* (Washington, D.C.: Brookings Institution, 1995).
7. Female genital mutilation is not practiced in the South, except in some small pockets where Islam has taken roots, such as western Bahr el-Ghazal and northern Upper Nile.
8. See Hutchinson, *Nuer Dilemmas.*
9. The Sudan National Television maintains a Monday morning Armed Forces program. In this program, footage of the war front and alleged victories are presented. Also presented in the government characterization of the living conditions in SPLA areas, where the SPLA is described as a "lawless" organization bent on ruling through violence, and whose soldiers live by looting the civilians.
10. African Rights, *Sudan's Invisible Citizens: The Policy of Abuse Against Displaced People in the North* (London: African Rights, 1995).
11. Mahmud and Baldo, *Human Rights Abuses in the Sudan.*
12. Keen, *The Benefits of Famine.*
13. Human Rights Watch, *Bahr el-Ghazal and the Famine of 1998* (Washington, D.C.: Human Rights Watch, 1999). Reports by the two Special Rapporteurs are available at the United Nations Commission on Human rights in Geneva, Switzerland. They are easily accessible on the agency's Web site.
14. A recent report described the town of Abu Matariq as "the hub of the slave trade in southern Dar Fur. Not only do some inhabitants initiate their own slave raids into Dinka areas, the small towns act as an important exit-entry point for the slave trade." See *Slavery in Sudan, 1986–1998: The Evidence.* Mimeo.
15. Mahmud and Baldo, *Human Rights Abuses in the Sudan.*
16. See the report entitled *Humanitarian Assistance: Consequences Beyond Relief,* written by a team of consultants for the European Commission Humanitarian Office (ECHO) (Brussels: European Union, 1999).
17. Damazo D. Majak, "Islam: A Factor in the Sudan Civil War," paper presented at the African Studies Association meeting, Seattle, Washington, 1992.
18. It is worth pointing out that the army's emphasis in the famous memorandum was on the search for peace rather than on war. War should be regarded as the last resort, the ultimatum stated.
19. *Sudan Democratic Gazette,* July, 1992.
20. See chapter 5 of the report, *Sudan: Unintended Consequences of Humanitarian*

Assistance, European Commission Humanitarian Office (Brussels: European Union, 1999).

21. Such statements are a part of popular political discourse. I do not have any documentation as to when and where these statements were made, but it is ordinary in Sudanese politics to attribute such statements to political leaders.

22. Human Rights Watch, *Children in Sudan.*

23. Jok Madut Jok and Sharon Hutchinson, "Sudan's Prolonged Second Civil War and the Militarization of Dinka and Nuer Ethnic Identities," *African Studies Review* 42, no. 2 (1999).

24. Ibid.

25. Human Rights Watch, *Famine in Bahr al-Ghazal.*

26. The Arabic term *abeed* is the plural of *abd* (slave).

27. ECHO, *Humanitarian Assistance.*

Chapter 6. The Political-Economic Conflict

Note to epigraph: Interview with an Aweil Dinka in Nyamlel, 1999.

1. The rather derogatory term *Fellata* is used in Sudan to refer to immigrants from northern Nigeria. These people are a mixture of Hausa pastoralists who entered Sudan through Chad to graze but settled in Darfur, and the Fulani who also entered Sudan through their seminomadic pastoralist activities. Some of these people were also pilgrims to Mecca who decided to work in the Gezira cotton scheme and settled in Sudan.

2. The Arab name for this river is Bahr al-Arab, meaning the Arab sea, and this in itself indicates the level of confrontation over the ownership of grazing valleys of the river.

3. Some South Sudanese have used this government concern to point out the possibility that the government is not planning in the interest of the South. "Why would a government fear that some citizens may be denied access to any areas in the same country by other citizens," Southerners have often wondered.

4. Chevron started oil prospecting and drilling oil wells in South Sudan in the late 1970s, but halted its operations in 1984 when the second round of war escalated. The withdrawal of the Chevron from Sudan was as much a response to the security situation as it was a political comment on the Sudanese conflict. The company withdrew in recognition of the North-South disputes over the oil reserves as well as in reaction to the killing of its workers.

5. Hutchinson, *Nuer Dilemmas,* 67.

6. Egypt has always claimed to have historic or "acquired" rights in the waters of the Nile, and many agreements have been signed throughout the last century with regards to distribution of the Nile waters between Egypt and upstream countries. The proposal to dig the canal was part of Egypt's continuous effort to put her interests above the interests and the rights of upstream peoples. This has indeed caused people in such places as Ethiopia to wonder why Egypt's historical right to Nile waters should be paramount over the lives of Ethiopians who have perished over the years due to drought. Why should Ethiopia not build a dam and increase irrigation?

7. The High Executive Council was the name of the semiautonomous government of the South following the Addis Ababa agreement. This government was based in Juba.

8. The phrase attributed to Nimeiri was a part of the popular political discourse

in the South during the years of turmoil, but there is no documentation as to when, where, and in what context he made this statement.

9. These were the two most prominent political figures in the Southern Regional Government. Abel Alier was the first president of the High Executive Council following the Addis Ababa agreement. Joseph Lagu was the head of the Anyanya movement who became a high-ranking officer in the national army, and later became president of the High Executive Council himself.

10. Nimeiri was unable to return to Khartoum and remained in exile in Egypt for the next fifteen years until May 1999.

11. This particular television appearance was in August 1988. The statement was made in the context of the floods, which had caused serious misery in Khartoum, especially for the displaced Southerners whose makeshift dwellings were hit the hardest. Garang had made a statement pointing out the government bias against Southerners in rendering relief services to flood victims.

12. *Sudan Times*, 3, no. 624, October 9, 1988.

13. See Mahmud and Baldo, *Human Rights Abuses in the Sudan*, p. 17.

14. The avoidance of the SPLA villages only changed in 1996–99 when the regular Sudan army and militias organized joint operations, such as the raid on Nyamlel in 1998, as explained earlier.

15. See Peter Verney, *Slavery in Sudan* (London: Sudan Update and Anti-Slavery International, 1997).

16. For more details, see *Slavery in Sudan (1986–1998): The Evidence*, mimeo, 1998, 12.

17. Alex de Waal, *Famine that Kills: Darfur, Sudan, 1984–1985* (Oxford: Clarendon Press, 1989).

18. A. Karim and McDuffield et al., *Operation Life-line Sudan (OLS): A Review* (Geneva: Department of Humanitarian Affairs, 1996), p. 204.

19. Tom Dodd and John Welten, *Mission Report: ed-Da'ein* (Khartoum: European Commission Delegation, 1998).

20. ECHO, *Unintended Consequences of Humanitarian Assistance.*

21. *Slavery in Sudan (1986–1998): The Evidence.* Mimeo.

Conclusion. Sudanese Slavery and International Opinion

1. David Livingstone, *Last Journals of David Livingstone in Central Africa, from 1865 to His Death*, edited by H. Murray Waller (London: 1874).

2. Eric Reeves, "Human Agony in Sudan Can't be Ignored." *San Francisco Chronicle*, August 12, 1999. Also see U.S. Committee for Refugees *Quantifying Genocide: War and Disaster in Sudan* (Washington, D.C.: USCR, 1998).

3. U.S. Committee for Refugees, *Quantifying Genocide.*

4. Human Rights Watch, *Famine in Bahr el-Ghazal, 1998* (New York: Human Rights Watch, 1999). This report on the 1998 disaster detailed the factors that caused it.

5. See the report on behalf of European Commission Humanitarian Office "Sudan: Unintended Consequences of Humanitarian Assistance" (Brussels: The European Union, November 1999).

6. Mark Duffield, "The Political Economy of Internal War: Asset Transfer, Complex Emergencies and International Aid," in *War and Hunger: Rethinking International Responses to Complex Emergencies*, ed. J. Macrae and A. Zwi (London: Zed Books, 1994).

7. Mary Anderson, *Do No Harm: Supporting Political Capacities for Peace Through Aid* (Cambridge, Mass.: Local Capacities for Peace Project, Collaborative for Development Action, 1996).

8. ECHO, *Sudan: Consequences Beyond Humanitarian Assistance.*

9. Steve Crawshaw, "Two Worlds Collide in a Wasteland Racked by War," *Independent*, April 15, 1999.

10. This is a suspicion that many people in South Sudan hold about the NGOs. It has been expressed in many forums before, and the issue of U.S. direct aid to the SPLA, in the minds of many South Sudanese, was this self-perpetuation.

11. Thomas O. Attiya, "Stand on South Sudan Wrong," *Daily Nation*, December 14, 1999.

12. This statement was made by the Executive Director of UNICEF, Carol Bellamy, in Geneva. See Reuters, March 12, 1999.

13. In 1987 and 1988, the Arabic press in Khartoum was preoccupied with this kind of thinking. Many editorials, too many to list here, dismissed the claims of slavery as unthinkable in Sudanese society since the law forbids it.

14. Mahmud and Baldo, *Human Rights Abuses in the Sudan.*

15. For more views on North-South relationships from the vantage point of laypersons, see Deng, *War of Visions.*

16. Bona Malwal himself, despite his prominence as a politician, a former minister, and a renowned journalist, was regularly picked up by state security agents and interrogated.

17. Bona Malwal's newspaper was always threatened with banning by the government of Sadiq al-Mahdi. The editor himself had received many threats of arrest and accusations of being part of a "fifth column" in support of the SPLA. The government was particularly angry over an article written by Alan Whitaker and reprinted by the paper in 1988.

18. Human Rights Watch, *Children in Sudan: Slaves, Street Children and Child Soldiers* (New York: HRW, 1995).

19. See the Special Rapporteur's report on human rights in Sudan, *Situation of Human Rights in the Sudan: A Report of the Special Rapporteur, Mr. Gaspar Biro* (Geneva: UN, 1994).

20. See "Africa's Dirty Secret: Slavery in Our Times," *Washington Times*, May 5, 1995.

21. For more historical analysis of the role of Arabs and Muslims in world slavery, see Gordon Murray, *Slavery in the Arab World* (New York: New Amsterdam Books, 1989). See also Bernard Lewis, *Race and Slavery in the Middle East: An Historical Enquiry* (New York and Oxford: Oxford University Press, 1990).

22. See a letter to the editor of the *Sudan Democratic Gazette* from Steve Wondu, the SPLA representative in Washington, January 1998.

23. See Bona Malwal's address to the Randolph Institute on the occasion of his award for human rights activities in Sudan, *Sudan Democratic Gazette*, September 1999.

24. Cameron Duodo, "Africa's New Slaves: Slave Trade Thrives in Sudan," *South Africa Mail and Guardian*, January 28, 2000.

25. Ibid.

26. Charles Jacobs and Rafael Abiem, "Of Human Bondage in the Twentieth Century," *Boston Globe*, June 4, 1996.

27. Sonia Levitin traveled from Los Angeles to Aurora, Colorado, to interview the children and their teacher for a novel on Sudan's slavery, *Dream Freedom* (San Diego: Silver Whistle, 2000).

28. See "Swiss Group Says it Freed 1,050 Slaves in Sudan," Reuters, January 28, 1999.

29. Author's interview with Garang Akok, a former slave, in the Warawar market in Aweil East County, summer 1998.

30. Karin Davies, "Slave Trade Thrives in Sudan." Associated Press, February 7, 1998.

31. UN Commission on Human Rights, *Situation of Human Rights in the Sudan: Visit of the Special Rapporteur, Mr. Leonardo Franco, to the Republic of Sudan, 13–24 February 1999* (Geneva: The UN, Addendum to E/CN.4/1999/38).

32. Clare Nullis, "UNICEF Criticizes Sudan on Slavery," Associated Press, March 12, 1999.

33. "Sudanese Government Summons UNICEF over Slavery Claim," news article by Agence France-Presse on March 17, 1999.

34. The United States Mission to the United Nations issued a statement entitled "U.S. Position on Sudan Human Rights Resolution on April 26, 1999"; it was circulated to various news media and is available at the mission's headquarters in New York.

35. See Gregory Kane, "America Chooses to Ignore Those Enslaved in Africa," *Baltimore Sun*, March 3, 1999.

36. It has to be noted that even the Libyan support for the SPLA was not necessarily to express solidarity with the South or to make a stand against injustice, but only to depose Nimeiri, whom Qaddafi had loathed for a long time.

37. See Barry Came, "Freeing the Slaves of Sudan: A Canadian Couple Spend Their Vacations Buying People out of Bondage in the African Savanna." *Maclean's*, April 10, 2000.

38. Eric Reeves, "The Last, Best Hope Sits on its Hands: We have the Economic Power to Push for a Just Peace; Millions of Sudanese are Dying in the Civil War," *Los Angeles Times*, February 10, 2000.

39. Ibid.

40. See Sebastian Mallaby, "Taking Foreign Policy Private," *Washington Post*, May 29, 2000.

41. Andrew England and Chris Logan, "Fury of Baroness as UN Attacks Her Mercy Missions," *Daily Mail*, October 29, 1999.

42. Alex de Waal of the London-based African Rights made this statement in an interview with Karin Davies, "Slave Trade Thrives in Sudan."

43. Richard Miniter, "The False Promise of Slave Redemption," *Atlantic Monthly*, July 1999.

44. Human Rights Watch, "Background Paper on Slavery and Slavery Redemption in the Sudan" (New York and Washington: HRW, March 12, 1999).

45. Fisher, "Selling Sudan's Slaves into Freedom," Associated Press, January 3, 1999.

46. See Bona Malwal, "UNICEF's Unjustifiable Condemnation of CSI over Slave Redemptions," *Sudan Democratic Gazette*, March 1999.

47. Andrew England and Chris Logan, "Fury of Baroness as UN Attacks Her Mercy Missions."

48. Robert Unruh, "Students Tackle Sudan Slave Trade," Associated Press, January 28, 1999.

49. Todd Bensman, "Efforts to Buy Freedom for African Slaves Drawing Criticism," *Dallas Morning News*, June 7, 1999.

50. See Davies, "Slave Trade Thrives in Sudan."

Bibliography

African Rights (1995) *Sudan's Invisible Citizens: The Policy of Abuse Against Displaced People in the North.* London: African Rights.

"Africa's Dirty Secret: Slavery in Our Times" (1995) *Washington Times,* May 5.

Albino, Oliver (1970) *The Sudan: A Southern Viewpoint.* London: Institute of Race Relations and Oxford University Press.

Anderson, Mary (1996) *Do No Harm: Supporting Political Capacities for Peace Through Aid.* Cambridge, Mass.: Local Capacities for Peace Project, Collaborative for Development Action.

Arou, Mom K. N., and B. Yongo-Bure, eds. (1988) *North-South Relations in Sudan Since the Addis Ababa Agreement.* Khartoum: Institute of African and Asian Studies and Khartoum University Printing Press.

Attiya, Thomas O. (1999) "Stand on South Sudan Wrong." *Daily Nation,* December 14.

Bales, Kevin (1999) *Disposable People: New Slavery in the Global Economy.* Berkeley and Los Angeles: University of California Press.

Bashir, Muhammad O. (1976) *The Southern Problem.* Khartoum: Khartoum University Printing Press.

Bensman, Todd (1999) "Efforts to Buy Freedom for African Slaves Drawing Criticism." *Dallas Morning News,* June 7.

Beny, Laura (1999) "Legal and Ethical Dimensions of Slavery in the Sudan: The Failure to Address Victims' Testimonies." Paper presented at the African Studies Association annual meeting, Philadelphia, November 1999.

Burr, Millard, and Robert Collins (1995) *Requiem for the Sudan: Famine and Disaster Relief on the Upper Nile.* Boulder, Colo.: Westview Press.

——— (1999) *Africa's Thirty Years' War: Chad, Libya, and the Sudan, 1963–1993.* Boulder, Colo.: Westview Press.

Came, Barry (2000) "Freeing the Slaves of Sudan: A Canadian Couple Spend Their Vacations Buying People out of Bondage in the African Savanna." *MacLean's,* April 10.

Collins, Robert (1971) *Land Beyond the Rivers: The Southern Sudan, 1898–1918.* New Haven: Yale University Press.

——— (1975) *The Southern Sudan in Historical Perspective.* Tel Aviv: Shiloah Center for Middle Eastern and African Studies.

——— (1983) *Shadows in the Grass: Britain in the Southern Sudan, 1918–1956.* New Haven: Yale University Press.

———— (1992) "Nilotic Slavery: Past and Present." In *Human Commodity*, edited by Elizabeth Savage. London: Frank Cass.

———— (1999) "Africans, Arabs, and Islamists: From the Conference Tables to the Battlefields in the Sudan." *African Studies Review* 42, no. 2, pp. 105–23.

———— (1999) "Slavery in the Sudan in History." In *Slavery in North Africa*, edited by Shaun Elizabeth Marmon. Princeton: Markus Weiner.

Crawshaw, Steve (1999) "Two Worlds Collide in a Wasteland Racked by War." *Independent*, April 15.

Daly, Martin (1986) *Empire on the Nile: The Anglo-Egyptian Sudan, 1898–1943*. Cambridge: Cambridge University Press.

Davies, Karin (1998) "Slave Trade Thrives in Sudan." Associated Press, February 7.

De Waal, Alex (1989) *Famine that Kills: Darfur, Sudan, 1984–1985*. Oxford: Clarendon Press.

Deng, Francis Mading (1995) *War of Visions: Conflict of Identities in the Sudan*. Washington, D.C.: Brookings Institution.

Duodo, Cameron (2000) "Africa's Forgotten War." *Mail and Guardian* (South Africa), January 28.

———— (2000) "Africa's New Slaves: Slave Trade Thrives in Sudan." *Mail and Guardian* (South Africa), January 28.

Duffield, Mark (1994) "The Political Economy of Internal War: Asset Transfer, Complex Emergencies and International Aid." In *War and Hunger: Rethinking International Responses to Complex Emergencies*, edited by J. Macrae and A. Zwi. London: Zed Books.

England, Andrew, and Chris Logan (1999) "Fury of Baroness as UN Attacks Her Mercy Missions." *Daily Mail*, October 29.

European Commission Humanitarian Office (1999) *Humanitarian Assistance: Consequences Beyond Relief*. Brussels: European Union.

European Commission Humanitarian Office (1999) *Sudan: Unintended Consequences of Humanitarian Assistance*. Brussels: European Union.

Finnegan, William (1999) "The Invisible War." *New Yorker*, January 25.

Fisher, Ian (1999) "Selling Sudan's Slaves into Freedom." Associated Press, January 3.

Gray, Richard (1961) *History of the Southern Sudan, 1839–1889*. London: Frank Cass.

Harker, John (2000) *Human Security in Sudan: The Report of a Canadian Assessment Mission*. Ottawa: Ministry of Foreign Affairs.

Human Rights Watch (1995) *Children in Sudan: Slaves, Street Children and Child Soldiers*. New York: Human Rights Watch.

———— (1999) "Background Paper on Slavery and Slavery Redemption in the Sudan." New York and Washington, D.C.: Human Rights Watch, March 12.

———— (1999) *Famine in Bahr el-Ghazal, 1998*. New York: Human Rights Watch.

Hutchinson, Sharon E. (1996) *Nuer Dilemmas: Coping with Money, War, and the State*. Berkeley: University of California Press.

Jackson, C. (1955) *Behind the Modern Sudan*. New York: Macmillan.

Jacobs, Charles, and Rafael Abiem (1996) "Of Human Bondage in the Twentieth Century." *Boston Globe*, June 4.

Johnson, Douglas (1989) "The Structure of a Legacy: Military Slavery in Northeast Africa." *Ethnohistory* 36, no. 1, pp. 72–88.

———— (1998) "Indigenous Religions in the Sudanese Civil War." Paper presented at the conference "Religion and Conflict in Africa," London.

Jok, Jok Madut (1998) *Militarization, Gender and Reproductive Health in South Sudan*. Lewiston, N.Y.: Edwin Mellen Press.

———— (1999) "Militarization and Gender Violence in South Sudan." *Journal of Asian and African Studies* 34, no. 4, pp. 427–42.

Jok, Jok Madut, and S. Hutchinson (1999) "Sudan's Prolonged Second Civil War and the Militarization of Dinka and Nuer Ethnic Identities." *African Studies Review* 42, no. 2.

Kane, Gregory (1999) "America Chooses to Ignore Those Enslaved in Africa." *Baltimore Sun*, March 3.

Karim, A., M. Duffield, et al. (1996) *Operation Life-line Sudan (OLS): A Review*. Geneva: Department of Humanitarian Affairs.

Keen, David (1994) *The Benefits of Famine: A Political Economy of Famine and Relief in Southwestern Sudan, 1983–1989*. Princeton: Princeton University Press.

Levitin, Sonia (2000) *Dream Freedom*. San Diego: Silver Whistle.

Lewis, Bernard (1990) *Race and Slavery in the Middle East: An Historical Enquiry*. New York and Oxford: Oxford University Press.

Livingstone, David (1874) *Last Journals of David Livingstone in Central Africa, from 1865 to His Death*. Edited by H. Murray Waller. London.

Magardie, Khadija (2000) "A One-sided View of Civil War." *Mail and Guardian*, February 4.

Mahmud, Ushari, and Suliman Baldo (1987) *Human Rights Abuses in the Sudan, 1987: The ed-Da'ein Massacre: Slavery in the Sudan*, Khartoum.

Majak, Damazo Dut (1990) "The Northern Bahr el-Ghazal: People, Alien Encroachment and Rule, 1856–1956." Ph.D. dissertation, University of California, Santa Barbara.

———— (1992) "Islam: A Factor in the Sudan Civil War." Paper presented at African Studies Association meeting. Seattle, Washington.

———— (1995) "Rape of Nature: The Environmental Destruction and Ethnic Cleansing of the Sudan." Paper presented at the American Historical Association Pacific Coast Branch 88th annual meeting. Maui, Hawaii.

Mallaby, Sebastian (2000) "Taking Foreign Policy Private." *Washington Post*, May 29.

Malwal, Bona (1999) Address to the A. Philip Randolph Institute on the occasion of his award for human rights activities in Sudan. October.

———— (1999) "UNICEF's Unjustifiable Condemnation of CSI over Slave Redemptions." *Sudan Democratic Gazette*, March 1999.

Miniter, Richard (1999) "The False Promise of Slave Redemption." *Atlantic Monthly*, July 1999.

Murray, Gordon (1989) *Slavery in the Arab World*. New York: New Amsterdam Books.

Nullis, Clare (1999) "UNICEF Criticizes Sudan on Slavery." Associated Press, March 12.

Patterson, Donald (1999) *Inside Sudan: Political Islam, Conflict, and Catastrophe*. Boulder, Colo.: Westview Press.

Reeves, Eric (1999) "Human Agony in Sudan Can't Be Ignored." *San Francisco Chronicle*, August 12.

———— (2000) "The Last, Best Hope Sits on Its Hands: We Have the Economic Power to Push for a Just Peace; Millions of Sudanese Are Dying in the Civil War." *Los Angeles Times*, February 10.

Ruay, Deng A. (1994) *The Politics of Two Sudans: The North and the South*. Uppsala: Nordiska Afrikaninstitutet.

Sikainga, Ahmad Alawad (1986) "British Policy in the Western Bahr al-Ghazal (Sudan), 1904–1946." Ph.D. dissertation, University of California, Santa Barbara.

—— (1989) "The Legacy of Slavery and Slave Trade in Western Bahr al-Ghazal, 1850–1939." *Northeast African Studies*, 2, no. 2, pp. 75–95.

—— (1991) *The Western Bahr al-Ghazal Under British Rule: 1898–1956*. Athens: Ohio University Press.

—— (1996) *Slaves into Workers: Emancipation and Labor in Colonial Sudan*. Austin: University of Texas Press.

"Slave Trade Thrives in Sudan" (1998) Associated Press, February 7.

"Slavery in Sudan" (1988) *Sudan Times* 3 (624), October 9.

Sudan Archives at Durham University. Various documents.

"Sudanese Government Summons UNICEF over Slavery Claim" (1999) Agence France-Presse, March 17.

"Swiss Group Says It Freed 1,050 Slaves in Sudan" (1999) Reuters, January 28.

UN Commission on Human Rights (1994) *Situation of Human Rights in the Sudan: A Report of the Special Rapporteur, Mr. Gaspar Bîro*. Geneva: UN.

—— (1999) *Situation of Human Rights in the Sudan: Visit of the Special Rapporteur, Mr. Leonardo Franco, to the Republic of Sudan, 13–24 February 1999*. Geneva: UN, Addendum to E/CN.4/1999/38.

U.S. Committee for Refugees (1998) *Quantifying Genocide: War and Disaster in Sudan*. Washington, D.C.: U.S. Committee for Refugees.

—— (2000) *The Nuba People: Confronting Cultural Liquidation*. Washington, D.C.: U.S. Committee for Refugees.

United States Mission to United Nations (1999) "U.S. Position on Sudan Human Rights Resolution on April 26, 1999." New York: Mission Headquarters.

Unruh, Robert (1999) "Students Tackle Sudan Slave Trade." Associated Press, January 28.

Verney, Peter (1997) *Slavery in Sudan*. London: Sudan Update and Anti-Slavery International.

Waal, Alex de (1997) *Famine Crimes: Politics and the Disaster Relief Industry in Africa*. Oxford: James Currey.

Index

Printed in the United States
71712LV00004B/203